Education for Disabled Children

Education for Disabled Children

Rashmi Agrawal
B.V.L.N. Rao

SHIPRA

(2011, First Published in 2007)

Rs. 995

ISBN: 978-93-88691-12-3

2019 Impression

Education for Disabled Children

Published by:
SHIPRA PUBLICATIONS
LG 18-19, Pankaj Central Market,
I.P. Ext., Patparganj, Delhi 110092, India
Ph.: +91 11 47322068, 9650028065, 9810522367
info@shiprapublication.com
www.shiprapublication.com

Preface

Swati joined as a school teacher for games in a government co-educational school. She soon observed that while other children played various games, one boy used to sit in a corner all alone watching the others play. Sometimes he would throw the ball back into the playground when it came to him. Swati saw a peculiar expression of delight when the boy had a chance to hold the ball and throw. She asked the boy, 'why don't you play'? The boy replied, 'I cannot play as I have only one leg. The other leg is artificial'. On this Swati said, 'So what, you can do it and I will teach you how to do it.'

This is only one case. There may be many, where children with some or the other disability keep aloof from others or sometimes others neglect them. The fact is that persons with disabilities have talents and capabilities, which are to be recognized, identified and nurtured. Disabled children can perform like others, only their needs may differ.

This book provides an insight into the world of the disabled, their needs, their problems and ways to cope with them. Mainstreaming of the disabled is a must, as countries cannot afford to waste the talents of a vast section of children just because they have some disability. There are instances where disabled children have excelled in various fields.

Over the past three decades, the concept of mainstreaming of disabled has gradually been taking root in the country's education system. While such a step is eminently desirable in the larger social perspective, the teachers need to acquire special abilities to identify the out of the ordinary needs of the individual child, develop among themselves appropriate management skills in a class comprising children of diverse levels of learning abilities, use special equipment, adopt special instructional methods and material, adapt the normal educational curriculum to suit the situation, and above all in displaying a humane approach in handling children with special needs. The school administration and the government as well as the society at large too have an important role to play in supporting the development of disabled by providing appropriate resources and in encouraging innovative efforts and experiments.

This book is an attempt to provide detailed guidelines to teachers in identification and effective education of children with special needs in a normal school setting. It is hoped that the material included in the book will help the teachers develop a sense of awareness about the requirements of children with special needs and in translating this awareness into effective methods of instruction. Specific illustrations have been included for curriculum modifications and teaching strategies to suit different types of disabilities. It is also expected that the book will be useful for normal as well as disabled children to understand each other and grow and learn together in a mutually beneficial manner.

The book also explains various concepts in the field of disabilities, indicates the size of the problem and outlines various current policies and programmes in the field of special education.

The authors are grateful to Shipra Publications who have given us a chance to write about a very challenging and socially relevant subject. Authors are also thankful to those children with disabilities who provided first hand information about their problems and needs and an experienced based book could take a shape.

Rashmi Agarwal
B.V.L.N Rao

Contents

1

Special Education: An Introduction

All children are not alike in relation to their mental and physical attributes. Some are highly gifted children while others are less talented; some have physical disabilities like blindness or low vision, deafness, speech disorders, lack of or non-functional limbs; some are retarded in intellectual development; some may be suffering from complications like epilepsy; some may be emotionally disturbed or are unable to make a proper adjustment in school, family or community; some may have learning disabilities.

While most persons are likely to be different from what is considered as the normal to some extent or other, in some persons the deviation may be so pronounced that it marks them as exceptional and needing special attention. Such children exhibit marked behavioural or communication disorders, or intellectual, physical or multiple disabilities. While all students require support to varying extents from teachers, classmates, family and the community at large in order to derive the fullest benefit from their school experience, these exceptional children have special needs that demand additional support beyond those ordinarily available in the normal school environment.

Such supports may be in the form of special educational services, special educational programmes or special infrastructural or learning facilities, and most importantly, special skills on the part of the teachers, in order to enable them to participate effectively in the learning process, in the school setting or outside it.

The term 'special education' refers not only to the process of teaching students with a learning disability, a developmental disability or a behavioural problem, but is also extended to cover children who display exceptional abilities and talents in one or more fields, who are also called gifted children.

Gifted children are more capable than others, have a higher level of intelligence, can absorb knowledge faster and retain it better. They are happy to undertake extra and complex work but get bored in the routine curricular activities. They may have natural talents and special aptitudes for creative and artistic work. Their educational needs are clearly different from those of children with disabilities or even normal children. Gifted children, though generally categorised as children with special needs along with children with disabilities, thus, form a group apart.

Children who are different from the normal children are termed as exceptional children. This book excludes the gifted children from its purview and deals only with the educational needs of the children with disabilities.

Definition of Exceptional Children

Crunchshank has given the definition 'An Exceptional child is who deviates physically, intellectually, emotionally and socially so marked from normal growth and development that he cannot be benefited from a regular classroom programme and needs special treatment in the school'.

Similarly Kirk said 'An exceptional child is one who deviates from normal or average child in mental, physical and social characteristics to such an extent that he require a modification in school practices or special education services or supplementary instruction in order to develop to his maximum capacity.'

The above definitions show that:

- Some children are different than others,
- These differences can be physical, psychological, or social,
- Their needs can not be met with normal curriculum of the school, and
- Modifications in school's services are required to develop them fully.

Historical Evolution of Education of the Disabled

In pre-historic and primitive ages, the disabled were treated with contempt. In those times, when physical abilities counted most for day-to-day living, such persons were generally victims of lack of proper care and concern. Frampton and Gall (1955) observed that while there was no conclusive evidence, but abandonment of the disabled was a universal practice in the ancient world, it was claimed that handicapped individuals were not being given due attention.

As social conscience developed, these practices yielded place to attitudes of compassion and desire for remedial measures. All great religions preached compassion for the disabled. In ancient India too, the society was required to treat the disabled with compassion and sympathy. Though, under the influence of religious prescriptions, persons with disabilities were, thus, treated in a more humane fashion right through the Middle Ages, it was only after 1500 A.D. that real progress has been made in the care and education of the exceptional children. The process of change was initiated by scientific and medical research that showed the way toward the solution of the problems posed by disabilities.

It was, however, only in the second half of Eighteenth Century that the concepts of education for the disabled took their root. The liberal, socialistic ideas sweeping across the western hemisphere, France and the United States of America in particular, provided the inspiration to political and social reformers and experts in medicine and education to focus on the children with special educational needs.

In France, the year 1785 witnessed the first school for the blind started by Valentine Huay in Paris. Father D'Lepse developed an early version of manual alphabet using finger spelling for the deaf. The case study of 'The Wild Boy of Aveyron' by Jean Marc Gaspard Itarde, a French physician, was pioneering work in the field of education for the mentally retarded. In Germany, Samuel Heinicke developed an oral method of instruction for the deaf children.

In the United States of America, the first permanent school for the deaf was set up in 1817 at Hartford, Connecticut. The year 1829, in which Louis Braille developed the system of raised point alphabet using six dots arranged in two parallel rows of three dots each, was a landmark in the education of the blind.

The first residential institute for people with mental retardation was founded Samuel Gridley Howe in Boston, Massachusetts in the year 1848. In 1869, the US Patents Office registered the first wheel chair patent.

In India, the first school for the deaf was set up at Bombay in 1883 and the first school for the blind at Amritsar in 1887. There are over 3,200 such special schools today run mostly by non-governmental organizations (NGOs).

The post Second World War years witnessed, under the influence and guidance of the United Nations, a rapid transformation in the humanity's approach towards the persons with disabilities and their education—from 'one of charity' to an 'issue in human rights'. The Universal Declaration of Human Rights (1948), The Convention (No.159) on Vocational Rehabilitation and Employment of the International Labour Organisation (1983), The Declaration of 1981 as the International Year of the Disabled, The Declaration of the Rights of Mentally Retarded Persons (1971), The Declaration on the Rights of Deaf-Blind Persons (1979), The World Programme of Action Concerning Disabled Persons

(1982) and the declaration of the decade 1983-92 as the 'Decade of Disabled Persons' were landmark intentional events in this process.

International action concerning the disabled got accelerated during 1990s. In 1992, United Nations adopted a resolution declaring 3rd December of each year as International Day of Disabled Persons. The objective was to promote awareness and understanding of issues relating to disabled persons and to mobilize support for practical action. In 1993, the UN General Assembly adopted "Standard Rules on the Equalisation of Opportunities for Persons with Disabilities".

Encouraged and assisted by the activities of the international bodies, a number of initiatives were taken by the national governments in a number of countries to promote the rights, and economic and social development and education of the disabled.

In the United States of America, Americans with Disabilities Act (ADA) is the most important general legislation concerning the disabled. The United States Congress also passed in 1975, in response to discriminatory treatment by public educational agencies against students with disabilities, the Education of the Handicapped Act (EHA) making special education programmes mandatory. The EHA was later modified to strengthen the protective provisions for disabled students and was renamed as Individuals with Disabilities Education Act (IDEA). IDEA seeks to ensure that every disabled student is entitled to a free, appropriate public education in the least restrictive environment. A team of professionals and parents meet to develop an individualized educational plan to determine the students' unique educational needs, develop annual goals for the student, and determine the placement and special services the student needs. The mandate of 'least restrictive environment' requires that the student be exposed to the maximum extent with non-disabled peers, while still providing appropriate education.

In the United Kingdom, the Disability Discrimination Act of 1995 ensures that the persons with disabilities are treated without discrimination. In the schools, a child is identified as one with Special Education Needs (SEN) and it is the responsibility of the Special Education Needs Coordinator (SENCO) in the school to ensure that all pupils in the schools with special needs receive the appropriate support to facilitate their successful education.

In Australia, the Disability Discrimination Act of 1992 aims to eliminate, as far as possible, discrimination against persons on the ground of disability in the areas of work, occupation, education, etc., and to ensure that persons with disabilities have the same rights to equality and other fundamental as the rest of the community. In the area of education, as in the United States of America and United

Body structures are anatomical parts of the body such as organs, imbs and their components.

Impairments are problems in body function or structure such as a significant deviation or loss.

Activity limitations are difficulties an individual may have in executing activities.

Participation restrictions are problems an individual may experience in his involvement in life situations.

Government of India formulated certain uniform definitions of various terms relating to disablement. These definitions are:

(a) *Impairment*: Impairment is a permanent or transitory psychological, or anatomical loss and/or abnormality. For example, a missing or ineffective part, tissue or organ or "Mechanism" of the body, such as an amputated limb, paralysis after polio, myocardial infarction, cerebro-vascular thrombosis, restricted pulmonary capacity, diabetes, myopia, disfigurement, mental retardation, hypertension, perceptual disturbance.

(b) *Functional Limitation*: Impairment may cause functional limitations which are the partial or total inability to perform those activities necessary for motor, sensory, or mental functions within the range and manner of which a human being is normally capable such as walking, lifting loads, seeing, speaking, hearing, reading, writing, counting, taking interest in and making contact with surroundings. A functional limitation may last for a short time or a long time, be permanent or reversible. It should be quantifiable whenever possible. Limitations may be described as "progressive" or "regressive".

(c) *Disability*: Disability is defined as an existing difficulty in performing one or more activities which, in accordance with the ubject's age, sex and normative social role, are generally accepted as ssential basic components of daily living, such as self-care, social elations and economic activity. Depending in part on the duration of e functional limitation disability may be short-term, long-term or ermanent.

(d) *Temporary Total Disability*: Temporary total disability is that riod in which the affected person is totally unable to work. During s time he may receive orthopaedic, ophthalmologic, auditory or ech or any other medical treatment.

(e) *Temporary Partial Disability*: Temporary partial disability is that od when recovery has reached the stage of improvement so that erson may begin some kind of gainful occupation.

Kingdom, the argument that all students have an equal right to experience a broad and enriching curriculum, while at the same time having their individual needs adequately met, found favour. South Australia was one of the first states to adopt a system of integrated education in normal schools in the early 1970s and is currently actively implementing inclusive practices in schools.

In India, the National Policy for Persons with Disabilities was adopted in 1993. It, *inter alia*, emphasized the need for mainstreaming of the persons with disabilities in the general education system through Inclusive Education. Sarva Shiksha Abhiyan (SSA) i.e. education for all, was launched by the central government with the goal of ensuring eight years of elementary schooling for all children, including children with disabilities, in the age group of 6 to 14 years by 2010.

The Persons With Disabilities (Equal Opportunities, Protection of Rights and Full Participation) Act, 1995, commonly known as the PWD Act, provides for the following in the area of education

- Every child with disability shall have the right to free education till the age of 18.
- Appropriate transportation, removal of architectural barriers and restructuring of curriculum and modification in the examination system.
- Children with disabilities shall have the right to scholarships, uniforms, free books and learning material.
- Special schools for children with disabilities will be equipped with vocational training facilities.
- Non-formal education shall be promoted for children with disabilities.

The Integrated Education for Disabled Children (IEDC) Scheme, which has been in operation since the 1970s, provides for free education of children with disabilities in the age group 15-18 years.

Concepts of Impairment, Disability and Handicap

The term 'disability' does not have an easy, commonly acceptable and precise definition. As mentioned earlier, most human beings are not perfect in all respects, mentally and physically, the extent of imperfection varying widely. Moreover, the term 'disability' is not a universal concept. Its meaning varies according to cultural and attitudinal differences prevailing in different societies.

A form of disability considered as disability in one cultural setting might not be considered so in another one. For example in Northern

Mali, (Mali, a country in African Continent), an ugly woman used to be considered to be most disabled. In some other societies, dwarfs are considered disabled, even though being a dwarf does not impose any limitations on the person's functioning. Referring to these complexities in evolving a uniform concept of disability, Dr. Einar Helander opined that the initial definition of a disabled person could be "a person who in his/her society is regarded as disabled, because of a difference in appearance and behaviour".

In simple terms, disability may be defined as a kind of impairment, physical or mental, that makes it difficult for a person to do what other people are able to do. It may be broadly understood as a "significant loss or want of abilities, temporary or permanent, due to disease, accident, genetic causes or any other reason" (Pandey and Advani). It hampers significantly an individual's capability to perform a particular task as per standards. Clearly, the extent of one's disability is a matter of degree.

World Health Organisation (WHO) distinguished between Impairment, Disability and Handicap as:

(a) An 'Impairment' means any loss or abnormality of psychological, physiological or anatomical structure or function,

(b) A 'Disability', is a restriction or lack of (resulting from impairment) ability to perform an activity in a manner or within the range considered normal for a human being, and

(c) A 'Handicap' is a disadvantage for a given individual resulting from an impairment or disability that limits or prevents the fulfillment of a role that is considered normal (depending on the age, sex and social and cultural factors) for that individual.

It may be observed that

- impairment may be corrected with appropriate aids and appliances and need not always lead to a disability or a handicap,
- a disability is a consequence of impairment leading to functional limitation or activity restriction. It may arise as a direct consequence of impairment or as a response, often psychological, on the part of the individual to the impairment.

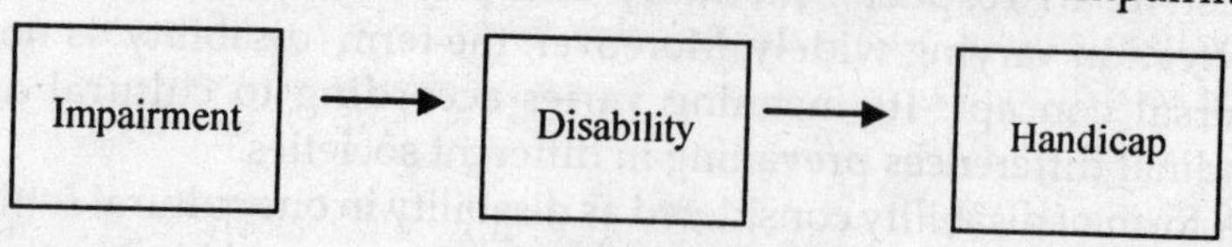

Fig. 1.1

The United Nations World Programme of Action Co
Disabled Persons adopted in 1982 defined 'handicap' as a fu
the relationship between disabled persons and their environ
occurs when they encounter cultural, physical or social barrier
prevent their access to the various systems of society that are av
to other citizens. Thus, handicap is the loss or limitati
opportunities to take part in life of the community or an equal
with others".

According to the International Labour Organisation (ILO):

"the term 'disabled person' means an individual wh
prospects of securing, retaining and advancing in suita
employment are substantially reduced as a result of a d
recognized physical or mental impairment". It may be observ
that while the WHO definition is formulated basically from th
point of view of health, the United Nations' definition i
formulated from the point of social equality and that of ILC
relates to equality in employment. (Convention No.159)

The United Nations Standard Rules on the Equalisation of
Opportunities for Persons with Disabilities, 1993, describe 'disabilit
as summarizing "a great number of different functional limitatio
occurring in any population in any country of the world. People m
be disabled by physical, intellectual or sensory impairment, medi
conditions or mental illness. Such impairments, conditions or illne
may be permanent or transitory in nature".

WHO brought out a second edition of the Internati
Classification of Impairments, Disabilities and Handicaps (IC
2) and, in May 2001 the 54th World Health Assembly endors
revised classification, giving it the title 'International Classif
of Functioning, Disabilities and Health.' The classification a
providing a unified and standard description of human fun
and disability as an important component of health.

In this revised classification, the earlier terms of 'disab
'handicap' (used in the 1980 Classification) have been re
'Activity Limitation' and 'Participation Restriction' respecti
using the term 'disability' in an umbrella sense to cover all in
activity limitations and participation restrictions. Th
attached to different terms used in the above terminolo
below:

Body functions are the physiological functions o
(including psychological functions).

Kingdom, the argument that all students have an equal right to experience a broad and enriching curriculum, while at the same time having their individual needs adequately met, found favour. South Australia was one of the first states to adopt a system of integrated education in normal schools in the early 1970s and is currently actively implementing inclusive practices in schools.

In India, the National Policy for Persons with Disabilities was adopted in 1993. It, *inter alia*, emphasized the need for mainstreaming of the persons with disabilities in the general education system through Inclusive Education. Sarva Shiksha Abhiyan (SSA) i.e. education for all, was launched by the central government with the goal of ensuring eight years of elementary schooling for all children, including children with disabilities, in the age group of 6 to 14 years by 2010.

The Persons With Disabilities (Equal Opportunities, Protection of Rights and Full Participation) Act, 1995, commonly known as the PWD Act, provides for the following in the area of education

- Every child with disability shall have the right to free education till the age of 18.
- Appropriate transportation, removal of architectural barriers and restructuring of curriculum and modification in the examination system.
- Children with disabilities shall have the right to scholarships, uniforms, free books and learning material.
- Special schools for children with disabilities will be equipped with vocational training facilities.
- Non-formal education shall be promoted for children with disabilities.

The Integrated Education for Disabled Children (IEDC) Scheme, which has been in operation since the 1970s, provides for free education of children with disabilities in the age group 15-18 years.

Concepts of Impairment, Disability and Handicap

The term 'disability' does not have an easy, commonly acceptable and precise definition. As mentioned earlier, most human beings are not perfect in all respects, mentally and physically, the extent of imperfection varying widely. Moreover, the term 'disability' is not a universal concept. Its meaning varies according to cultural and attitudinal differences prevailing in different societies.

A form of disability considered as disability in one cultural setting might not be considered so in another one. For example in Northern

Mali, (Mali, a country in African Continent), an ugly woman used to be considered to be most disabled. In some other societies, dwarfs are considered disabled, even though being a dwarf does not impose any limitations on the person's functioning. Referring to these complexities in evolving a uniform concept of disability, Dr. Einar Helander opined that the initial definition of a disabled person could be "a person who in his/her society is regarded as disabled, because of a difference in appearance and behaviour".

In simple terms, disability may be defined as a kind of impairment, physical or mental, that makes it difficult for a person to do what other people are able to do. It may be broadly understood as a "significant loss or want of abilities, temporary or permanent, due to disease, accident, genetic causes or any other reason" (Pandey and Advani). It hampers significantly an individual's capability to perform a particular task as per standards. Clearly, the extent of one's disability is a matter of degree.

World Health Organisation (WHO) distinguished between Impairment, Disability and Handicap as:

(a) An 'Impairment' means any loss or abnormality of psychological, physiological or anatomical structure or function,
(b) A 'Disability', is a restriction or lack of (resulting from impairment) ability to perform an activity in a manner or within the range considered normal for a human being, and
(c) A 'Handicap' is a disadvantage for a given individual resulting from an impairment or disability that limits or prevents the fulfillment of a role that is considered normal (depending on the age, sex and social and cultural factors) for that individual.

It may be observed that

- impairment may be corrected with appropriate aids and appliances and need not always lead to a disability or a handicap,
- a disability is a consequence of impairment leading to functional limitation or activity restriction. It may arise as a direct consequence of impairment or as a response, often psychological, on the part of the individual to the impairment.

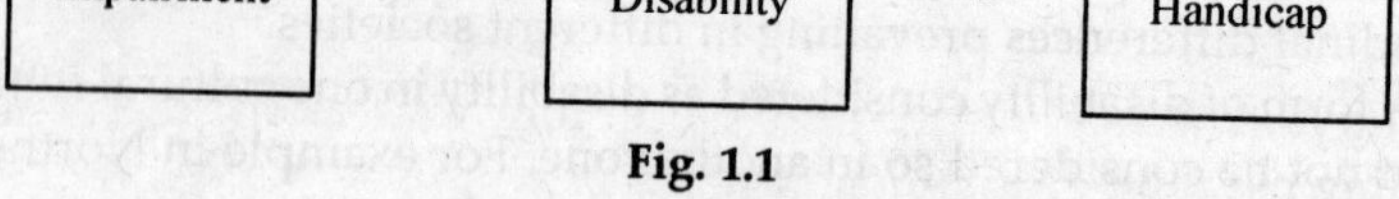

Fig. 1.1

The United Nations World Programme of Action Concerning Disabled Persons adopted in 1982 defined 'handicap' as a function of the relationship between disabled persons and their environment: "It occurs when they encounter cultural, physical or social barriers which prevent their access to the various systems of society that are available to other citizens. Thus, handicap is the loss or limitation of opportunities to take part in life of the community or an equal level with others".

According to the International Labour Organisation (ILO):

> "the term 'disabled person' means an individual whose prospects of securing, retaining and advancing in suitable employment are substantially reduced as a result of a duly recognized physical or mental impairment". It may be observed that while the WHO definition is formulated basically from the point of view of health, the United Nations' definition is formulated from the point of social equality and that of ILO relates to equality in employment. (Convention No.159)

The United Nations Standard Rules on the Equalisation of Opportunities for Persons with Disabilities, 1993, describe 'disability' as summarizing "a great number of different functional limitations occurring in any population in any country of the world. People may be disabled by physical, intellectual or sensory impairment, medical conditions or mental illness. Such impairments, conditions or illnesses may be permanent or transitory in nature".

WHO brought out a second edition of the International Classification of Impairments, Disabilities and Handicaps (ICIDH – 2) and, in May 2001 the 54th World Health Assembly endorsed the revised classification, giving it the title 'International Classification of Functioning, Disabilities and Health.' The classification aimed at providing a unified and standard description of human functioning and disability as an important component of health.

In this revised classification, the earlier terms of 'disability' and 'handicap' (used in the 1980 Classification) have been replaced by 'Activity Limitation' and 'Participation Restriction' respectively, while using the term 'disability' in an umbrella sense to cover all impairments, activity limitations and participation restrictions. The meanings attached to different terms used in the above terminology are shown below:

Body functions are the physiological functions of body systems (including psychological functions).

Body structures are anatomical parts of the body such as organs, limbs and their components.

Impairments are problems in body function or structure such as a significant deviation or loss.

Activity limitations are difficulties an individual may have in executing activities.

Participation restrictions are problems an individual may experience in his involvement in life situations.

Government of India formulated certain uniform definitions of various terms relating to disablement. These definitions are:

(a) *Impairment*: Impairment is a permanent or transitory psychological, or anatomical loss and/or abnormality. For example, a missing or ineffective part, tissue or organ or "Mechanism" of the body, such as an amputated limb, paralysis after polio, myocardial infarction, cerebro-vascular thrombosis, restricted pulmonary capacity, diabetes, myopia, disfigurement, mental retardation, hypertension, perceptual disturbance.

(b) *Functional Limitation*: Impairment may cause functional limitations which are the partial or total inability to perform those activities necessary for motor, sensory, or mental functions within the range and manner of which a human being is normally capable such as walking, lifting loads, seeing, speaking, hearing, reading, writing, counting, taking interest in and making contact with surroundings. A functional limitation may last for a short time or a long time, be permanent or reversible. It should be quantifiable whenever possible. Limitations may be described as "progressive" or "regressive".

(c) *Disability*: Disability is defined as an existing difficulty in performing one or more activities which, in accordance with the subject's age, sex and normative social role, are generally accepted as essential basic components of daily living, such as self-care, social relations and economic activity. Depending in part on the duration of the functional limitation disability may be short-term, long-term or permanent.

(d) *Temporary Total Disability*: Temporary total disability is that period in which the affected person is totally unable to work. During this time he may receive orthopaedic, ophthalmologic, auditory or speech or any other medical treatment.

(e) *Temporary Partial Disability*: Temporary partial disability is that period when recovery has reached the stage of improvement so that the person may begin some kind of gainful occupation.

(f) *Permanent Disability*: Permanent disability applies to permanent damage or loss of use of some part/parts of the body after the stage of maximum improvement from any medical treatment has been reached and the condition is stationary.

Types of Disabilities

Persons with disabilities are a heterogeneous group encompassing a variety of disabilities and varying degrees of disability in each. Disabilities can be broken down into a number of broad sub-categories, which include the following:

- Physical impairments affecting movement, such as muscular dystrophy, post polio syndrome, *spina befida* and cerebral palsy.
- Sensory impairments, such as visual or hearing impairments
- Cognitive impairment, such as Autism or Down Syndrome.
- Psychiatric conditions such as Depression and Schizophrenia

An alternative way of classifying the disabilities is

- Visual disability
- Hearing disability
- Loco motor disability
- Mental disability

Visual disability may be further divided into sub-categories

(a) total blindness, and
(b) low vision.

Similarly, mental disability includes

(a) mental retardation, and
(b) mental illness.

According to the Persons with Disabilities (Equal Opportunities, Protection of Rights and Full Participation) Act, 1995, 'Disability' includes the following categories:

(i) *Blindness*: refers to a condition where a person suffers from any of the following conditions, namely:
(a) Total absence of sight; or
(b) Visual acuity not exceeding 6/60 or 20/200 (Snellen) in the better eye with correcting lenses; or
(c) Limitation of the field of vision subtending an angle of 20 degree or worse.

(ii) *Low vision*: Persons with low vision are those with impairment of visual functioning even after treatment or standard refracting correction but who uses or is potentially capable of using vision for the planning of execution of a task with appropriate assertive device.

(iii) *Leprosy-cured*: Leprosy cured person means any person who has been cured of leprosy but is suffering from:

(a) Loss of sensation in hands or feet as well as loss of sensation and paresis in the eye and eye-lid but with no manifest deformity;

(b) Manifest deformity and paresis; but having sufficient mobility in their hands and feet to enable them to engage in normal economic activity;

(c) Extreme physical deformity as well as advanced stage which prevents him from undertaking any gainful occupation, and the expression "leprosy cured" shall be construed accordingly.

(iv) *Hearing impairment*: Hearing impairment_means loss of sixty decibels or more in the better ear in the conversational range of frequencies.

(v) *Loco motor disability*: Loco motor disability means disability of the bones, joints, muscles leading to substantial restriction of the movement of the limbs or any form of cerebral palsy.

(vi) *Mental retardation:* Mental retardation means a condition of arrested or incomplete development of mind of a person, which is specially characterized by sub normality of intelligence and

(vii) *Mental illness:* Mental illness means any mental disorder other than mental retardation.

According to the Act, a person with disability is a person suffering from not less than 40 per cent of any disability as certified by a medical authority.

Learning Disabilities

Some persons may have more than average intelligence as measured by higher than average Intelligence Quotient, but yet exhibit a lack of ability to interpret and understand properly what they see or hear. For example, one may not remember faces, words, names of people ore may have difficulty in seeing the difference between similar objects, say, for instance 3 and 8 or p and q; or, one may have difficulty in remembering what is said or knowing the difference between similar sounds; or, there may be problems of hand-eye coordination resulting in poor handwriting; or, may be poor in managing his time, space available and tasks to be done; or difficulties in understanding non-verbal communications; or may have poor social skills. Such disabilities, resulting from neurological disorders of the brain, are categorized as learning disabilities.

All types of disabilities have been detailed in later chapters of this book.

Degree of Disability

If the degree of disability is not considered, almost every human being may have to be considered disabled to some extent or other. In general terms, disabilities can be broadly classified as mild, moderate, severe and profound, depending on the degree of the disability. For practical purposes, particularly in extending various services, concessions and other facilities, certain standards defining the degree of disability of each category are required that can be measured. The degree of visual disability is usually defined in terms of total absence of light, visual acuity and/or field of vision. Hearing disability is likewise measured in terms of decibels or loss of hearing. Locomotor disability is judged in terms of percentage loss of usage of the limbs, while mental disability is assessed in terms of Intelligence Quotient (IQ). The standards prescribed for a person to be considered as disabled vary across countries. Even within the country different standards may be adopted for different purposes. In India, for example, the Uniform Definitions prescribed by Government of India in 1986, classified the visual, hearing and orthopaedic disabilities as mild, moderate, severe or profound as follows:

(a) Mild	Less than 40% disability
(b) Moderate	40% and above but below 75%
(c) Severe	75% and above but below 100%
(d) Profound/Total	100%

The criteria for determining the percentage of disabilities in the case of hearing and visual disabilities has been established by the government which would be discussed later. The Uniform Definitions also prescribe the criteria for determining the percentage of disability in the case of locomotor disabilities in upper and lower limbs, trunk (spine), amputees, neurological conditions, and cardio-pulmonary diseases and mental disorders. The degree of disability determines the eligibility of a person to various facilities. For example, only those persons who have disability of more than 40 per cent shall be eligible for registration in Employment Exchanges in the category of handicapped and considered against jobs in public sector reserved for them.

The Changing Terminology

Various alternative expressions have been in vogue at different time points in history to signify disability. People with disabilities used to be called successively with terms ranging from the most derogatory one of 'crippled' to 'handicapped', 'disabled', 'persons with disabilities', 'physically/mentally challenged' to 'persons differently-abled' as the society's approach to the disabled gradually changed from one of contempt to recognizing their human rights. In United Kingdom, for example, people engaged in fighting for disability rights use the term 'disabled' to signify a person who is disabled by the society's inability to accommodate all of its members in the mainstream, thus, shifting the problem from the individual to the social system. Then there is also the 'Person First' movement arguing that the disabled should first be recognized as persons. Thus, it would be preferable to use the phrase 'a woman who is blind' to 'a blind woman' and generally 'persons with disabilities' to 'disabled persons'.

Concepts of General, Special, Integrated and Inclusive Education

The term 'general education' refers to the system of education (including the institutions, curricula, teachers and teaching and evaluation methods) adopted in the normal school system catering to the educational needs of normal children. In the case of education of children with exceptional needs, there are various models that have been tried.

The first, and historically the oldest and the one still prevailing, is that of 'special education' by segregating the children with exceptional needs in a totally different learning environment in special educational institutions, like the schools for the blind, for the deaf, for the mentally retarded, etc. The curricula adopted and the teachers and the teaching methods followed in these special institutions are specific to the disability concerned and are different from those in the normal schools. This approach has been considered unacceptable by social activists on the grounds that

(a) the long-term exclusion of the children with disabilities from the mainstream is socially and educationally harmful to both groups,

(b) segregation in the childhood eventually leads to segregation in the adult life violating human rights,
(c) the breaking of relationships, which is an inevitable result of segregation, is the most serious form of social deprivation that further damages the children's ability to learn, and
(d) 'special needs' is not another term for the needs of the disabled but signify needs which are currently unmet in the mainstream education.

An improvement over the segregated education is the system of integrated education, which gained popularity in the early years of the second half of twentieth century. This system brought the disabled children into the normal school system, but still viewed the disabled child as the problem. This model considers that the disabled child has special problems and needs special teachers, environment, curriculum and equipment, and is different from the other children. All over the world, there is now a growing trend to move away from the special schools model to an 'inclusive education' model for the education of the disabled children.

Inclusive education system views that if a child is not learning, the problem lies in the education system and not in the disabled child. The difficulties arise because of rigid methods and curriculum, inaccessible environment, untrained teachers and poor quality of teaching, lack of proper attitudes on the part of the teachers, lack of support from public agencies, etc. Thus, the focus shifts from making the disabled child responsible for his problems to making the education system responsible. The Salamanca Statement adopted at the World Conference on Special Needs Education: Access and Quality in 1994 states that

> "Regular schools with this inclusive orientation are the most effective means of combating discriminatory attitudes, creating welcoming communities, building an inclusive society and achieving education for all; moreover, they provide an effective education to the majority of children and improve the efficiency and ultimately the cost-effectiveness of the entire educational system".

Concept of Education for All and Equal Opportunities of Education: A Differentiation

India has a low literacy rate. The concept of 'Education for All' relates to increasing the literacy rates in the country through adopting various methods. These include opening new schools after every few miles so that children could easily go to school, giving incentives to children like mid-day meal, free books etc. The basic focus of 'Education for All 'is to provide facilities of schools in every part of the country and enhance the literacy rate.

India is a vast country with various socio-economic and cultural variations. All parts of the country are not developed alike. There are many areas, which are still backward, and people are not aware of the advantages of education. They are off the mainstream. Children belonging to such areas cannot compete with the rest of the children who are in the mainstream. The concept of 'Equal Opportunities of Education' is concerned with taking these disadvantaged groups to the mainstream so that children of such groups are able to compete with their counterparts. For this purpose a number of efforts have been initiated such as reservation of Schedule Castes/ Schedule Tribes and Other Backward Classes, special schools for children with special needs, special or remedial classes for the marginalized groups, special facilities for the disabled in the normal schools etc.

Objectives of Special Education

- To make disabled children be useful citizens of the country
- To prepare them to adjust with the environment
- To identify their talents and provide opportunities for their development
- To help them in accepting their disability and develop confidence and positive self- esteem to handle it
- To provide education in a way so that they could earn their livelihood
- To help parents in dealing with their disabled child
- To help their mainstreaming in the society

Need for Special Education

It has been recognized that problems and needs of the disabled children are different from their counter parts; the educational planning for them should be to meet their special needs and problems.

- Children with various categories and types of disabilities like blinds, deaf or dumb require special attention and assistance of specially trained teachers to make them learn. Hence special schools or resources in the normal schools are needed.

- Proper learning may not take place in normal classes. There is a need to have special classes in terms of remedial classes and provisions of resource centers, itinerant teacher to develop disabled children to their full capacities.
- Special education provides disabled full opportunities in making them self- dependent.
- Disabled children may require special support to develop socially desirable behaviours and meet their emotional needs. Special education provides such support
- Disabled children may require help in developing good relations with others and interacting with peer groups. This need can be met with differently planned educational services.
- Special education helps in generating awareness about various disabilities, needs of disabled and helps in their mainstreaming.

2

Incidence of Disabilities

Concepts of Prevalence and Incidence of Disabilities

How many are the disabled and how acute is the problem of disability? Two different concepts are used to answer this question. The most obvious measure is the actual number of disabled persons in the country at a particular point of time, which indicates the 'prevalence' of disability in the country. Prevalence of a particular condition, such as disease, disability, etc indicates the number of persons having that condition at a particular point of time.

While this measure is useful in understanding the overall dimension of the problem and in determining the scale of operations of beneficial programmes, the total number, by itself, will not be useful in comparing the extent of disability in different countries/regions that have different sizes of population. For example, the number of disabled in a country with a population of a billion like India cannot be compared to the number of disabled in a much smaller country like Sri Lanka. The concept of prevalence rate is more useful for this purpose. The prevalence rate of a disability is the percentage of the population with disabilities to the total population of the country. One can compare the prevalence rates of different countries or regions of a country to compare the extent of the problem in different countries/regions or prevalence rates of the same country at different times to study how the prevalence is changing over time.

The concepts of 'Incidence' and 'Incidence Rate' correspond to the concepts of 'Prevalence' and 'Prevalence Rate', but with an essential difference. While prevalence of disability indicates the total number of persons with disabilities at a particular time, incidence indicates the number of persons who are either born with disabilities or become disabled within a particular span of time, usually a year. Similarly, prevalence rate of disability indicates the percentage of persons with disabilities to the total population at particular point of time, while incidence rate indicates the percentage of persons who are either born with disabilities or become disabled for some reason or other during a specified year to the total population in that period. Clearly, prevalence is the accumulated result of the incidence over a number of years in the past.

Thus, while prevalence is 'stock' measure, incidence is a 'flow' measure. Conditions, which are either permanent or are of long duration, such as disabilities or diabetes will have high prevalence rates and lower incidence rates. On the contrary, in the case of conditions like common cold, which are of short duration or are easily curable, the rates of incidence would be high and the rates of prevalence would be low.

As observed in the previous Chapter, there is considerable variation in understanding what constitutes disability in different countries. This makes it extremely difficult to arrive at comparable data on disabled population in different societies. Even within the same country, accurate statistics on disabled persons are difficult to gather for two reasons. Firstly, the sources of such data are the household surveys, either general population censuses or sample surveys. In either case, the investigators usually are not equipped or fully trained to ascertain the disability and the extent of the disability, which requires proper equipment and specialized medical personnel. What can be obtained through these surveys are data on prevalence or incidence of certain easily observable disabilities based on simple operational definitions.

The second problem arises out of the unwillingness on the part of the disabled persons and other members of their households, for social and cultural reasons, to admit that they or their relatives have disability. For example, in India, households may not admit that their children, particularly the girls, are disabled as such admission could lead to a social stigma and hamper the prospects of the marriage of such girls. This again, leads to recording of only persons with clearly visible disabilities.

The data from national censuses and household surveys, therefore, generally underestimate the prevalence or incidence of disability. Even though data collection systems have been improved over the subsequent years, disability statistics continue to suffer from limitations and only reflect persons who report themselves as disabled. Many disabled persons may not consider themselves to be disabled or prefer not to report as such. As a result, disability statistics tend to be underestimates of the real situation.

Prevalence of Disabilities in the World

Estimates of the numbers of the persons with disabilities obviously vary with the categories of disabilities included and the definitions and norms adopted for judging disabilities. At the global level, Dr. Helander of WHO estimated in 1974 that about 10 per cent of the world population was disabled. If this percentage is applied to the current world population, one would conclude that there are about 600 to 650 million persons with disabilities in the world today.

An International Labour Organisation (ILO)'s Press Release of 2001 states that there are approximately 610 million persons with disabilities, of whom 80 per cent lived in developing countries, predominantly in the rural areas. Many countries still adopt the percentage of 10 as indicative of the prevalence of disabilities. Developed countries have more accurate data collection systems through their censuses and surveys. The data for some of these countries (Paciello, 2000) are given below.

- 8.5 million in United Kingdom
- 52.6 million in United States of America
- 37 million in European Union
- 4.2 million in Canada
- 3.7 million in Australia

According to Pravda (3rd December 2002), the Russian Ministry of Labour and Social Development reported about 10 million disabled persons, of whom 592,000 were disabled children. In the USA, data for 2002 indicate that 18 per cent of the American population suffered from disabilities. In Canada, the disability prevalence rate was 12 per cent in 2001. Available data show considerable variation in the prevalence rates, from as low as 2 per cent in India to 18 per cent in the USA. Such wide variation can only be the consequence of definitional, attitudinal, and reporting differences.

The statistic on disabled for selected Asian countries may be seen in the Table 2.0. It is to be observed that estimates are on the lower side.

Prevalence of Disability in India

In India, estimates of disabled population come from two different sources, both adopting the household survey approach. These are the Population Censuses conducted once in ten years and the sample surveys of the disabled conducted, again more or less once in ten years, by the National Sample Survey Organisation (NSSO) in the Ministry of Statistics and Programme Implementation.

Table 2.0: Disability Statistics for Selected Asian Countries

Sl. No.	*Country*	*Year*	*No. of disabled (million)*	*Prevalence Rate (% of total population)*	*Categories covered*
1.	Pakistan[1]	1998	3,293,155	2.49	Visually impaired, hearing impaired, physically impaired, mentally handicapped, mentally impaired, multiple disabilities and others
2.	Thailand[2]	2001	1,100,761	1.75	Physical, hearing and communication, intellectual and learning, visual, mental and behaviour
3.	Philippines[3]	2000	942,098	1.2	Low vision, oral defect, partial blindness, mentally ill, mentally retarded, quadriplegic, hard of hearing, others
4.	Nepal[4]	2001	103,795	0.46	Physical disability, blindness, deafness, mentally retarded, multiple disability
5.	Bangladesh[5]	1991	518,649	0.47	Visual impairment, hearing impairment, intellectually disabled, lepers and physically disabled
6.	Indonesia[6]	2000	1,449,900	3.09	Physical, brain lesion, visual, hearing and speech, mental retardation, development (autism), mental, kidney and heart

1. National Population Census of Pakistan, 1998
2. Report of the Disabled Person survey, 2001, National statistical Office, Thailand
3. Census of Population and Housing, 2000, National Statistical Office, Philippines
4. Census 1991, National Planning Commission and Central Bureau of Statics, Nepal
5. Census, 1991, Bangladesh Bureau of Statistics (Data from 2001 Census not available)
6. National Survey SUSENAS, 2000, Indonesia
7. Korean Institute of Health and Social Affairs

Sources: As cited in the website of Asia Pacific Development Centre on Disablity.

(a) *Population Census Data*

Information on the disabled persons (persons with infirmities, as they were termed at that time) was collected in the very first census of India conducted in 1872. That Census covered both physical and mental disabilities and leprosy as well, the categories covered being insanity, deaf-muteness, blindness and leprosy. Collection of such information continued till the 1931 Census, but was not undertaken in 1941 to 1971 Censuses, primarily, as mentioned earlier, because of the difficulties in collecting accurate information.

In the year 1981, declared as International Year for the Disabled, most countries of the world included questions of disability in their censuses, and so after a gap of 50 years, the 1981 Census of India again collected data on disabilities, covering only three categories — totally dumb, totally blind and totally crippled. The 1981 Census results substantiated once again the feeling that it would be difficult to get accurate data on disabilities due to complexities involved in the concepts and reluctance on the part of the respondents. The question on disability was not included in the 1991 Census. However, collection of these data was resumed in 2001 Census in the wake of sustained pressures from organizations in the field of rights and welfare of the disabled and the requests made by the Government as a follow up of the enactment of the Persons with Disabilities Act 1995.

The concepts of disability mentioned in the PWD Act, 1995 being too complex and infeasible to apply in a Census like operation, a simple and operationally feasible definition of disability (see Box 2.1) was adopted in the 2001 Census, which covered five types of disabilities—In Seeing, In Speech, In Hearing, In Movement and Mental.

Table 2.1: Disabled Persons in Undivided India 1881 to 1931

Census Year	*Population with Infirmity by Type (in thousands)*					*Total Population (thousands)*	*Prevalence Rate (Percent of Disabled to Total Population)*
	Insanity	*Deaf-mute*	*Blind*	*Leprosy*	*Total Disabled*		
1881	81.13	197.21	526.75	131.97	937.06	253,896.33	0.37
1891	74.28	196.86	458.87	126.24	856.25	287,314.67	0.30
1901	66.20	153.17	354.10	97.34	670.82	294,361.06	0.23
1911	81.01	199.89	443.65	109.09	833.64	315,156.40	0.26
1921	88.30	189.64	479.64	102.51	860.10	318,942.48	0.27
1931	120.30	230.90	601.37	147.91	1,095.68	352,837.78	0.31

Source: Census of India, 1931: Vol. II

The 1981 Census recorded 0.48 million totally blind, 0.36 million totally crippled and 0.28 million totally dumb, making a total of 1.1 million totally disabled persons or just 0.2 per cent of the total population of 655 million in that year. It would be seen that the Censuses right from 1881 to 1931 and 1981 grossly underestimated the disabled population due to conceptual and enumeration errors.

Box 2.1

Disability type	*2001 Census definition*
1. In Seeing	A person who cannot see at all (has no perception of light) or has blurred vision even with the help of spectacles will be treated as visually disabled. A person with proper vision only in one eye will also be treated as visually disabled. Persons with blurred vision but had no occasion to test whether eye sight would improve by using spectacles would also be treated as visually disabled.
2. In Speech	A person will be recorded as having speech disability, if he/she is dumb. Persons whose speech is not understood by a listener of normal comprehension and hearing would also be considered to have speech disability. Persons who stammer but whose speech is comprehensible would not be classified as disabled in speech.
3. In Hearing	A person who cannot hear at all (deaf) or can hear only loud sounds will be considered as having hearing disability. A person who is able to hear using hearing aid will not be considered as disabled in hearing. If a person cannot hear through one ear but his/her other ear is functioning normally, would also be considered having hearing disability.
4. In Movement	A person who lacks limbs or is unable to use the limbs normally will be considered having movement disability. Absence of a part of a limb like a finger or a toe will not be considered as disability, but absence of all the fingers or toes or a thumb will make a person disabled by movement. If any part of the body is deformed, the person would also be treated as disabled. A person who cannot move him/herself or without the aid of another person would be treated as movement disabled. A person unable to move or lift or pick up any small article placed near him/her or a person who may not be able to move normally because of problems of joints like arthritis and has to variably limp while moving would also qualify to be covered as disabled.

(*Contd.*)

(*Contd.*)

5. Mental	A person who lacks comprehension appropriate to his/her age will be considered as mentally disabled. This would not mean that a person is not able to comprehend her/his studies appropriate to his/her age and is failing to qualify examinations is mentally disabled. Mentally retarded and insane persons would be treated as mentally disabled. A mentally disabled person may generally depend on his/her family members for performing daily routine. It is left to the respondent to report whether the member of the household is mentally disabled and no tests are required to be applied to judge the disability.
Multiple disabilities:	If a person suffered from two or more types of disabilities, only one of them would be recorded. In such cases, it would be left to the respondent to decide about the type of disability to be recorded.

According to the 2001 Census, there were a total of 21.91 million disabled persons (of the five types mentioned above) out of a total population of 1028 million. The prevalence rate of disability was, thus, 2.13 per cent of the total population, a significant improvement over the past censuses, but still well below Helander's estimate of 10 per cent for the world as a whole and still lower than the rates for USA (18 per cent) and UK (12 per cent). Break-up of the 21.91 million disabled by type of disability is shown in Table 2.2.

Table 2.2: Number of Disabled Persons by Type of Disability (2001)

Type of disability	*No. of disabled persons*	*Percentage to total disabled*	*Percentage to total population (Prevalence Rate)*
1. In Seeing	106,34,881	48.55	1.03
2. In Speech	16,408,68	7.49	0.16
3. In Hearing	12,617,22	5.76	0.12
4. In Movement	61,054,77	27.87	0.59
5. Mental	22,638,21	10.33	0.22
Total	219,06,769	100.00	2.13

Source: Census of India, 2001

Thus, about half of the enumerated disabled persons had disability in seeing and a little over one-fourth had disability in movement. The prevalence rates were about 1 per cent for visual disability and 0.6 per cent for movement disability.

Thus, according to the 2001 Census, in every population of 10,000, on an average, there were 213 disabled persons—103 persons per with disabilities in seeing, 16 with disabilities in speech, 12 with disabilities in hearing, 59 with disabilities in movement and 22 with mental disabilities.

Table 2.3: Number of Disabled Persons by Type of Disability and Sex (2001)

Type of Disability	*No. of Disabled Persons*			*Percentage to Total Population (Prevalence Rate)*		
	Male	*Female*	*Persons*	*Male*	*Female*	*Persons*
1. In Seeing	57,32,338	49,02,543	106,34,881	1.08	0.99	1.03
2. In Speech	9,42,095	6,98,773	16,408,68	0.18	0.14	0.16
3. In Hearing	6,73,797	5,87.925	12,617,22	0.13	0.12	0.12
4. In Movement	39,02,752	22,02,725	61,054,77	0.73	0.44	0.59
5. Mental	13,54,653	9,09,168	22,638,21	0.25	0.18	0.22
Total	126,05,635	93,01,134	219,06,769	2.37	1.87	2.13

Source: Census of India, 2001

The prevalence rates for females were lower than for males in all types of disabilities (Table 2.3). This could be due to relatively higher non-reporting of disabilities in the case of females. Similarly, the prevalence of disabilities was lower in the urban areas Table 2.4), probably due to better awareness of and facilities for corrective action, in all types of disabilities, with the sole exception of mental disabilities.

From the point of view of education, persons with disabilities in the age group below20 years would be important. Table 2.5 shows the distribution of the disabled persons by type of disability and age group.

Table 2.4: Number of Disabled Persons by Type of Disability and Residence (2001)

Type of Disability	*No. of Disabled Persons*			*Percentage to Total Population (Prevalence Rate)*		
	Rural	*Urban*	*All*	*Rural*	*Urban*	*All*
1. In Seeing	78,73,383	27,61,498	106,34,881	1.06	0.97	1.03
2. In Speech	12,43,854	3,97,014	16,408,68	0.17	0.14	0.16
3. In Hearing	10,22,816	2,38,906	12,617,22	0.14	0.84	0.12
4. In Movement	46,54,552	14,50,925	61,054,77	0.63	0.51	0.59
5. Mental	15,93,777	6,70,044	22,638,21	0.21	0.23	0.22
Total	163,88,382	55,18,387	219,06,769	2.21	1.93	2.13

Source: Census of India, 2001

Table 2.5: Number of Disabled Persons by Type of Disability and Sex (2001)

Type of Disability	*Number of Disabled Persons in the Age Group (years)*					
	0 -4	*5-9*	*10-19*	*20-29*	*30 and above*	*All*
1. In Seeing	8,31,408	9,86,168	17,87,977	14,55,363	55,73,965	106,34,881
2. In Speech	35,851	2,57,201	4,82,509	2,88,415	5,76,892	16,40,868
3. In Hearing	23,723	80,024	1,86,705	1,14,433	8,56,837	12,61,722
4. In Movement	2,34,199	5,44,088	14,85,654	9,70,700	28,70,836	61,05,477
5. Mental	74,691	1,89,562	5,32,436	4,42,138	10,24,994	22,63,821
Total	11,99,872	20,57,043	44,75,281	32,71,049	109,03,524	219,06,769
Percentage in each age-group	5.48	9.39	20.43	14.93	49.77	100.00

Source: Census of India, 2001

About half of all disabled persons were below 30 years in age – one tenth in the age group 5 to 9 and one fifth in the age group 10 to 19, both important from the point of view of education of the disabled.

(b) *National Sample Survey*

The National Sample Survey Organisation (NSSO) conducts sample surveys on various socio-economic subjects on a regular basis through their annual Rounds. Even though data on disabled population had been collected by the NSSO in the past years also, the first comprehensive survey on the subject was conducted in their 36th Round (July-December 1981), then again in its 47th Round (July-December 1991) and most recently in its 58th Round (July-December 2002). The first two surveys (1981 and 1991) covered only physical disabilities, while the latest survey (2002) covered mental disabilities as well. The categories of disabilities covered are

1. Mental Disabilities
   (a) Mental retardation
   (b) Mental illness
2. Physical Disabilities
   (a) Visual Disabilities
      (i) Blindness
      (ii) Low vision
   (b) Hearing Disability
   (c) Speech Disability
   (d) Locomotor Disability

The NSSO adopted its own operational definitions of various types of disabilities. These definitions are shown in Box 2.2.

While in the 2001 Population Census, a person with multiple disabilities was counted only once in the type of disability the respondent decided, the NSS survey counted him in each of the types of disabilities.

In the 2002 survey, it was found that about 8.4 per cent of the households in the rural areas and 6.1 per cent of those in the urban areas reported to have at least one disabled person. The number of disabled persons (having any disability, counting each disabled person only once) was estimated at 18.49 million during July – December 2002. This formed 1.8 per cent of the total population. There were 14.09 million disabled persons in rural areas and 4.40 million in the urban areas. There were 10.89 million men and 7.60 million women amongthe disabled. Table 2.6 compares the NSS data with those obtained from the 2001 Census.

Thus, the estimates based on data from NSS survey for 2002 were lower, in all categories (male, female, rural and urban), than the corresponding figures counted at the 2001 Census. The differences could have arisen due to a variety of reasons, definitional, operational and inaccuracies in reporting. While one cannot be too sure about the exact number, these figures are good enough for purposes of policy formulation. Both sets of figures, which indicate a prevalence rate of the order of 2 per cent, are, however, disputed as too low. For instance, The National Centre for Promotion of Employment for Disabled People (NCPEDP), an NGO, argues that the percentage of disabled persons in the population is 5 to 6 and the number would accordingly be 60 to 70 million.

Box 2.2: Definition of Disabilities Adopted by NSSO

Disability: A person with restrictions or lack of abilities to perform an activity in the manner or within the range considered normal for a human being was treated as having disability. It excluded illness/injury of recent origin (morbidity) resulting into temporary loss of ability to see, hear, speak or move.

Mental disability: Persons who had difficulty in understanding routine instructions, who could not carry out their activities like others of similar age or exhibited behaviours like talking to self, laughing / crying, staring, violence, fear and suspicion without reason were considered as mentally disabled. The "activities like others of similar age" included activities of communication (speech), self-care (cleaning of teeth, wearing clothes, taking bath, taking food, personal hygiene, etc.), home living (doing some household chores) and social skills.

Visual disability: By visual disability, it was meant, loss or lack of ability to execute tasks requiring adequate visual acuity. For the survey, visually disabled included (a) those who did not have any light perception - both eyes taken together and (b) those who had light perception but could not correctly count fingers of hand (with spectacles/contact lenses if he/she used spectacles/contact lenses) from a distance of 3 metres (or 10 feet) in good day light with both eyes open. Night blindness was not considered as visual disability.

Hearing disability: This referred to persons' inability to hear properly. Hearing disability was judged taking into consideration the disability of the better ear. In other words, if one ear of a person was normal and the other ear had total hearing loss, then the person was judged as normal in hearing for the purpose of the survey. Hearing disability was judged without taking into consideration the use of hearing aids (i.e., the position for the person when hearing aid was not used). Persons with hearing disability might be having different degrees of disability, such as profound, severe or moderate. A person was treated as having 'profound' hearing disability if he/she could not hear at all or could only hear loud sounds, such as, thunder or understands only gestures. A person was treated as having 'severe' hearing disability if he/she could hear only shouted words or could hear only if the speaker was sitting in the front. A person was treated as having 'moderate' hearing disability if his/her disability was neither profound nor severe. Such a person would usually ask to repeat the words spoken by the speaker or would like to see the face of the speaker while he/she spoke or would feel difficulty in conducting conversations.

Speech disability: This referred to persons' inability to speak properly. Speech of a person was judged to be disordered if the person's speech was not understood by the listener. Persons with speech disability included those who could not speak, spoke only with limited words or those with loss of voice. It also included those whose speech was not understood due to defects in speech, such as stammering, nasal voice, hoarse voice and discordant voice and articulation defects, etc.

Locomotor disability: A person with—(a) loss or lack of normal ability to execute distinctive activities associated with the movement of self and objects from place to place and (b) physical deformities, other than those involving the hand or leg or both, regardless of whether the same caused loss or lack of normal movement of body—was considered as disabled with locomotor disability. Thus, persons having locomotor disability included those with (a) loss or absence or inactivity of whole or part of hand or leg or both due to amputation, paralysis, deformity or dysfunction of joints which affected his/her "normal ability to move self or objects" and (b) those with physical deformities in the body (other than limbs), such as, hunch back, deformed spine, etc. Dwarfs and persons with stiff neck of permanent nature who generally did not have difficulty in the normal movement of body and limbs was also treated as disabled.

Table 2.6: Number of Disabled Persons from

Area	Census (March 2001)			NSS (July – December 2002)		
	Males	Females	Persons	Males	Females	Persons
Rural	9,410.2	6,978.2	16,388.4	8,310.2	5,774.8	14,085.0
Urban	3,195.4	2,322.9	5,518.4	2,581.1	1,824.9	4,406.0
Total	12,605.6	9,301.1	21,906.8	10,891.3	7,599.7	18,491.0

Source: 2001 Census and NSS Report No. 485

Classification of the number of the disabled persons estimated from NSS survey showed that about 0.99 million were mentally retarded and 1.10 million were suffering from various forms of mental illnesses, making up a total of 2.09 million persons with mental disabilities. Of the estimated 2.82 million with visual disabilities, 2.01 million were blind and 0.81 million had low vision. About 3.06 million had hearing disabilities, 2.15 million had speech problems and 10.63 million had locomotor disabilities (Table 2.7).

Table 2.7: Estimated Number of Disabled Persons by Type of Disability

Type of disability	Males	Females	Persons
Any disability**	10,891.3	7,599.7	18,491.0
Mental disability	1,290.3	805.4	2,095.7
(a) Mental retardation	625.8	368.9	994.7
(b) Mental illness	664.5	436.5	1,101.0
Visual disability	1,298.0	1,528.7	2,826.7
(a) Blindness	928.7	1,084.7	2,013.4
(b) Low vision	369.3	444.0	813.3
Hearing disability	1,613.3	1,448.4	3,061.7
Speech disability	1,291.1	863.4	2,154.5
Locomotor disability	6,633.9	4,000.1	10,634.0

Source: NSSO Report No. 485

The prevalence rates of disability, according to NSS survey were 1.8 per cent for any type of disability, 2.0 per cent among males and 1.5 per cent among females. As in the Census, it was found that the prevalence rates were lower for females than for males and in the urban areas in comparison to rural areas. The prevalence rates were around 0.5 per cent for the age group 0 – 4 in both rural and urban areas. They, however, rise to vary between 1 to 2 per cent up to the age of 50 and then increase significantly, attaining the highest level for the age-group 60 and above (Table 2.8).

Table 2.8: Prevalence Rates (No. of Persons with any Disability per 100 population) by Age-Group

Age –Group (Years)	*Prevalence Rates*	
	Rural areas	*Urban areas*
0 - 4	0.52	0.49
5 - 9	1.17	1.02
10 - 14	1.55	1.32
15 - 19	1.75	1.34
20 - 24	1.63	1.24
25 - 29	1.49	1.00
30 - 34	1.45	1.05
35 - 39	1.44	1.14
40 - 44	1.59	1.31
45 - 49	1.91	1.48
50 - 54	2.28	1.86
55 - 59	3.02	2.57
45 – 59	2.31	1.86
60 and above	6.40	5.51

Source: NSSO Report No. 485

A comparison of the 2002 survey data with those from the earlier surveys in 1981 and 1991 does not indicate any definite trends in the prevalence rates (Table 2.9). It must, however, be noted that the comparability of the latest survey with the two previous surveys is affected by the facts that mental disability was not covered in the latter and certain age restrictions for the hearing and speech disability imposed in the earlier surveys were removed in the latest survey.

Table 2.9: Changes in Prevalence Rates of Disability (1981 to 2002)

Residence/sex	*36th Round (July – Dec. 1981)*	*47th Round (July – Dec. 1991)*	*58th Round (July – Dec. 2002)*
Rural Males	2.04	2.28	2.12
Rural Females	1.63	1.69	1.56
Rural Persons	1.84	2.00	1.85
Urban Males	1.53	1.77	1.67
Urban Females	1.30	1.35	1.31
Urban Persons	1.42	1.58	1.50

Source: NSSO Report No. 485

Certain other important results given by the NSS survey of 2002 are:

- The prevalence rates of disability are the highest for Orissa being over 2.5 per cent. In Kerala too, the rate exceeds 2.0 per cent. At the other extreme, Assam had the lowest prevalence rate at 1.0 per cent.
- About 13.3 per cent of the disabled cannot take self-care even with aid/appliances, 17.2 per cent can take self-care only with aid/appliances, 60.3 per cent can take self-care without aid/appliance and 9.0 per cent either had no access to aid/appliance or did not try one.
- About 55 pr cent of the disabled persons were illiterate, 25 per cent had education up to primary level, 11 per cent up to middle level, while 9 per cent continued up to or beyond the secondary level.
- Only 1.5 per cent of the disabled in the rural areas and 3.5 per cent of those in the urban areas completed a vocational course, about 70 to 80 per cent of them in non-engineering trades.
- The enrolment ratio for the disabled in the age group 5 to 18 years in a normal school was 475 per 1000 in the rural areas and 444 per 1000 in the urban areas. The ratio was, thus, better in the rural areas.
- About 11 per cent of the disabled in the age-group 5 to 18 years were enrolled in special schools in the urban areas. The corresponding percentage for the rural areas was less than 1.

Incidence of Disability

In contrast to the prevalence rate of disability which indicates the position as on a particular date, incidence rate throws light on the number of persons acquiring disability, either at birth or subsequently, in a specific time interval, usually a year. While the Census does not provide data on incidence of disability, the NSS surveys do. The incidence rate is measured with reference to the 365 days preceding the survey.

According to the 2002 survey, the rate of incidence of any disability was 69 per 100,000 population. It implies that each year, 69 persons in every 100,000 population were either born with a disability or become disabled each year.

As in the case of prevalence rates, the incidence rates were also lower for females than for males. They were also lower in urban areas than in rural areas. Among the States, Andhra Pradesh had the highest incidence rate of any disability between 100 to 120 per 100,000 population. Kerala had the second highest rate at about the same level as Andhra Pradesh.

As in the case of prevalence rates, Assam had the lowest incidence rate for any disability at less than 20 per 100,000 population.

Table 2.10: Rates of Incidence of Disabilities (No. per 100,000)

Type of Disability	*No. of Persons becoming Disabled during 365 days Preceding Survey*								
	Rural Areas			*Urban Areas*			*All Areas*		
	Male	*Female*	*Persons*	*Male*	*Female*	*Persons*	*Male*	*Female*	*Persons*
Mental retardation	1	0	1	1	1	1	1	1	1
Mental illness	4	2	3	4	3	4	4	2	3
Blindness	7	11	9	4	7	6	7	10	8
Low vision	3	5	4	3	3	3	3	5	4
Hearing disability	9	7	8	8	6	7	8	6	7
Speech Disability	3	2	3	4	2	3	3	2	3
Locomotor disability	58	40	49	60	43	52	58	41	54
Any disability	77	61	69	75	58	67	76	60	69

Source: NSSO Report No. 485.

State wise population of disabled by types of disability has been given in Annexure I of the book.

3

Children with Mental Retardation

The American Association on Mental Retardation defines Mental Retardation as referring to "substantial limitations in present functioning. It is characterized by significantly sub average intellectual functioning, existing concurrently with related limitation in two or more of the following applicable adaptive skill areas: communication, self-care, home living, social skills, community use, self-direction, health and safety, functional academics, leisure, and work." (1992)

Page (1976) defined the concept, as "Mental deficiency is a condition of sub-normal mental development, present at birth or early childhood and characterized mainly by limited intelligence and social inadequacy".

Fox and Gregory say "Mental retardation refers to a chronic condition present from birth or early childhood which is characterized by both impaired intellectual functioning as measured by standardized tests and impaired adaptation to the daily demands of the individual's social environment."

Dunn (1970) defined mentally retarded persons as "who are so deficient in general intellectual ability that their inability to care for themselves, coupled with their disruptive behaviour in some cases, is so severe when, compared with their age mates in the community, that they require assistance, care and protection in excess of that which average parents can be expected to provide during their childhood or that which average communities should be able to provide during their adulthood."

American Association of Mental Deficiency (1973) stated mental retardation as:

> "significantly sub average general intellectual functioning, concurrently with deficits in adaptive behaviour and manifested during the developmental period."

Reddy (1983) described a mentally disabled as a "person who lacks general alertness, initiative, creative attitude, sentiments and ideas.

Furthermore, he looks slow in development as compared to others in the same age and experience difficulties in undertaking his responsibilities unlike normal person."

The American Psychiatric Association (1968) defined mental retardation as "subnormal general intellectual functioning, which originates during the developmental period and is associated with impairment of either learning and social adjustment or maturation or both".

The above definitions show that:

1. Level of functioning gets limited in mentally retarded children.
2. Mentally retarded children have lower levels of intelligence
3. It affects one or more areas of functioning
4. It affects social behaviours
5. Mental Retardation manifests itself in early childhood
6. Mental Retardation is measurable
7. Adoption to various skills is difficult in mentally retarded children.

National Sample Survey Organisation has estimated that 3 per cent of the total Indian population is mentally retarded which comes to around 20 million.

Categories of Mental Retardation

There are four categories of mentally retarded—profoundly retarded, severely retarded, trainable and educable retarded. Profoundly retarded children have very low levels of intelligence and may suffer from more than one handicap. Such children need support of special institutions. Severely retarded category children also have very low levels of intelligence and constantly require supervision or care in special homes. The trainable retarded children can be trained to take care of themselves in routine and repetitive jobs. However, they have difficulty in reading or doing mathematics. Some such children have some other special ability like that of singing. They are capable of performing some activities in sheltered workshops such as candle making, sorting jobs etc. Special training facilities are required for such children.

The educable mentally retarded children are those children who are borderline cases so far as intelligence levels are concerned. The physical appearance of these children is generally normal. These are termed as mildly retarded children. They require special programmes and extra classes to handle school curriculum. They are generally aggressive and need special and individual attention. They can learn to do simple routine jobs and study up to a certain level. Some of these children are very good in languages, physical activities, making craft items etc. Categories of mental retardation according to intelligence level have been specified as under:

Categories	IQ levels
1. Profound mental retardation	below 20
2. Severe mental retardation	20-34
3. Moderate mental retardation	35-49
4. Mild mental retardation	50-69
5. Borderline deficiency	70-79

How to Identify Mentally Retarded

Some indications of mentally retarded children are as follows:

1. Cannot remember things
2. Start walking and speaking later than the normal children
3. Show excessive aggression
4. Find it difficult to solve mathematical problems
5. Incoherent speech
6. Make sounds that do not convey any thing
7. Not conscious of their behaviour
8. Learning is very slow
9. Show tantrums, are impulsive
10. Dependent on others for doing routine tasks
11. Show difficulty in finding similarities and discrimination in things. Also lack analytical ability.
12. Academic achievement is poor
13. Some mentally retarded children may have physical deformities. They are unable to perform certain physical acts such as functions involving motor coordination.
14. Children with severe mental retardation have very limited or no mobility, they are unable to pick up things. Their language skills are poor and they find it difficult to maintain personal hygiene or doing routine daily works such as drinking, eating etc.

The Assessment

Initially, the behaviour of the child, his growth, learning pace etc. should be observed. As soon as some abnormal behaviour in the child is observed, he should be taken for a physical and mental check up. There is a stigma attached with the Mental Retardation and, therefore, parents do not want to disclose the problems of the child. There are cases where such children are kept in confinement, which is not proper. Early assessment and diagnosis can help the child to get adequate training. Assessing the range of his retardation, training programmes can be formulated to make him self-dependent or provide him institutional help wherever necessary. Intelligence is measured through psychological tests, which are available. A trained psychologist who can administer and interpret the results of the test logically should do such assessment. To identify specific potential in the child various other tests can be used. Various hospitals in the country have facilities for assessing the degree of mental retardation. Some of the intelligence tests used are Stanford Binet Test, Draw – A – Man test, projective tests like CAT. For seeing the damage to the brain, child should be taken to a medical doctor

Causes of Mental Retardation

There are several hereditary and socio-economic causes that lead to mental retardation:

1. *Genetic Factors*

'Mental retardation tends to run in families' Coleman, 1976. There are genetic chromosomal defects that are associated with mental retardation. These defects may cause the retardation from moderate to severe degrees. Down's syndrome is also because of chromosomal defects.

2. *Infections and Pollutants*

If the fetus of the pregnant mother has virus diseases, it may lead to retardation in the off spring. Toxic and other pollutants may also cause brain damage in the child. Typhoid vaccine, various drugs taken by the mother during pregnancy, alcoholism, etc., all may cause damage in the brain of the child. Incompatibility in the blood types between mother and fetus i.e. Rh or ABO system incompatibility should also be diagnosed as it also relates to mental retardation in the child.

3. *Injuries*

Kennedy, 1963 and Rothchild, 1967 reviewed research studies and found that pre-mature births are linked with high incidence of neurological problems and mental retardation is also associated with it. Accidents during the delivery, lack of oxygen to the child and other complications during pregnancy may damage the brain of the child.

4. Radiation

Too much exposure to x-rays can be harmful. It has been found that radiation damages sex cells and other body tissues. It affects badly on fertilized ovum leading to defective off springs. Parents may be exposed to radioactive material which can also harm the offspring.

5. Malnutrition

Protein deficiencies and lack of proper nutrition can result in physical and mental damage of the child. Specifically lack of protein diet for the mother and child has been found to be directly related to lowered intelligence.

6. Socio-Cultural deprivation

Earlier it was believed that mental retardation occurs due to genetic or brain problems. Of recent it has come to light that lack of stimulation of the brain due to socio cultural deprivation also results in mental retardation. This deprivation is due to poverty, illiteracy and lack of opportunities of interaction with others. The environment that does not provide adequate intellectual stimulation can cause mental retardation. Tarjan and Eisenberg, 1972 described this phenomenon in the following manner:

> "They are raised in homes with absent fathers and with physically or emotionally unavailable mothers. During infancy they are not exposed to the same quality and quantity of tactile and kinesthetic stimulations as other children. Often they are left unattended in a crib or on the floor of the dwelling. Although there are noises, odors, and colors in the environment, the stimuli are not as organized as those found in middle-class and upper-class environments. For example, the number of words they hear is limited, with sentences brief and most commands carrying a negative connotation."

A report by the American Psychological Association (1970) reported that

> "Mental retardation is primarily a psycho-social and psycho-educational problem – a deficit in adaptation to the demands and expectations of society evidenced by the individual's relative difficulty in learning, problem solving, adapting to new situations, and abstract thinking."

Generally socio-cultural deprivation results in mild forms of mental retardation.

Preventive Measures

Proper self-care, adequate health facilities and maintaining good health can be preventive measures for mental retardation.Due to illiteracy in the country people are not aware of the causes of mental retardation specially in rural areas. Health facilities also do not reach to each and everyone. Some of the precautions that are necessary to prevent mental retardation are as follows:

(i) *Precaution during Pregnancy*

Proper care should be taken during pregnancy time. Good and healthy food, prevention from injuries during pregnancy, avoidance of smoking and drinking alcohol, medication as per Doctor's advice should be followed to prevent the birth of a mentally retarded child.

(ii) *Marriages and Birth of the Child at Right Age*

These days especially in urban areas individuals prefer to marry at a later age. After the age of 35, the birth of a child is very risky and the child born may suffer from mental retardation. Children should be born before the age of 35.

(iii) *Regular Health Checkups*

A regular health check up of the pregnant mother is essential. It is also necessary for the woman who is planning to have a child. Supplements like multi-vitamins, calcium etc. should be provided as per need. In India observing fasts is very common among females. Women should ensure that they get adequate nutritional food to give birth to a health child. Proper nutrition is necessary for healthy mental and physical growth of the child. Frequent abortions also make a woman weak.

(iv) *Delivery by Trained Person*

In developing countries, in many cases delivery of the child takes place at home by untrained persons, which can cause problems. Safe delivery by a trained Doctor can prevent cases of mental retardation.

(v) *Discouraging Marriages among Close Relatives*

Marriages among close relatives result in health problems of the offspring including mental retardation. These marriages are known as consanguineous marriages. In many societies and tribal areas such marriages are very common and traditional. People are not aware of its consequences. Such practices should be discouraged.

Disorders relating to Mental Retardation

1. *Down's Syndrome*

This is also known as 'mongolism' as persons with Down syndrome have almond shaped slanting eyes. Langdon Down explained the term in 1986, therefore it is known as Down's syndrome. This syndrome has life long implications for physical appearance, intellectual achievement and general functioning (Golden and Davi's 1974). This syndrome is because of chromosomal disorders associated with mental retardation.

2. *Phenylketonuria (PKU)*

It is a metabolic disorder in which children look normal at birth but are unable to have an enzyme needed to break down phenylalanine. This is found in protein as amino acid. This condition leads to brain damage. The symptoms like vomiting, a peculiar odor, seizures & infantile eczema, appear during 6 to 12 months after the birth of the child. If the disease remains unidentified it can lead to severe mental retardation.

3. *Cretinism*

This disorder takes place due to imbalance of endocrine gland. Cretinism is because of thyroid deficiency resulting in brain damage. This thyroid deficiency comes due to lack of iodine but sometimes it may occur due to injuries during the birth or some other diseases like measles, diphtheria etc. In such cases one has dwarf like body, bent legs and a curvature of spine. Head is large and skin is dry. Thought process is sluggish in such cases. Early detection can help.

4. *No. 18 Trisomy Syndrome*

It is because of Autosomal anomaly of chromosome 18. Person suffering from it has malformed ears, flexion of fingers and also heart defects.

5. *Niemann-Pick's Disease*

This is because of disorder of lipoid metabolism in which loss of weight takes place and paralysis can occur gradually

6. *Turner's Syndrome*

It is due to sex chromosome anomaly. It causes webbing of neck, increased carrying angle of forearm and sexual infantilism.

Helping the Mentally Retarded

The borderline retarded children can be taught to manage their daily routine activities and also to pursue academics up to a certain level. These children should be provided some vocational training along with the educational syllabus. This vocational training should involve repetitive work. Such children should be treated with care and concern. Sometimes a mentally retarded child acts in such a way that is not considered normal. He may make different poses or may be aggressive without any valid reason. Other students generally laugh at such activities. The teacher has to organize community awareness programmes so that others may know about the status of the child and could deal with him with empathetic attitude.

Teaching for mentally retarded has to be extremely gentle. Such children take a long time in learning an activity. Specific and continued training with patience may be helpful. The concept of gentle teaching has emerged from the Psychology of Interdependence. The concept of Psychology of Interdependence is based on the assumption that each individual wishes to have a feeling of companionship, which can modify the individual's behaviours in the desired direction.

The parents and other family members have to play an important role in the development of a retarded child. Most of the times, parents scold the child for not learning or behaving in the desired manner. Counselor should help the parents in understanding the needs of the child. Parents may take professional or institutional help on a life long basis in cases of high degree of retardation.

The syllabus has to be adapted according to the needs of the child in the school. For example, generally, the retarded child is unable to do mathematical problems. Extra tutorials may also be arranged in the school so that the needs of the children could be met.

Educating the Mentally Retarded

As discussed earlier, there are various categories of mental retardation. Some borderline children can manage themselves and their daily routine activities while other mentally retarded children need help in doing the daily life activities. With special and specific education and training, independence up to a certain extent can be developed. A plan of action for educating the mentally retarded should include the following:

1. *Motor Development*

In many cases mentally retarded children are unable to control their motor development. While standing or walking, they may frequently fall. As Woods (1975) stated that these children find difficulty in controlling their head, sitting or walking. To train such children in balancing their movements, help of physiotherapist is required. In case the physiotherapist is not available in the school, child may be referred to the clinic. Parents of such children should also be trained to supervise the child's movement. In case of hyperactive retarded child, safety precautions are also needed. While sitting on a chair, the child may fall down and injure himself.

2. *Language Development*

The mentally retarded child may be slow in speech development or learning language than other children. Some children only make sounds and are not able to speak. In other cases speech may not be clear and understandable. Special efforts are required to develop speaking ability in such children. There are speech therapist or speech therapy clinics, which can provide help. Parents and teachers both should put efforts in developing language skills in the child. One word at a time should be pronounced with clarity and child should be encouraged to repeat it. Practice is needed in such cases. New word should be taught only when the child learns the one word.

3. *Daily Activities*

Extensive training is needed in teaching the child doing his daily routine tasks. Schools can make a plan on how to train the mentally retarded children. Children should be encouraged to do their activities. These should be taught one by one dividing a job into various small tasks. Children should perform under strict supervision. Amount of supervision should be decreased when a child learns an activity. Training in taking bath, maintaining hygiene, toiletry training, eating, holding things all should be taught gradually. A lot of patience is required. Parents also need training in such cases. Severely mentally retarded children need constant supervision. Those who do not develop speech at all or have multiple disabilities are trained to communicate through eye – movement or finger movement.

Piaget a well-known psychologist provided certain activities that may serve as guidelines in training the mentally retarded children. Some of these suggestions, which can help teachers and parents in dealing with mentally retarded child, are as under:

(a) Touch the child with your own fingers and play with your own and the child's fingers. Hide fingers and hands;

(b) Flash a torch, focusing in different directions and see if the eyes of the child follow the light. Play with it alternately hiding and showing the torch;

(c) Play with hand gestures;
(d) Bulge out your face and burst your lips and let the child feel them;
(e) Use a handkerchief and perform various activities with it;
(f) Suspend toys, which make noise when touched, in front of the child's eyes when the child is lying down;
(g) Hang toys near the feet of the child so that the child has to try to stretch out to touch them;
(h) Hang a toy which makes noise and tie a handkerchief at the same time on to a piece of string, within the child's reach;
(i) Hang ribbons of various colours;
(j) Play with sounds made in front of, behind and at the side of the child at varying distances;
(k) Comb your hair, put on cream, lipstick, etc. closely in front of the child;
(l) Sing daily and keep a record of songs;
(m) Carry or wheel the child to several different positions in the room on any one day;
(n) Play with a pan and lid;
(o) Give the child different objects, like paper, card board, cloth and plastic toys, to handle;
(p) Tap different objects with a stick in front of the child, behind him, near him and far away from him;
(q) Place small objects on the child's palm and play by giving the objects and taking them if the child lets them go;
(r) Hang brightly coloured material on a string and blow at them using a tube or fan;
(s) Place a mirror in front of the child;
(t) Play holding games with a pencil or a stick.

4. *Behaviour Management*

Mentally retarded children need to be trained in managing their behaviours. These children often are aggressive and impulsive. They threaten other people. They may also physically abuse others. Some of them are very talkative. Their talks may not have much meaning in it. They can throw things and can be destructive. Behaviour interventions are needed. These can be done introducing role models, showing pictures, encouraging good behaviour, interactions, organizing group activities, diverting the attention of the child, giving responsibility etc. Teacher has to show confidence in the child. When the retarded child is kept busy in some or the other activity, his aggressiveness reduces.

5. *Dealing with Difficulties*

Retarded children learn at a slow pace. They find it difficult to learn abstract and complex concepts. The subjects that need abstract ability are difficult for mentally retarded. Basic academic skills can be developed. It has been found that poor learning in case of mentally retarded children is because of their diverted attention to unimportant aspects of learning. Child has to be taught on which aspect of learning he has to concentrate. Another difficulty in dealing with mentally retarded is non-awareness of their entering behaviour. In a class if the teacher believes that everybody can communicate verbally or has writing skills, the retarded child who is yet to develop such skills would lag behind than other normal children. The retarded child compares his achievements with other normal children and when he finds that he has not achieved as others are doing, he develops a feeling that ' he cannot do'. He becomes withdrawn. A special plan of teaching the mentally retarded is needed to deal with their specific difficulties.

6. *Teaching of Subjects*

Operant conditioning technique can be used to develop skills in mentally retarded. Social behaviour, personal behaviour, occupational skills, academic skills can be developed in mentally retarded children by dividing each skill into simple components. Skills must be functional and related to real life situations. Step by step progress must be reinforced. A favourable atmosphere at home can do wonders for such children. Repetition of each task is important in their case.

How to divide skills into specific tasks – Example.

Skill development—child eats independently

Activities: (1) Use of Spoon

(2) Use of Napkin

(3) Eating in socially approved manner

Tasks for Activity (1)—Use of Spoon

→ selection of spoon

→ holding it in hand

→ Taking food in spoon

→ Take spoon to the mouth

→ Take spoon out and pick up more food

Instructions and Functional Strategy

Place various spoons before the child and ask to select the appropriate one. Tell him how to hold it, take food and eat.

Above instructions should be given one by one. First stage is that child learns to take appropriate spoon for eating various items. Once he practices it, at second stage he should be taught how to hold it. Next stage would be taking food in the spoon, lastly eating habits.

For teaching the child above instructions, teacher should demonstrate, or show a film, child can personally be helped by correcting his tasks if he is not performing well. Encouragement should be given when the child performs well.

For Activity two and three, tasks can be identified like use of Napkin would involve taking out the napkin from the Box, wipe out the face and cleaning of hand. Similarly eating in socially approved manner would involve good eating habits like drinking without noise, taking small bites, eating with closed mouth, no spilling of food around, behaviour with others during eating.

Demonstrations and practice are helpful in skill development of the child. Later he can be taken out for eating for further refinement of learning.

4

Children with Hearing and Speech Impairment

As is evident from the name, children with hearing and speech impairment cannot hear or have difficulty in hearing and communicating through verbal language. Various scholars have defined the hearing impairment in the following terms.

> "Deafness means a hearing impairment that is so severe that the child is impaired in processing linguistic information through hearing, with or without amplification, that adversely affects a child's educational performance" (Individuals with Disabilities Education Act, 1990, of United States of America).
>
> Moores (1987) differentiates between 'deafness and 'hard of hearing'- " A deaf person is one whose hearing is disabled to an extent (usually 70 db or greater) that precludes the understanding of speech through the ear alone, without or with the use of a hearing aid. A hard of hearing person is one whose hearing is disabled to an extent (usually 35 to 69 db) that makes difficult but does not preclude, the understanding of speech through the ear alone, without or with a hearing aid."

A person with normal hearing can hear the sounds ranging from a very low frequency of 60 Hz to about 16,000 Hz. The hearing impaired child is not able to hear any of these sounds in this range. The hard of hearing children according to Alice Streng "are those with reduced hearing although defective, is functional with or without a hearing aid." In medical terms, hearing disability has been defined in terms of the degree of loss of hearing or defect in the ear. The medical model categorises the hearing disabled children as below:

Table: Medical Model Categorises the Hearing Disabled Children

Sl. No.	Category	Level of hearing loss (decibels)	Needs
1.	Mild	20-30 db	Hearing equipment
2.	Marginal	30-40 db	Hearing and speech therapy
3.	Moderate	40-60db	Adaptation of instruction with better visual instructions
4.	Severe	60-75 db	Use of special methods
5.	Profound	75 and above	Intensive special methods for teaching.

Thus, it is evident from the above that deaf children are those who can not listen even with the help of auditory apparatus.

Causes of Hearing Disability

There can be hereditary or environmental factors that cause deafness or other hearing malfunctioning. A child may be born deaf by birth due to some disorder in the ear. Ear has various parts containing outer ear, middle ear, inner ear and eustachian tube. These parts contain membrane, eardrum, canals, nerves etc. which all collectively work to listen to sounds. When somebody speaks vibrations are created in the air, the air touches the outer ear and these waves are passed through the other parts of the ear to brain, which understands the sounds. Any damage in any part of the ear at birth can cause deafness.

Hearing problem may also occur due to some illness after birth—like infections in the ear, unhygienic conditions of the ear, severe and prolonged colds, sinus, measles, mumps, loud continued noises, jaundice etc.

Any accidents a child may meet with during play or travel may result in hearing difficulties or total loss of hearing.

The causes of hearing disability can be summarized in the following chart.

Genetic causes are also termed as 'endogenous' causes while causes relating to injury etc. are known as 'extrogenous'.

Hearing Disability, Speech and learning

Hearing and speech has a direct correlation. A child develops speech through observing and hearing other people talking. If a child is deaf by birth and has never heard any sound, he may not develop verbal communication. He has to adopt alternative methods of communication like sign language. But as discussed earlier, some children may develop hearing disorders at a later stage than at birth. If by that time, they have picked up the verbal communication they

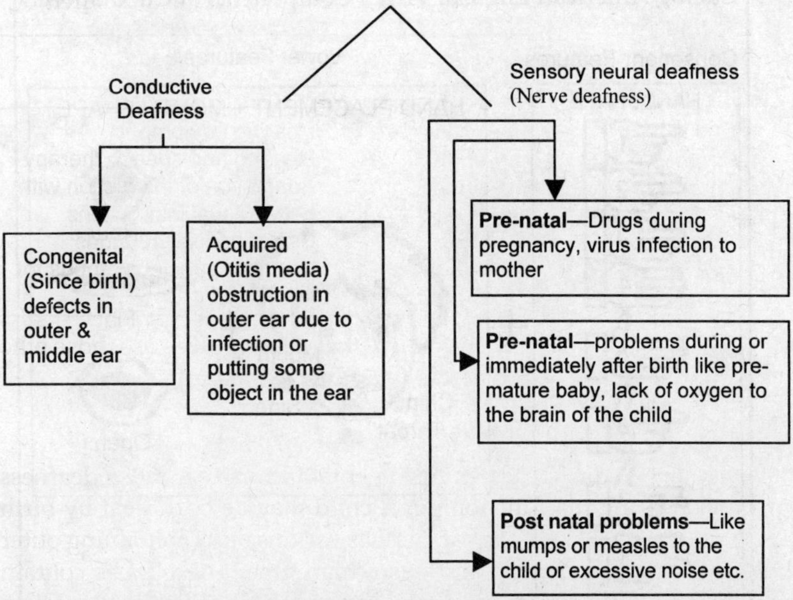

can speak well. The children who are not totally deaf can hear with the help of hearing aids. The totally deaf can be taught to read lip movements to understand the language and can respond through speech. The deaf children are, thus, of two types—pre-language deaf (those who become deaf before learning a language) and post-language deaf (those who become deaf after learning a language).

Various methods have been developed for deaf children so that they can be taught to pick up language. Some of these are:

Cued Speech

Cued Speech is a sound-based visual communication system, which uses eight hand shapes in four different locations (cues) in combination with the natural mouth movements of speech. These cues were developed for English language by Dr. R. Orin Cornett and Professor Emeritus of Audiology of Gallaudet University, USA, in 1966. It has now been adapted into 59 languages and dialects.

The visual components of the Cued Speech System include:

- eight (8) hand shapes to distinguish consonant features
- four (4) hand placements combined with
- three (3) mouth shapes to distinguish the vowel features of American English

Cueing American English: Visual Components of Cued Speech

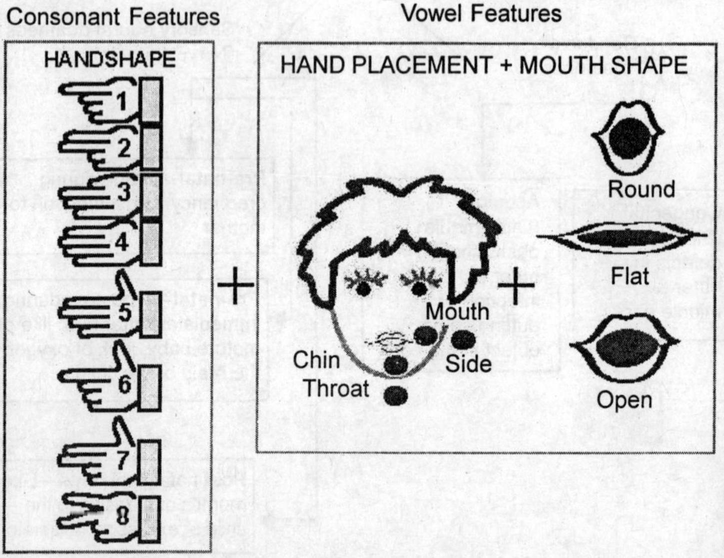

Cued speech has quite a number of benefits. It can be learned in a relatively short period of time. It takes about three to twelve months of consistent cueing to achieve fluency.

Sign Language

A Sign Language is a language, which uses manual communication instead of sound to convey meaning- simultaneously combining hand shapes, orientation and movement of the hands, arms or body, and facial expressions.

When people using different sign languages meet, communication is significantly easier than in the case of people who speak different languages. It is believed that Sign language in this respect gives international access to deaf community.

But sign language is not universal. Wherever communities of deaf people exist, sign languages develop naturally, but as with spoken languages, these vary from region to region. They are not based on the spoken language in the country of origin; in fact their complex spatial grammars are markedly different. However, various signed "modes" of spoken languages have been developed, such as *Signed English* and *Walpiri Sign Language*. Hundreds of sign languages are in use around

The Fingerspelled Alphabet

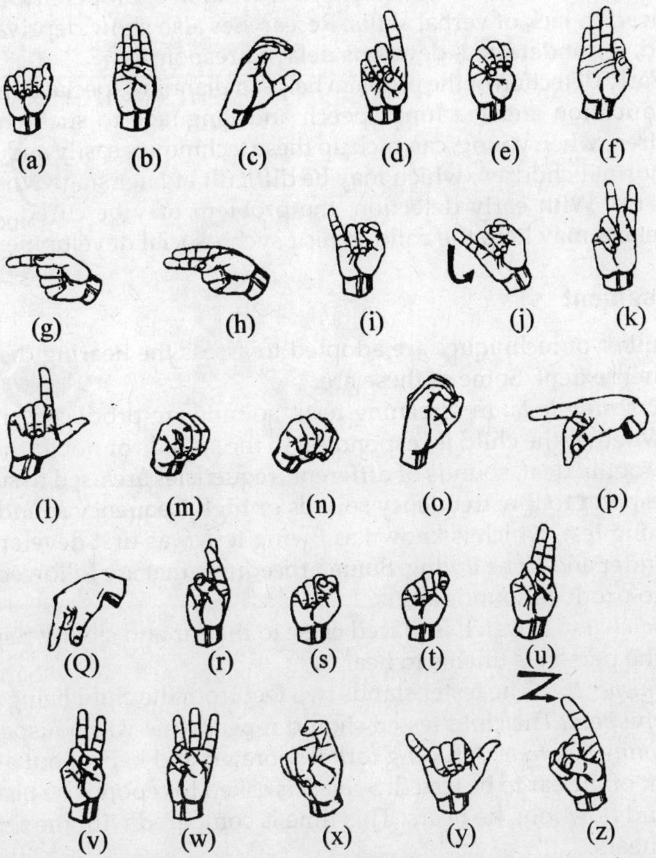

the world and are at the core of local deaf cultures. Some sign languages have obtained some form of legal recognition, while others have no status at all.

Lip-reading is another method but it is said to be of limited help because it is estimated that lip-reading is only to an extent of as little as 30 per cent of what is said, while the rest of the communication is guessed.

Early Detection

Early detection of the problem is necessary. When a child's problems are ignored as, for example, when a child is not performing well in the class, it is routinely thought that he is not concentrating well, or is not attentive, or has no interest in studies or is retarded, the problems may increase in due course. In such situations, the child develops a sense of guilt and self-insufficiency. Deprivation of proper hearing may also lead to lack of verbal skills. Researches also show deprivation of sound, if not detected, develops delayed responses.

Early detection of the problem helps in planning special techniques for education and teaching speech and language to such children. Children, when young, can pick up these techniques easily and behave like normal children, which may be difficult at later stage when they grow up. With early detection, the problem may be cured, and its awareness may help the child in his psycho-social development.

Assessment

A number of techniques are adopted to assess the hearing disorders and their extent. Some of these are:

Screening tests: In screening tests, sounds are produced and it is seen whether the child is responding to the sounds or not. If the child is not totally deaf, sounds of different frequencies are used to see if he can respond to low frequency sounds or high frequency sounds. The screening test, which is known as Ewing test, was first developed by Alexander and Irene Ewing. Some procedures that are followed these days to produce sounds are:

Watch test: A watch is placed close to the ear and slowly removed until the person is unable to hear it.

Whisper test: The tester stands two feet from the child being tested and whispers. The child tested should repeat what was whispered.

Tuning fork tests: A tuning fork is vibrated and kept about an inch in front of the ear to be tested. Subject is asked to report if he hears the tone and how long he hears. This time is compared with the time the tester hears.

Sound instrument test: The child is seated at a table on which an appropriate toy has been placed. The toy should be a simple one like rings on a peg or carom coins in a cup. The child should be playfully engaged in putting the rings on the peg or carom coins or marbles in a cup. The examiner then produces a sound with one of the instruments (bell, drum, whistle or rattle). The production of the sound is not visible to the child. The child must not be deeply engrossed in the play itself. The primary response given by the child consists of a cessation of the play activity or he momentarily ceases his play and assumes an attitude of searching awareness. For mentally retarded child it is important to select an instrument that is familiar to him. Unusually long duration of sound stimulus is necessary for such children because it is difficult for them to shift from their foreground visual sensations.

The sound toy test: The toys, which are used, include a squeaking doll, quacking duck, xylophone, ringing telephone etc. If the child responds to these sound toys, it suggests that the child lack of speech is not due to deafness. It may also suggest that with the amount of hearing he has got, his speech could be developed. To see the responses to sound toys, one procedure is to simply present the toy to the child and encourage him to play with it. As he plays with it and sound occurs, his response (surprise, immobilization, amusement or apprehension) is noted. This test is applicable even to very young children. If two toys are identical except that one produces a sound and another does not, the child might respond to the absence of sound in the toy also.

The voice tests: Simple voice tests are applicable to many children in various ways For example, as the child is engaged mildly in a playful activity, the examiner hums at a low intensity. Normal children listen to voice at about two months of age. This test does not require child's active cooperation. Voice tests can also be used to elicit imitative responses from the child. Initially the child is permitted to see the face of the examiner and after some training period sounds are given alternately without visual clues. This could be done at varying intensities and distances from the child. This test has been useful with children who are mentally retarded. Normal children imitate vocalizations of adults beginning at approximately nine months of age.

Various other instruments are available in modern days that can measure the degree of hearing loss. These are known as audiometric techniques. If any problem is observed in the child relating to hearing and speech development, a doctor should be contacted immediately.

Identification of Hearing Impaired (Characteristics)

- High pitched tone
- Distorted sounds
- Excessive nasality
- Lack of comprehension
- Same pattern of voice
- Problems in making sentences or understanding concepts
- Abnormal emotional behaviour
- Aloofness and withdrawal symptoms, specially when the child is not disabled at birth.
- May not be able to follow directions
- Stammering
- Tilts head consistently to get better sound
- Avoids talking to other children

- Speaks louder than required
- Watches the speaker to understand what he is saying
- Blank facial expressions
- Deformity of the ear or discharge from the ear
- Ear aches, headaches or dizziness
- Noise in the ear or head.

Educating the Hearing Disabled

Special educational plans are needed to educate the hearing disabled child according to the degree of deafness and speech disability. If the child is hard of hearing, special aids and appliances can be used to correct his problem and education can be more or less similar as is for normal children with certain precautions. But if the child is totally deaf and dumb different kind of educational planning would be necessary. There are special schools for deaf and dumb and for partially deaf children where they are taught to have communication through sign language or lip movement. Their integration in the normal schools requires special teacher who is trained in dealing such children, a resource room where facilities required for hearing impaired children are available.

Language development and speech development are two basic tasks, which require attention in case of hearing disability. In such cases emphasis should be more on visual learning than hearing. Hearing disabled children require visual stimulus to learn about the world which is possible by taking them outside to various places like museums, art galleries, exhibitions, markets, places of historical importance, cultural places, etc. Speech therapist should accompany these children to help them in learning. Louis Fond (1963) indicated the method to develop language and concept development:

(i) *Reception*: Most of the information to the child should be given to brain using other senses than vision.

(ii) *Symbols*: Words, signs, gestures are used in receiving the information.

(iii) *Encoding*: Symbols are arranged in such a way that these convey the meaning

(iv) *Transmission*: Encoded information is transmitted to others.

(v) *Decoding*: Sent message is decoded to understand the information.

Several techniques are used for hearing disabled children to pick up language. Various sounds are produced to stimulate the child's auditory sense. In case the child is not responding hearing aids are used.

This technique is known as 'oralism' or 'auditory stimulation'. Another form of this technique is using multi-sensory approach. In this technique sounds are produced and other senses are also stimulated through use of touch or providing visual stimulation. Mildered Groht, 1985 and Hart 1964 discussed another technique of oral stimulation. In this technique teachers are required to introduce such activities which demand talking on the part of the child. Activities should be such that children could ask various questions and their curiosity is generated. For example they may be taken to a Zoo. Children may be stimulated to talk about the animals.

This is to be understood that hearing disabled children require individual attention and multi-faceted approach. This would include providing signals, showing pictures & objects, body and facial gestures, tactual symbols, auditory stimulation, lip movement, sign language, outside visits, stimulation of brain through generating curiosity and Braille language teaching in case of deaf-dumb-blind child.

While teaching the hearing disabled in the normal class, there may be a need for the interpreter. Teacher should face the student while talking. Small sentences should be spoken with clarity. Students should sit in the front benches so that they could see the teacher speaking. While writing on the chalk- board, the teacher should not speak. Cause and effect relationship of the concepts can be taught through demonstration or asking the children 'Do it yourself'. New word should be used on several occasions and in various situations so that the disabled child could memorise it and could understand the meaning and usage of the word. Hearing disabled children should be taught simple language without using many prepositions, phrases or idioms.

Glossary of terms used in Speech Pathology and Audiology

Audiogram : A record of the test of a person's hearing showing graphically the level of hearing at each frequency.

Audiometer : An instrument used in the measurement of hearing levels in decibels.

Auditory feedback : Hearing one's own speech.

Auditoryperception : Listening or mental perception of sound.

Auditory memory span : The number of related or unrelated items that can be recalled immediately after hearing them presented.

Auditory training : A method applied to a hearing impaired

	child or adult, which has the purpose of teaching him to use more effectively his remaining hearing ability with or without a hearing aid.
Decibel (db)	: A unit for measuring hearing levels
Deaf	: Individual whose hearing is nonfunctional for communication purposes with or without a hearing aid. As distinct from the 'deaf', all those individuals with some amount of hearing loss are called Hard of Hearing. Hearing aids are beneficial for Hard of Hearing.
Hearing aid	: A device which amplifies sounds—useful for persons with hearing loss.

5

Children with Visual Impairments

Visually impaired children may be of various types. They can be totally blind, partially sighted or colour blind. In the category of totally blind are those children who are not able to see anything, while partially sighted children require special arrangements for vision. Colour-blind children are those who cannot differentiate various colours.

Blindness may occur in some children by birth while in others it may be caused due to some accident. In some children it may develop as they grow.

Blindness in legal terms has been defined as the vision of the child in the better eye, after correction is 20/200 or worse than this. A person does not come under the category of blind if the one eye has 20/200 or worse and the other eye has better than 20/200. A person is not visually impaired if he can do his normal work after using glasses. This means that a legally blind individual would have to stand 20 feet from an object to see it with the same degree of clarity as a normally sighted person could from 200 feet. In many areas, people with average acuity who nonetheless have a visual field of less than 20 degrees (the norm being 180 degrees) are also classified as being legally blind.

In educational terms, a child is designated as visually impaired if he cannot read through sight and is required to use Braille system or any other system to read. Partially sighted children, can read the normal books, but have sight problems up to the extent that requires special arrangements for instructions e.g. writing in big print etc.

Approximately ten percent of those deemed legally blind, by any measure, are fully sightless. The rest have some vision, from light perception alone to relatively good acuity. Those who are not legally blind, but nonetheless have serious visual impairments, possess low vision. According to the 10th Revision of the WHO, International Standard Classification of Diseases, Injuries and Causes of Death, low vision is defined as visual acuity of less than 6/18, but equal to or better than 3/60, or corresponding visual field loss to less than 20 degrees, in the better eye with best possible correction.

Causes of Blindness

Most visual impairment is caused by disease. According to WHO, the most common causes of blindness around the world are:

- *Cataracts*: Loss of transparency of the lens of the eye.
- *Glaucoma*: Glaucoma is a group of diseases of the optic nerve involving loss of retinal ganglion cells in a characteristic pattern of optic neuropathy. The pink rim of disc contains nerve fibers. The white cup is a pit with no nerve fibers. As glaucoma advances, the cup enlarges until it occupies most of the disc area.
- *Age-related Macular Degeneration*: Macular degeneration is a medical condition where the light sensing cells in the macula malfunction and over time cease to work.
- *Trachoma*: The bacteria Chlamydia Trachomatis cause an eye disease, which may result in blindness. Derived from the ancient Greek, "Trachoma" means "rough eye." Ulceration and consequent scarring of the cornea cause the blindness.
- *Corneal*: The cornea is the curved, transparent layer that covers the front part of the eye and protects its inner structures. Together with the lens, the cornea refracts light and consequently helps the eye to focus. If this does not work adequately, it may cause blindness.
- *Diabetic Retinopathy*: Diabetic retinopathy is damage to the retina caused by complications of diabetes, which could eventually lead to blindness.
- *Anophthalmia*: In this, the eyes do not develop. When the eyeballs are small it hinders sight, the problem is then termed as Microphthalmia.
- *Aniridia*: In this disease, Iris is not developed, which results in rapid movement of the eyeball.

It has also been seen that in a large number of cases, the incidence of blindness is due to heredity and genetic disorders. Visual impairments also occur due to developmental disorders if proper care is not taken at initial stages. Sometimes, some other general health related problems such as typhoid, measles etc. may result in visual impairment. Injuries in the eyes, burns, accidents may also cause visual inadequacies.

Children in poorer communities are more likely to be affected by blinding diseases than are their more affluent peers, as, because of poverty, they are not able to get proper treatment. Sometimes the access to treatment is also difficult in remote areas.

Of the estimated 40 million blind people located around the world, 70–80 per cent can have some or all of their sight restored through treatment.

How to Identify a Visually Impaired Child

Children with visual impairment may be identified from the following:

1. Having watery eyes
2. Rubbing eyes frequently
3. Reddening of eyes frequently
4. Covering one eye and tilting the head forward
5. Holding objects and books close to the eyes
6. Asking help from others when taking notes from the blackboard
7. Blinking frequently—Squinting eyelids together
8. Complaining about headache and closes eyes frequently
9. Bumping into people or objects
10. Skipping words or lines while reading or tries to guess words
11. Having poor eye-hand coordination
12. Moving head forward and backward while looking at distant objects
13. Watching T.V. from a very close distance
14. Difficulty in reading small print
15. Complaint of tiredness after reading one Para or page
16. Sensitivity to light
17. Confuses between alphabets such as c and e, g and q etc.

The above characteristics may be identified by observing the child. Children with total blindness are easy to detect as they will not have any sight and would find difficulty in movement or responding to the directions. Partially blind children can be identified through observation of the above characteristics. Whenever one or more than one characteristic is observed, the child needs to be taken for the medical examination. Early detection may help the child in getting appropriate corrective measures.

Colour Blindness

As said earlier, colour blindness is a condition in which a child is unable to differentiate between certain colours. The most common cause of colour blindness is hereditary (genetic) photoreceptor disorders, but it can also be acquired due to damage to the retina, optic nerve, or higher brain areas. For example, it is possible to acquire colour blindness only in a portion of the visual field but maintain normal color vision elsewhere. Some forms of acquired colour blindness are reversible. Transient colour blindness also occurs (very rarely) in the aura of some migraine.

The different kinds of color blindness result from one or more of the different cone systems either not functioning at all, or functioning in an unusual way. The most frequent form of human color blindness results from problems with either the middle or long wavelength sensitive cone systems, and involve difficulties in discriminating reds, yellows, and greens from one another. They are collectively referred to as 'red-green color blindness'. Other forms of colour blindness are rare. They include problems in discriminating blues from yellows, and the rarest forms of all, complete color blindness or monochromacy, where one cannot distinguish any color from grey.

How to Diagnose Colour Blindness

Colour blindness is most often tested using the *Ishihara color test*, which consists of a series of pictures of coloured spots. A figure (usually a number) is embedded in the picture as a number of spots in a slightly different colour, and can be seen with normal colour vision, but not with a particular colour defect. The full set of tests has a variety of figure/background colour combinations, and enable diagnosis of which particular visual defect is present.

However, the *Ishihara color test* is criticized for containing only numbers and thus not being useful for young children. It is often stated that it is important to identify these problems as soon as possible and explain them to the children to prevent possible problems and psychological traumas. For this reason, alternative colour vision tests were developed using only symbols (square, circle, pictures like that of a car).

Prevention and Remedies for Visual Impairment

Preventive and remedial measures can be adopted if the child is identified early as having some problem. Some of the measures can be as follows:

1. *Balanced Diet:* Malnutrition, particularly deficiency of Vitamin A, is one of the causes of sight problems. Even if a mother is suffering from malnutrition, the child can have visual defects. A balanced diet is necessary.
2. *Prevention of Injuries:* Some injuries can be caused in a natural manner while playing or moving. Some precautions are

necessary to prevent injuries. For example, children should be kept away from the place of fire, electric switches etc. While working in laboratories they should be provided adequate safety devices such as sunglasses, welding helmets etc.

3. *Treatment:* After identification of the problem of the child, he should get immediate treatment. It can prevent further complications.
4. *Exercise:* If the problem is identified at initial stage, exercise can help in preventing aggravation of the disease or even eradication of it. A trained doctor can prescribe various exercises according to the problem of the vision. It has been seen that exercises can help in getting back normal vision, if the problem is detected at early stage.

Other techniques that are used for vision improvement are surgery, use of glasses, grafting of eyes. Precautions include taking proper care of the eyes such as cleaning with water, reading in adequate light with proper seating arrangement etc.

Tools Helpful for Visually Impaired

A number of tools and techniques have been developed for visually impaired. Some of these are as under:

Stick for Mobility

People with serious visual impairments can travel independently using a white cane. It is an international symbol of blindness through which others know that a blind person is moving. A long cane is used to identify obstacles in the path.

Guide dogs

Some blind people employ guide dogs. These companion dogs are trained to lead blind individuals to their places. Though highly intelligent, guide dogs neither interpret street signs nor determine when the person should cross a street. Visually impaired people who employ these animals must already be competent travelers.

Reading and Magnification Equipments

Visually impaired people read print, through the use of magnification devices. A variety of magnifying glasses are available which can make reading easier for those with decreased visual acuity.

The totally blind persons read through Braille and Moon type or rely on talking books and readers. They use computers with special hardware such as scanners and refreshable Braille displays as well as software written specifically for the blind, like optical character recognition applications and screen reading software.

Closed-Circuit Televisions, equipment that enlarge and contract textual items, are more high-tech alternatives to traditional magnification devices. So too are modern web browsers, which can increase the size of text on some web pages through browser controls or through user-controlled style sheets.

Computers

Access technology, such as Freedom Scientific's JAWS for Windows screen reading software, enables the blind to use mainstream computer applications.

Experimental approaches such as seeing with sound project are beginning to provide access to arbitrary live views from a camera.

Braille Keyboard

Braille Key Boards are available to help blind persons. Picture Braille software enables the user to create pictures in Braille format using a simple drawing programme. The user can draw free hand using the mouse supplied. Braille Key Boards can work with most IBM-compatible computers.

Speaqualizer

A hardware attachment for some IBM PCs and compatibles, which enables the user to hear data being displayed on the video monitor.

Braille Printer

Braille printers do the actual embossing of Braille onto paper. The first step in converting computer files into a Braille document is to choose the type of Braille. Grade I Braille consists of letters, numbers and punctuation marks while grade II Braille includes contractions of common combinations of letters and words. To print Grade 2, a Braille translation programme must be used to take the computer file, insert the contractions, and format the document for the Braille page.

Braille Translator

Blind or visually impaired people who read Braille can use the specialized equipment to get the print in Braille. Braille translators are available in hardware and software.

Low Vision Projection Screen

This low vision projection system allows inspection of images, which can be magnified up to 720X. A video camera is used with closed circuit television or CCD camera and monitor.

Other aids

People may use talking thermometers, enlarged or marked oven dials, talking watches, talking clocks, talking scales, talking calculators, talking compasses and other talking equipment. Devices have been adapted to make life for blinds comfortable. Adaption of banknotes is one such example.

Dealing with Children with Visual Impairment

Role of the School and the Teachers

1. Children with visual impairment may be seated in the front rows so that they can read the books and writing on the blackboard without any difficulty or pressure.
2. Books with bold letters may be provided to such children.
3. Radio and T.V. broadcasts may be arranged
4. Efforts may be made to procure cassettes in different curricular areas. State Institutes of Education or State Councils of Educational Research and Training or District Institutes of Education and Training or Centres or Institutes of Educational Technology may be approached for this purpose.
5. Blind children need Braille script books.
6. School doctor may be consulted from time to time.
7. Cooperation of the parents should be sought in the follow-up work.
8. Use verbal communication along with the writings or indicating towards an object, picture or sign.
9. See that the visually impaired child is adjusted with his vision aid/equipment.
11. The visually impaired children should be made familiar in the classroom, the furniture in the class and other equipments placed in the classroom. They should also be made familiar of the school premises. A school map indicating the various places may be given to the blind students in Braille language or a replica may be prepared for them so that they could be familiar with the school environment and move freely.
12. Their chairs and desks should not be changed frequently. The places of other equipments should also be fixed.
13. The sitting arrangement should be such that they can enter easily and go out without much hindrance.

14. For partially sighted children, adequate illumination in the classroom is extremely important. Proper lighting should be available and they should be kept away from the rear of the sunlight.

Education for the Visually Impaired

A number of models have been tried to educate the visually impaired. For partially sighted children a special class was tried in the normal school where the teacher could handle all the partially sighted children. This method was tried in Boston initially but, as it was observed that these children remain aloof from the other school children, was gradually abandoned. Another model, which was tried, was named as Cooperative Plan. Under this plan, children had to study in the regular normal class with other children but wherever a closed eye activity was involved they had to go to a special class.

In America an Itinerant Teacher plan was initiated, under which an Itinerant Teacher visits various schools to distribute special equipments and material to help all the visually impaired children and look after their adjustment in the normal school. Under this plan the children study along with the other children.

Another plan, which was tried, had been the resource room plan. In this plan also the children remain in the normal school but go to a resource room for choosing the special material required for education. In case of need some special teaching is arranged in this resource room.

Usually for blind children, going to school implies admission to a residential school for the blind (Braille classes). Of late some attempts have been made to integrate them with the normal children by admitting them to normal schools but the coverage of blind population of the students in this respect is not significant. A blind school aims at assisting the blind child, through the use of special methods and aids in his adjustment to the world in which he has to live as an adult. But such arrangements keep these children aloof and they are unable to enter the main stream.

Schools for the blind usually provide for activities such as dancing, scouting, and dramatics. Special equipment and methods of teaching are employed for the education of the blind. Particular attention is given to practice on typewriter because it permits written communication with the seeing.

It is essential that an effective system of delivery of services is established in the normal schools to cater to the special needs of the visually disabled children. Availability of qualified and experienced teachers who have regular classroom experience and in addition are competent to adapt materials, teach Braille, use visual aids and technological devices and plan, develop, deliver, and monitor all aspects of schooling for those affected by visual impairment should be ensured.

It has been seen that many students can follow the curriculum with adaptation of learning resources or instructional methods. When necessary, however, the curriculum should be modified to reflect individual needs.

At the secondary level, school districts may develop and approve orientation and mobility programmes or Braille programmes for visually impaired students as locally developed. As mentioned earlier, most students with visual impairment require specialized equipment (e.g. Braille books, closed-circuit televisions, cassette recorders, optical aids etc.) and adapted learning resources (e.g., Braille texts, enlarged print books, tapes). The schools should be equipped with such facilities.

Pre-Requisites for Education of Visually Disabled

Education of the blind depends upon certain pre-requisites. Some of these are:

- Willingness on the part of the schools to admit blind students. The laws can be there but if the schools are not willing to take blind children in the school, normal interaction of such students with the school would not be possible even if they get admission in the school.
- After the willingness, it is necessary that the schools, which are ready to take blind students in the school, are equipped with necessary facilities. These facilities include availability of trained teachers so that they could deal with such students, necessary equipments and apparatus needed for blinds, architectural barriers free environment and other resources like Braille books etc.
- If blind students are admitted in a school with the normal children, orientation programme for teachers as well as normal children is needed to develop harmonious relationship among blind children and others. Peer group should not treat blind children as 'others' or 'aliens'. Normal children should be oriented towards the behaviours they must adopt. For example

instead of using the words like 'Can you see this' they have to practice saying 'can you feel this'. If children are taken to a garden, teachers instead of saying 'Flowers here are beautiful' can say 'come and touch the softness of flowers'.

- A transportation facility is another area where schools that are admitting blind students, must concentrate. These children would require transport for coming to school and going back home. This arrangement can be made either by school or a group of parents can hire a transport. In case there is a bus available for normal children, in the same bus blind children can come to school. But in such case some seats should be made available to these children in the front. The other children and attendant of the Bus should be oriented to help blind children in case of need.

In other words a climate has to be evolved in the school where blind children are accepted.

Teaching Plan

Education is to be imparted according to the specific needs of the individuals; therefore educational plans are to be prepared according to the needs of the individual or individuals (where problems are common). Educational plan for such children in general would include:

1. *Orientation*

Orientation and familiarity with the school environment and its structure is essential. Blind students should be taken to each area and place of the school such as classroom, principal's office, staff room, library, recreational place, resource room etc. Hazards in school (if any) should be explained and precautionary measures to be taken should be told. Such orientation would help the blinds in developing mobility skills and be independent.

2. *Use of Resource-room*

Blind children must be taught how to use resource room available in the school. They should be provided information about availability of the equipments in the resource room, where are these kept, how to take them and keep at a proper place after the use. It must be told to the students where Braille books, enhanced print material, CCTV etc. are being kept. These may either be in the resource room or in the library. Cataloging system of keeping these items must be explained. Schools should make arrangements to keep material/equipment useful for the blinds at such a place, which is easily accessible to them, may be near the classroom.

3. *Maintenance of Equipment and Material*

Children must be trained to maintain the equipment and material they use. For example if child is using specs, training should be given on how to keep it clean. Some children might be using contact lenses; they should be trained and supervised in maintaining the hygiene, cleaning lenses, washing of hands etc. Lack of such training may further cause problem to the children. While the older children can be trained easily, smaller children should constantly be supervised. Training in operation of other equipments like tape recorder, computers etc. is also necessary. Parents of the children coming from backward areas also may require training in maintenance of equipment their children are using. Eyes are the sensitive parts of the body. Cleanliness and hygiene are extremely necessary. Regular check ups should also be conducted to see improvements / deterioration.

4. *Safety Training*

Education of visually handicapped involves training in safety measures. Schools have various activities besides teaching theoretical topics. Teaching of theory is followed by practical work in laboratories. There are chemicals and other equipments that may hurt the blind students if they are not trained in observing safety rules. Instruction on using the equipments and other material should be written in Braille also. Verbal instructions should also be provided. For sometime, blind students should work in the laboratories under strict supervision of the instructor. Once they are use to and practice being safe, supervision can be reduced. Schools also have co-curricular activities. While all children should be encouraged to participate, safety training here also is necessary.

5. *Life Skill Training*

One important component of education is making a child self-dependent and be able to cope with problems. Such skills are to be developed in each and every child. Development of life skills are more essential in case of blind students because they suffer from low self-esteem and feeling of insecurity and neglect because of their handicap. Blind children may face more problems than the normal children in their daily living. They should be trained to meet their daily needs independently which includes movement in the house and outside, keeping the things at their place, locating the items of need, shopping, playing, finding out resources available for them, communication abilities, decision making, confidence building etc. Traffic rules, interaction with public, application of learned knowledge are areas in which these children require training.

6. *Social Skills*

Children have to develop as adults and responsible citizens of the society. Just because of some handicap they cannot be out casted from the community or be aloof and alone. Aim of the education is to develop social skills in the children to have proper interaction with others and develop harmonious relationships. Interaction with normal children can take place only if both understand the needs, strengths and weaknesses of each other. Awareness about handicap can give way to develop relations among normal and blind children. They should be helped to develop good manners and pleasant personality.

7. *Preventive Measures Skills*

Children with visual problems should be taught to take preventive measures so that their problems do not magnify. It can be observed that children watch T.V. from a very near distance, watch for long hours, read keeping the books near their eyes, do writing and reading without proper postures. Working on computers for long hours can also affect adversely specially to those children who already have eye-problem. Teacher should keep a watch on such activities and train the children to have proper posture and distance while reading, writing or watching T.V.

8. *Vocational Training*

Some visually handicapped children may go for higher studies while many of them may like to take up vocational streams after a certain level of education. Vocational training should be a part of school curriculum. It helps the children in knowing the world of work as well as being familiar with the skills that are required doing a job. Vocations should be identified which can easily be performed by visually impaired. Vocations, which require use of other sensory organs or body parts instead of vision, can be helpful and skills relating to these vocations may be the options to be given to blinds. They may choose from these options. Some of the areas are: work relating to music like composing, singing; writing poetry/ songs; doing work with hands like doing craft work, canning work, teaching etc.

9. *Education through Exploration*

Since blind children do not experience with sight, opportunities should be provided to them to explore and learn things by experience through other techniques. These can be taking out to these children to various places so that they could touch, feel, listen, and learn. Activities can include debates, ratio programmes, picnics, discussions, plays, visits to various places. These should be followed by verbal communication.

10. *Teaching of Subjects*

Teaching of various subjects to the blind and very low vision students requires extensive planning and patience on the part of the teacher. For teaching specific subjects, teachers have to use more verbal clues to give concepts and prepare objects that can be touched by children to have clarity of concepts. For example, teaching mathematics, the concepts of size and shape are unknown to blind students. Therefore, giving the concept of size and shape, teacher must use replicas of items, the child should touch the object of one size, it should be explained to him with verbal communication - the mathematical term used for a particular size or shape must be told. The objects can be various toys, counting beads, embossed diagrams etc. Objects should be so chosen which have a functional utility and children use them in their daily lives. It would make learning and remembering easy as and when they come across with that object, they will try to remember its mathematical term.

Geometry can be taught using embossed diagrams. For teaching history and geography embossed maps can be used. Models can teach historical development. A visit to museum can be arranged. Children can visit mountains, river belts, and ocean areas to explore the geographical concepts.

For teaching science subjects, multi-sensory approach should be followed. Senses of hearing, touch & feel, smell and taste should be used. Visits can be arranged to gardens, Zoological parks, Botanical garden to learn about various living beings etc. After such visits they should be encouraged to share their experiences and clear their doubts.

Computer technology has made revolution in facilitating teaching of the blind and low vision children. VISTA, ZOOMTEXT, LUNA etc. are softwares that can enlarge screens and low vision children can read easily. DECTALK, ECHO, SYNPHONIX etc. are voice synthesizers. ALVA, BRAILLEX, POWER BRAILLE are Braille displays of computers that are extremely helpful in the teaching blind and low vision children. Computers are very popular these days among children. Computer applications can be taught to blind students using Braille keyboard. Specially designed word processing computer programme for blinds is available. Facility of printing in Braille is also there which can help these children learning computers easily.

Computer is one such equipment, which brings children together very easily. Thus, it can facilitate mainstreaming of blinds.

It has been seen that visually handicapped children are endowed with certain other special abilities. These abilities can be their extra-ordinary creativity in composing poetry or music, singing, flair for arts & crafts like making models etc. These should be identified and developed. School should provide facilities to develop special skills in blind students. At initial stages in teaching music, different types of tones, pitch, the meaning of octaves, notes, differentiation of sounds, rhythms, etc. should be explained through demonstrations. Many blind children are gifted with excellent memory. The students who have a flair for composing songs or writing poetry or stories should be encouraged through explaining the rules of composition by citing various examples. Other students may help the blind child to note down the thoughts. Assistance can be provided to edit the written material so that the blind child could gradually develop his skills. Pottery making, model making etc. can also be taught as blind children can develop these skills through touch.

6

Orthopaedically Handicapped

Any person who has defects that cause physical deformity and as a consequence interfere with normal function of bones, muscles or joints is deemed orthopaedically handicapped. The impairment of physical capacity to perform normal function could have been caused by loss, deformity or paralysis of one or more limbs. The orthopaedically handicapped persons do not have complete control over their muscles and nerves. This lack of controls hinders their capacity to move about freely. They are unable to use their limbs in a manner most other people do.

Ministry of Social Welfare, GOI, has categorized orthopaedically handicapped as all these who have a condition which prevents them from having complete control of their muscles and the nerves which in turn control their ability to move about and use their limbs in a normal way.

Kurt Jonson defined the concept of Orthopaedic handicapped "in modern rehabilitation, a physical disability is considered to be an impairment of an anatomical nature, which may, or may not constitute a handicap.... A handicap is combined effect of physical, mental and environmental obstacles caused by the disability".

Samuel and Romaine stated—"The child may be considered handicapped, if his physical condition prevents full participation in childhood activities of a social, recreational, educational and vocational nature".

It can be observed from the above definitions that orthopaedic handicapped children have such a physical condition due to which they are not able to function normally in various activities, which other children can do. This may create further problems in seeking employment, having social acceptability or difficulty in getting along with others.

Causes

Orthopaedic impairments are caused by a variety of causes. Some anomalies like clubfoot are congenital. Diseases such as bone T.B. or

Poliomyelitis cause yet another type of orthopaedic handicaps. Fractures or burns cause contractures. Orthopaedic anomalies affect the individual in varying extents. While some impairments may be mild, others could be severe. In case of mild impairments, students may have just manageable difficulties in adjusting to general classrooms. Limb deficiencies could be present at birth or occur later in life. A person may be born with an entire limb or a part of the limb missing. An accident or illness may sometimes necessitate amputation, leaving the person orthopaedically impaired. Poliomyelitis is a disease caused by the poliovirus. The disease is, however, not so severe in incidence as it used to be in the early years of the preceding century. The polio vaccine developed in 1955 has the potential to virtually wipe off the disease. The vaccine can be taken orally and is more than 90 % effective.

Physical structure could also be adversely affected as a result of problems in the neurological system. Various body functions are coordinated by the nervous system. The system comprises the brain, the spinal chord and the peripheral nervous system. A variety of motor disorders surface if any of these parts is impaired.

Orthopaedic impairment may or may not be accompanied by mental retardation. This fact must not be lost sight of that orthopaedic-handicapped student with mental retardation need special education services.

Orthopedic disability includes a number of conditions of disabilities with a wide range of causes which in general can be divided in three basic categories:

1. *Hereditary factors*: Shape of the body is determined by genetic factors. Certain deformities are passed on from one generation to other. Some of such deformities are claw hand, spider hands, fused fingers, double joints, cleft palate etc. Dislocation of hip, clubfoot etc. is also caused by genetic factors. The chemicals in the atmosphere, nuclear explosions and other experiments also cause abnormalities in the child's physique.

2. *Congenital Defects*: These defects involve infections, malnourishment of the mother and the child, various diseases, doses of drugs etc. Congenital defects may cause missing bones, webbed fingers, cleft lip etc. Malnutrition, for example, can lead to defects in eyes and palate defects. Infections like rubella or German measles during pregnancy period can lead to microcephalia, hydrocephalia or cataract in the child.

3. *Defects after Birth*: After birth defects are acquired defects which can be due to various injuries, accidents, amputations due to diseases, defective postures or due to consequences of fights and

wars. Sometimes during the birth of the child improper use of forceps or anesthesia may cause deformities. Tuberculosis of bones or joints, sinus, certain fevers may result in physical disability. Polio is another disability, which is acquired after birth. Doing stunts for amusement is proving another important cause of physical deformity. Watching films or cartoons or advertisements where actors are shown flying or jumping or doing other extra-ordinary physical stunts effect the brain of the child. Children very easily identify themselves with such actors and try to imitate them. This causes permanent injuries or even death.

Artificial Limbs Manufacturing Corporation of India (ALIMCO) set up in 1972 and Jaipur Foot, Sawai Man Singh Hospital, Jaipur are helping the Orthopaedic handicapped in providing artificial limbs.

Disorders related to Orthopaedic Handicap

- *Cerebral plasy*: It is a group of neuro-muscular disorders resulting from damage to the brain and spinal chord before, during or after birth. Spastic cerebral plasy is most common. In its mild form it can be detected by careful neurological examination. Children with Athetold cerebral palsy suffer from involuntary movements like sharp jerks that impair voluntary movements. Ataxic cerebral palsy is rare. Its characteristics are under-active reflexes, muscle weakness, tremor and a wide gait as the affected person starts walking.
- *Muscular Dystrophy:* In this group of disorders the skeletal muscles progressively degenerate. About 50 per cent cases of muscular dystrophy relate to pseudo-hypertrophic type. In this disorder, the children are in the wheel chairs by the time they are teen-agers.
- *Autism*: It is a brain disorder, which affects communication, thought process and attention.

Guidelines to evaluate various disabilities and categorization of disabilities according to their degree has been detailed by Ministry of Social Justice and Empowerment which can be seen in Annexure III.

Effects of Orthopaedic Impairments

The disadvantage suffered by children with orthopaedic impairments is their inability to mix freely and independently in their peer group. A number of social and emotional behaviours are formed while young children interact with each other. Since social interaction is impeded, orthopaedically handicapped students are more prone to remain secluded. Their behaviour could be retarded in response to the expectations of those around them.

Prevention

In spite of long strides in scientific research, it has still not been possible to prevent congenital disabilities. However, man-made factors have also been responsible for causing orthopaedic disabilities. The two most important of these are (i) road accidents and (ii) injuries caused by agricultural implements. Both these are unfortunately negligent acts on the part of men and are preventable if greater caution is exercised. Road accidents are preventable only with the total involvement of the community, wherein the individuals realize the need for greater patience on the road, follow safety rules and have consideration of the safety and convenience of others. As for the agricultural implements, there is need for machines with safety arrangements and training in safety measures to the users of these implements.

Characteristics

Orthopaedically handicapped show the following characteristics:

- Inaccurate co-ordination of the limbs, which may affect mobility, posture & manual dexterity. This is the most visible and significant feature.
- Difficulty in perception and concentration where the impairment is neurological in character.
- Difficulty in verbal communication in case of muscular dystrophy and facial burns
- Limited ability in facial expressions in cases of cerebral palsy.
- Deformity in the child can be observed. This could be in arms, hands, legs, neck, waist etc.
- May suffer with pain in joints
- Amputated limbs

Measurement

The Government of India, Ministry of Welfare has given detailed guidelines for evaluation of various disabilities. These include measuring the disability in respect of locomotor functioning, strength of muscles, and coordination of activities.

Role of Teachers

The teachers of students with orthopaedic disabilities not only need to understand the special needs of such children but also communicate the same to all class members. For example, the student may need special assistance while eating or going to the toilet. The classroom and class work needs to be organized in a manner that these are accessible to the handicapped students. While the limitations should be recognized, expectations should be held high for all students.

How to Deal with Orthopaedic Children

The key to success in respect of orthopaedically challenged students is the same as for people with other kinds of disabilities. They have to be trained to be independent to the extent possible and the possibilities should not be underestimated. The learning environment has to be supportive and socialization has to be encouraged. Once sensitized, the peers would be more than willing to socialize with these children and this inherent capacity among normal children should be fully exploited to the advantage of the orthopaedically handicapped. A general strategy to encourage orthopaedically handicapped students is to bring to their attention lives of those who have overcome similar disabilities and succeeded in life and who can serve as role models.

Writing Aids

Students with orthopaedic impairments may need instruments like special pencil holders or slated boards that support their arms. While computers are helpful, keyboards may need modifications to suit the special needs of orthopaedically handicapped students.

7

Learning Disabilities

Children with learning disabilities are known as 'slow-learners'. Generally, the teachers consider these children as mentally retarded. But that is not a correct assumption. These slow learners are not necessarily mentally retarded children but suffer from some other problems. These problems could be due to difficulty in memorizing, writing, concentrating etc. Some Children may have difficulty in reading or they may lack motor coordination. Children with learning difficulty are to be identified. Generally these children have normal or sometimes even above average intelligence. Golick (1970) has classified learning disabilities in the following categories.

1. *Poor body awareness*: child cannot locate various body parts, difficulty in telling between right and left
2. *Poor ability to combine vision and movement*: poor eye-hand coordination.
3. *Visual inefficiency*: Even with normal vision, child may not be able to give selective vision
4. *Poor listening ability*: easily distracted towards noise.
5. *Poor integration of information from sensory channels*: child is not able to integrate the alphabets with their sounds.
6. *Poor grasp of sequence*: child is not able to remember the sequence of things like counting from 1 to 10, he will not count in order.
7. *Poor sense of rhythm*: difficulty in narrating a poem.
8. *Problems with concepts*: child has difficulty in identifying the similarities and variations in various objects. Poor concepts of time or number.
9. *Problems in learning*: like difficulty in arithmetic, remembering numbers or names, difficulty specially in memorizing
10. *Poor general knowledge*: child has difficulty in learning general information like home address, occupation of parents, names of friends, etc.

Learning disabilities have been defined as "a disorder in one or more of the basic psychological processes involved in understanding or in using language, spoken or written, that may manifest itself in imperfect ability to listen, think, speak, read, write, spell or to do mathematical calculations. The term includes such conditions as perceptual disabilities, brain injury, minimal brain dysfunction, dyslexia, and developmental aphasia. The term does not apply to children who have learning problems that are primarily the result of visual, hearing or motor disabilities, of mental retardation, of emotional disturbance, or of environmental, cultural, or economic disadvantage" (National Advisory Committee, USA,1969).

Kirk, S.A. states that "The term learning disability is not meant to be used for children with minor or temporary difficulties in learning but with a severe discrepancy between abilities and achievements in educational performance and such severe discrepancies described as learning difficulties with significant learning problems that cannot be explained by mental retardation, sensory impairment, emotional disturbance or lack of opportunity to learn."

The definitions show that:

1. Learning disabilities are not the same as mental retardation
2. It is due to some damage of the brain or dysfunction of the nervous system
3. Academic performance is not according to the intelligence of the child
4. The disability may show in the process of learning in one or more areas such as writing, speech, learning maths, or language, etc.

Causes of Learning Disabilities

Learning disabilities are due to constitutional disorder of the child's brain. These may also occur due to some accident or injury to the brain after birth.

How to Identify Learning Disabled

- School performance not up to mark.
- Cannot learn alphabets or remember names or numbers.
- Can read but cannot write.
- Poor hand writing.
- Can write but not good in verbal communication.
- Poor in solving mathematical problems.

- Difficulty in differentiating visual and or auditory perceptions
- Poor memory.
- Lack of perception of body image.
- Lack of eye-hand coordination.
- Difficulty in learning the concepts, symbols, abstract material etc.
- Good performance on intelligence tests but poor academic achievement.
- Lack of attention and social adjustment.
- Hyper-activity.

Assessment of Learning Disability

A child suffering from learning disability can be identified through the characteristics explained earlier. Parents and more importantly teachers can observe these characteristics when the child is not able to learn. At the smallest indication of learning disability, the child should be referred to the doctor and a psychologist. There are standardized psychological tests available, on the basis of which disabilities can be identified. Doctors can help in diagnosing the dysfunction of the brain.

Parents generally do not understand the concept of learning disability and, therefore, scold the child for not learning. They feel that the child is not paying attention to studies. In such cases a guidance worker should interact with the parents and explain the facts. Parental training programme can also be organized in the school on 'How to deal with learning-disabled child'.

Learning Disabilities and Attention Deficit Hyper-activity Disorder (ADHD)

A common disorder in the children with learning disabilities is prevalence of Attention-Deficit-Hyperactivity. Such children lack attention, are impulsive and hyper-active. They also have lower levels of self-esteem, a negative self-concept, mood instability and temper tantrums. Due to lack of attention they are slow learners and show poor academic performance.

Such children need their energies to be channelised in desired activities. They should be made to work in smaller groups. Such children in school should be given seats in the front and be given interesting activities to do. Such children get easily bored with a continued activity of the same nature, so variety should be introduced. Since they cannot concentrate for long, small tasks should be given. Instructions should be followed by visuals or activities that do not require continuous sitting.

How to Deal With Learning Disabled Children

As a first step, it is important to identify children with learning disability and to identify their specific problem. Some might be facing problems in reading or understanding, others in writing. Some children may have problem with solving mathematical problems. Apart from learning difficulties themselves, learning disabled children may face difficulty in having inter-personal relations or social interactions. There may be various categories of learning disabilities ranging from mild to extremely severe. Children with severe learning disabilities require intensive intervention, may need special schools or constant supervision or continuous tutorials. In the regular classroom, special tutorials with direct instructions would be helpful. Social skill training, use of equipment to overcome learning problems, practice in speaking and writing, and adapted curriculum should be provided. Behaviour management is another area which should be given due attention. Patience is required to deal with such students. They should be encouraged for appropriate behaviours. Simple assignments should be given and these students should not be punished because of their slow pace of learning. The special assistance should be reduced in a phased manner.

It may be mentioned that a person with learning disabilities in one area may be very successful in other areas.

Pre-Requisites to Educate Learning-Disabled Child

1. *Identification of disability*

One essential pre-requisite in educating a learning disabled child is to identify his disability. When the child scores on intelligence tests but does not perform accordingly, he is scolded thinking that he is not giving due attention to studies. Parents also have the same view and insist the child to study more and more. In such cases diagnosis of the problem is extremely important.

2. *Identification of specific problem*

When it is diagnosed that child is suffering from learning disability, his specific problem area must be identified. This may be learning language or writing or problems in solving mathematical questions. His writing may be illegible. He may not be able to sequence the concepts. He may have problem in speech or remembering dates or figures. Remedial measures can be taken only when problem area and specific problem of the child are identified.

Summary Table of Learning Disabilities

Category	*Conditions*	*Examples*
1. Visual Problems	Poor visual memory	Not remembering faces, words, people's names, reversals in writing (41 instead of 14)
	Poor visual perception	Difficulty in seeing the difference between similar objects (b and d)
	Figure ground discrimination	Inability to find the place to write one's name on an application form
	Poor visual tracking	In ability to follow a line on a page
2. Auditory Problems	Poor auditory memory	Difficulty in remembering what has been said, information or instructions
	Poor auditory discrimination	Difficulties in telling the difference between similar sounds, e.g. bee and pea or seventy and seventeen
	Poor auditory sequencing	Confusion with number sequence, lists or directions
	Poor auditory figure ground	Trouble hearing sounds over background noises
3. Motor Problems	Poor eye-hand coordination	Difficulties with handwriting
	Poor small muscle control	Misjudging where to place things
	Poor large muscle control	Clumsiness
4. Organisational Problems	Poor time management	Inability to be punctual, to meet deadlines
	Poor ability to organize tasks	Not understanding the steps required to carry out a task
	Poor ability to organize space	Inability to arrange things in a cupboard, a desk, arranging matter in a page
	Impairment of executive function	Unable to analyse things or apply information in a new situation
5. Conceptual Problems	Difficulty in interpreting non-verbal language	Facial expressions or body language
	Difficulty in understanding figures of speech	Idioms, metaphors, similes
	Difficulties in anticipating future	Doing things without assessing consequences
	Rigid thinking	Unable to be flexible in thinking
	Poor social skills and peer relations	Not maintaining eye contact during conversation, using inappropriate tone or language, lacking social graces

3. *Special educator*

To deal with learning disable child, there is a need to have a special educator who is aware of the learning problems and techniques to deal with them. Learning-disabled children require individual attention and therefore individual educational plan is needed. Learning disabled children can be integrated with the normal children but special educators should be there along with the normal school teacher in the class. Team teaching can be planned in such cases. In case, this is not economical remedial teaching after the normal class can be planned and provisions can be made for an itinerant teacher.

4. *Interaction with parents*

Parents should be made aware of the learning disabilities the child is facing so that they can be supportive and cooperative. They should also be trained in how to deal with the child. Like other disabilities like blindness or deafness, learning disabilities are not apparently visible. It is difficult to convince the parents that even after having good intelligence, child is unable to perform.

5. *Learning material*

Schools should have adequate teaching material where children can 'do themselves' instead of listening to instructions. Multi-sensory approach has to be used to educate learning-disabled child. Schools should be equipped with using such techniques.

Educating the Learning Disabled

Special techniques are to be used to educate the learning disabled depending upon their specific problems. In case a student is having the problems in mathematical ability, it should not be ignored and adaptation of the curriculum as well as various types of methods of teaching are to be used. The learning disabled students may have trouble in remembering the basic number facts. In stead of counting 3+2 = 5 or 6-3 = 3 or 2 x 3 = 6, through memory they try to count on fingers or through some objects like beads. They find it difficult to do the four basic operations of mathematics i.e. counting, subtraction, multiplication and division. In such cases instead of insisting upon that the child should do these operations mentally they should be allowed to keep beads or some other objects for this purpose or they can use small chart for conducting these operations so that they could move further along with the class. Intensive practice is required for disabled students to do mastery on the learning of concepts. Instead of giving long sessions, practice should be given for short duration sessions, for example, 10 to 15 minutes practice at one stretch instead of asking the child to practice half an hour or one hour. Emphasis should be given on simple and reverse operations, for example, 2+3 = 5 and 3+2 = 5. After practicing one operation, two operations at a time like 2+3 = 5, 2+4 = 6 should be taught. Some other disabled children easily understand the mathematical concepts but are weak in calculations. The curriculum involves the sequencing of steps which they may forget. This weakness of the students should be recognized. Sometimes only emphasis is given on calculations but in case the child is weak in calculations but otherwise has ability, his efforts should be given due importance and teacher should try to strengthen his weakness. A self-monitoring system can be developed or double check system should be taught to the child so that he could find out mistakes he is making in the calculations.

Some other learning disabled children lack visual -spatial – motor coordination or difficulty with the material that is depicted through pictures. They confuse in numbers, in signs and other symbols.Such students require very specific clear verbal instructions. Instead of presenting the concepts through pictures or diagrams or charts it is better to explain them verbally. The verbal instructions may follow the replicas of objects. For example they may be given a square and can count that a square has four lines. Sometimes it is difficult for the learning disabled children to apply their daily routine knowledge of mathematical ability to the methods which is in the syllabus of the school. In such cases, examples should be used with which a student comes across during his daily living. The models, the structures, etc. may be used with which the student is familiar.

The children suffering with speech problems or reading skills should be taught with patience and using multi-sensory techniques. To explain the words, material can be used, for example, to teach the child the names of the vegetables, the models of different vegetables may be brought to the classroom. Story telling is another method with which children identify themselves and can learn language. A small sentence or word speaking may be demonstrated and child should be asked to repeat the word or sentence. The researches also show that music helps in developing skills in language. Researches conducted in Stanford University have found that the people who listen music can differentiate miner differences in word syllables. It has also been found that musical training helps in efficient working up of the brain to process the language as there are rapidly changing sounds. Gabrieli said that the brain is plastic, adaptable and trainable.

The children who have writing disability or a poor handwriting should be helped in a number of ways. They should be taught the hand and finger exercises so that there muscles could be strengthened. Multiple materials should be provided to them to practice the writing. First of all they may be given some small beads and be asked to write alphabets or words using the beads. They can be given clay and be asked to prepare alphabets using the clay. Afterwards they may write using a board and chalk on which some lines may be made and child be taught to write using these lines as boundaries. The child should be taught how to hold a pen or pencil, how to keep the copy before him, the direction, etc. and should be helped in writing to practice the alphabets. Another method of helping can be that various alphabets can be kept in a box and child be asked to find out a specific alphabet, keep that alphabet on the copy and draw lines with the pen. As a second step he may keep this alphabet before him and try to write on the copy on his own. The child should not be asked to proceed further till he masters writing alphabet in the proper manner because once he moves further he may not be able to improve his handwriting or the mastery over the alphabets. He should be taught how much distance he should leave while writing another alphabet or word. Copy with lines may be used for developing good handwriting. Alphabets in various colours, material of different shapes should be used with learning-disabled children to motivate them and attract towards these materials.

Many disabled children lack abstract reasoning and thinking abilities. This reasoning can be developed through providing opportunities to these children to explore the world themselves. They may read a small story along with pictures in them and then small simple questions can be asked. First they can answer the question, seeing the pictures and in the next step pictures should be removed and children should be allowed to answer on their own. They may be provided with two pictures of similar kind with some variations and be asked to find out similarities and variations in the picture. To make it simpler the models of similar kind may be given with some variation. Other method can be to keep the things of similar nature in a box with one or two variations and asked them to sort out those things according to the similarity. For example, the models of fruits and vegetables be put together in a box and students may be asked to bifurcate fruits on one side and keep the vegetables on the other.

Some learning disabled children remain in their own world, try to draw some pictures on the paper or make stories on their own which may not have much meaning into it. Such children should be encouraged by asking what they have drawn on the copy or should be encouraged to make stories. Some small questions in between may be asked to give direction to their thought process.

Precautions for the Teachers

(*a*) *What a Teacher should do*

For behaviour modifications of disabled child, he should be observed in various situations to understand about his strengths and problems. These situations can be- interactions with other students, group activities, play, the class, the group discussions, etc. When the child shows the positive social behaviour it should be recognized and reinforced. This reinforcement can be through verbal or non-verbal communication. Verbal communication may include like 'you are doing good' or 'it was excellent'. The non-verbal communication can be a pat on the back of the child, a smile or other body gestures. Some signaling system should be established which a child could understand, to be used when the child is not behaving in a socially desirable manner. This does not mean that the teacher should punish the child. It can be just showing a signal like touching the child with hand or touching of your own finger or any other symbolic gesture, which the child can follow to stop the behaviour.

In many cases learning-disabled children forget to bring the desired material like pencil or a scale or an eraser to the school. These children should not be scolded. The child should be given one set that can be kept in the school.

Social skills can be taught through T.V. shows, dramas, role-play, etc. To get the attention of all the children playfulness on the part of the teacher is very encouraging. The teacher can introduce some games to start the lesson or can tell some small story, can show some coloured pictures or models. Children will easily be attracted to such playfulness and listen what the teacher is saying. While teaching and using the chalkboard, a laser point should be used to focus on the point. While using overhead projector in the classroom, the points one by one should be shown through the projector and other material should be covered. Teacher should involve all the students in the class, group activities should be given according to the abilities of the students. These activities may not be common for all the students.

(*b*) *What a Teacher should not do*

The teacher should not force the student to participate in every activity if he is not willing. The learning disabled should not be compared with other normal children. Failures or slow progress of these children should not be commented upon. Punishment should not be used in general in modifications of the behaviour of the children. In rare circumstances, when child shows behaviours which are harmful to him or others, can be punished but this punishment should not include corporal punishment; it can be verbal-warning to modify the behaviour. In no case corporal punishment should be used.

Types of Learning Difficulties and Symptoms

	Area of difficulty	*Symptoms*	*Examples*
Dyslexia	Processing Language	Reading, writing and spelling	Letters and words may be written or pronounced backwards
Syscalculia	Maths skills	Computation, remembering math facts, concepts of time and money	Difficulty learning to count by 2s, 3s or 4s
Dysgraphia	Written expression	Handwriting, spelling, composition	Illegible handwriting, difficulty organizing ideas
Dyspraxia	Fine motor skills	Co-ordination, manual dexterity	Trouble with scissors, buttons, drawing
	INFORMATION PROCESSING DISORDERS		
Auditory Processing Disorder	Interpreting auditory imformation	Language, development, reading	Difficulty anticipating how a speaker will end a sentence
Visual Processing Disorder	Interpreting visual information	Reading, writing and maths	Difficulty distinguishing letters like 'h' and 'n'
Attention deficit Hyperactivity Disorder	Concentration and focus	Over-activity, distractibility and impulsivity	Can't still, loses interest quickly

Source: Learning Matters

NCERT has developed a mannual elaborating how to deal with children with disabilities with special reference to learning disabilities. This Mannual is helpful for teachers who are supposed to deal with disabled students. The Mannual is based on the psychological principles of uniqueness of each individual.

A number of methods and approaches have been mentioned to deal with learning disabled with problems like restlessness, poor comrehension ability, difficulties in interaction etc.

The mannual for example explains "The curriculum in preparatory schools can be structured around areas like attenting and listening, perception, language development, creative expression, mathematics and physical education. While learning difficulties of most children are easily identifiable at the elementary stage, the main focus should be on promoting success by assigning them appropriate tasks that can be accomplished by these children. For example, by providing a study guide for a subject like social studies, giving extra time for tests, taking shorter tests, learning spellings of different words than their peers are just one of the few ways of helping the kids to improve their performance gradually."

The manual also emphasises on the use of visual and graphic presentation of contents for better understanding and mnemonic devices for better grasp of content besides training faculty to employ special instructional strategies especially at secondary level.

8

Adjustment Problems of Disabled and Coping Strategies

In a class of VI grade students a new-comer was admitted. The new-comer was orthopaedically challenged. His both legs had some disorder and he was using a wheel chair. Since the school structure was not handicapped friendly, he left his wheel chair outside the classroom and walked on the ground using his hands. After entering the classroom he tried a number of times to sit on the chair. At this stage, teacher called the peon and asked him to help the child to sit on his seat. The other children who were not physically challenged were watching curiously the child walking using his hands. One or two children sitting behind were also seen smiling. In another case a child with visual impairment was sitting in the back of the classroom and whenever the teacher was writing anything on the blackboard he used to come to the front and note down something in his notebook and go back to his chair. In another class, one girl child was not able to express herself. Whenever she tried to speak, she stammered and the whole class laughed. The child felt embarrassed and avoided speaking.

The above examples show that children suffering from some or the other kind of disability face a lot of problems not only in the school but also in the family, among the peer group and in the community. There are instances where children suffering with disabilities, for example, mental retardation are labeled as mad children. Attitudes of the society towards such children are not very positive and favourable. This hampers the normal development of these children, specially their emotional development.

Some Specific Problems of Disabled

1. *Emotional Adjustment*

Disabled children are often not dealt with care and concern and, therefore, encounter emotional adjustment problems. They find it difficult to make friends and are mal-adjusted in making relationships and so they feel very lonely. In due course, they may develop symptoms of withdrawal and anxiety. Their insecurities are reflected in their physical behaviours also. They may start biting their nails, show aggression and indulge in mannerisms for getting attention from others. They can be impulsive and irritable. This non-adjustment may lead to lack of concentration in their studies. They are restless and not able to adjust with environmental difficulties because of their emotional hang-ups. Emotional adjustment problems of the disabled may lead to development of low self-esteem and low levels of self-confidence.

2. *Dependence and Lack of Security*

Disabled children feel themselves dependent on others if they are not made aware of their disabilities and coping strategies. However, this depends upon the type of disability and its degree. For example, in case of vision problems, spectacles can take care of the vision if the child is not totally blind, but if the child is totally blind he has to depend for his movement etc. either on somebody or on some equipment/ apparatus. Similarly, in case of orthopaedically handicapped, where children are not able to use their legs, they have to depend upon some apparatus. Such children are to be made aware about their disabilities. They should be trained to live with their disability and reduce dependency. Sometimes the parents also are over protective of their disabled children. They always try to accompany such children and do not allow them to be on their own. This further enhances the feeling of insecurity and dependency.

3. *Adjustment with the Environment*

The disabled children are non-adjusted towards their environment in two ways. On one hand, the structures and buildings of the schools as well as house and other places are not generally disabled friendly and on the other hand, the attitudes of the peer group and the other people of the society are not favourable towards them. If the school structure does not have any ramp for moving the wheel chairs, the facility of Braille system for the blind children, availability of hearing aids etc., it becomes difficult for the children with various kinds of disabilities to adjust with the environment. Schools or the houses, which have multi-storey buildings and do not have disabled friendly lifts, create problems for the children with disabilities. Even if the lifts are available, signs are not available in the Braille system and if there is no announcement system, it is difficult for blind children to reach to the desired floor.

The attitudes of the people towards disabilities are generally unfavorable. 'You cannot do' is the common phrase used for disabled children. Sometimes, because of curiosity and lack of awareness, the children in the peer group ask undesirable questions from the children with disabilities, which make the later feel embarrassed and neglected. It has been observed that teachers also make undesirable remarks about such children. Teachers do not encourage the disabled children to participate in the curricular activities and in other group activities. Such attitudes leave a feeling of neglect among the children with disabilities.

It is also a common phenomenon that in families, in which there is a disabled child, parents avoid taking him or her along with them on outings or on family visits. There have been cases where families with a mentally retarded child do not disclose that they have such a child. They sometime do not even count him or her in the number of children they have. Such situations create obstacles in the development of children with disabilities, as such children can be made to become self-dependent and lead a normal life also. Children can be trained to deal with their day-to-day work. The educable mentally retarded children can even be taught in normal school subjects with some extra help.

4. *Feeling of Guilt*

A disabled child in the school and in the family, when constantly reminded about his disability, develops a feeling of guilt, which hampers his normal adjustment with the society. It has been seen that the disabled children possess some or the other ability. For example, some blind children are gifted with musical sense, the hearing handicapped are good painters, the orthopaedically handicapped are sometimes extraordinarily gifted with mathematical ability. Instead of reminding such children about what they cannot do, their specific abilities must be identified and nurtured to take them out of the sense of inferiority and guilt.

5. *Jobs and Disabled*

The Government has introduced 3% reservations in jobs for disabled but there are a number of problems when it comes to implementation. Firstly all the categories of disabled are not covered, secondly the attitude of the employers is apathetic towards employing the disabled. Even if the employers employ them, their capabilities are not given due respect. Facilities that are required by the disabled are not provided and sometimes no duties are assigned to them. They are considered as liability. Disabled are not occupationally handicapped; jobs for them must be identified. For example where lot of noise is there at the workplace, the deaf and dumb can do excellent jobs

6. *Lack of Awareness about Disabilities*

Disabled children face a lot of problems in making adjustments due to lack of awareness about various disabilities in the society. Parents are ignorant about how to deal with a disabled child. They sometimes do not know what facilities are available for their disabled child and how to avail these.

Role of the Family

Family is the first home for every child. Therefore, development of the child depends upon how he is handled by the family members including parents, siblings and other members of the extended family. Family provides a kind of support system to the children. In the modern days, when joint family system is cracking and nuclear families are emerging, role of parents and brother- sisters is very important in the overall development of the children. Children with disabilities have special needs and they require to be handled with greater care and concern. If, since the beginning, the disability of the child is accepted in the family and he is given proper support, he can develop as a normal person. The following are some of the precautions that should be taken in dealing with disabled children at the family level.

(i) Understanding the Disability

If, in a family there is a disabled child, parents should try to get more and more information about the disability. Precautionary measures should be taken so that the disability would not increase and adequate measures could be taken to deal with the disability. The information so collected should be shared with other family members.

(ii) Acceptance of the Child with his Disability

If the family members accept the child with his disability, it provides a lot of support to the child and he can face the challenges with greater self-confidence, acceptance and awareness. Parents and other family members should not pass negative comments about the disability of the child, rather they should encourage him to cope with his disability and help him in adjusting to his problems.

(iii) Identification of Specific Skills

Family should try to identify the capabilities of their disabled child.

Each and every person is endowed with some kind of specific skill, which should be identified and nurtured. For example, the blind child with a flair for music should be encouraged by the parents. Arrangements should be made for providing training in music to him. The school authorities should also be informed about the special ability of the child so that school may provide special training to the child.

(iv) Guidance and Supervision

Parents or family members should know how much their disabled child requires guidance and supervision. In case of need, some special institutional help may be sought so that family could deal with their child adequately. Parents should neither be over protective nor under protective because of the disability of the child. Family should try to make the child self-dependent. In the early childhood more supervision and guidance may be necessary and as the child grows up the extent of supervision should be reduced. Such experiments have been conducted in the developed countries. To quote, a few parents used to visit the school daily along with their disabled children initially. As a second step they asked the children to go on their own while they were supervising from a distance and at a later stage when they were confident that children can manage themselves, they did not accompany the children at all. Such practices make the disabled child self-dependent.

(v) Providing Proper Facilities

When the disability of a child is identified, family should support the child in its assessment and measuring residual capacity the child has. Appropriate aids and appliances should be provided so that the child could manage his life by himself to the extent possible. Family should also facilitate the integration of the child in the society as well as in the school by interacting with the concerned people.

(vi) Family and the Emotional Needs of the Disabled

Family has to deal with the disabled child's feelings of guilt and dejection. Parents and other members should explain to the child that there are individual differences and variations and what special abilities the child had. They should be encouraged to pursue normal education. The parents have to divide their time between the disabled child and the other children in the house according to their respective needs. If the parents are adaptive to the situation, the disabled child could be made to feel normal and that would enable his development as a normal personality. It should be remembered that these children require normal love and affection and not pity or sympathy.

Role of the School

School is the second home for the children. Whatever the child learns at home is strengthened and complemented in the school, which results in total personality development of the child. School environment has to be friendly and harmonious for the disabled child. There can be two types of disabled children entering the school – those who are coming from the special schools for the disabled and those who are directly getting admission in the normal schools. In both the cases their mainstreaming and integration with the other school children is necessary. The children who are coming from the special schools require special attention because in the special schools they were being given specific attention and curriculum etc. according to their disability. The children who are directly coming to the normal schools from the home may not be having any preferential treatment earlier but require special help. School can play a positive role in the development of disabled children in the following manner.

1. *Creating Awareness*

Children with disability have to live with other normal children but the other children may not understand the special needs of the disabled. It is the responsibility of the school that a proper atmosphere is created for the integration of the disabled children with their normal peers. It is possible through awareness generation programmes. On the one hand, it would provide information to each and all about various types of disabilities and, on the other, this awareness would be helpful in responding to the special needs of the disabled. The peer group also would learn to welcome the children with disabilities in to their fold. This awareness generation may be done through showing films, organizing dramas, providing written material, etc. The teachers may also ask the students some questions to assess their knowledge about disabilities and how would they deal with it. There are a lot of misconceptions about various disabilities, which can be overcome in the school situation through awareness generation programmes.

2. *Group Participation*

Keeping the disabled child aside, when other children are participating in group activities, is not a very healthy proposition. The school should encourage the disabled to participate in various activities, be it group discussions, other group work or extra curricular activities. There are instances when the disabled children, if encouraged, can do wonders one cannot think of. The child, whose both hands were cut, won the painting competition by painting with his foot and also holding the brush in the mouth. The only thing required is the motivation generated by encouragement from the concerned.

3. *School and Physical Barriers*

School should provide a physical structure free of barriers to facilitate the mobility of the disabled, especially the visually impaired and orthopaedically handicapped children. In a multi-storey building of the school with lifts, special lift should be there for the physically handicapped, with arrangements of Braille system, announcement system and the wheel chair to enter the lift. School should be equipped with other apparatuses which may be required by the disabled. For easy movement of the disabled using wheel chairs, there should be ramps in different parts of the school building. Such facilities would help in mainstreaming of the disabled in the school.

4. *Adaption of the School Curriculum*

Some modifications are required in the school curriculum and also in the teaching styles. If there are blind children in the class, the writing on the blackboard should be followed by the verbal communication. The scripts may be given to the blind children in Braille or they should be allowed to use a tape-recorder. Computers with Braille may be provided to such students for taking notes, etc. The adaption of curriculum has been discussed in detail in another chapter.

5. *Teacher's Training*

Special training for teachers to deal with disabled is extremely necessary, which the school should arrange. The disabled children do not require sympathy but need empathy. Pity does not help in the development of the children with disabilities. Encouraging participation without discrimination, normal communication with disabled, their acceptance and care on the part of the teachers are important factors. Special training for teachers may be arranged to make them aware about the specific disabilities and how the disabled children should be integrated with normal children in a school setting.

6. *Medical Facilities*

Most schools have some first-aid facilities. Some schools have arrangement for a medical center and a provision for a regular doctor.

Wherever a regular doctor is not available the visits of the doctor on certain days may be fixed. Some schools also keep contact with a nearby hospital. The disabled children who require medical facilities should be identified and referred to the doctor/hospital or other referral services. The school can maintain a record of such services available and whenever required these sources can be contacted and disabled children can be helped.

7. *Counselling*

A disabled child may face difficulties during its interaction with the peer group in the school. Provision should be made for a Counsellor to deal with emotions and hang-ups of the disabled children. While in some of the schools advisory services of a Counsellor are available, others with no such regular facilities can take the help of Counsellors posted in other schools.

8. *Identification and Assessment of Disability*

In the ideal situation, the family would know about the disability of the child and would be providing all sorts of needed help. But in a number of cases the family is unaware of the disability of the child or, even when aware, due to ignorance they do not pay much attention to the disability. Nor do they help the child in the assessment of his disability and finding out the residual capacity of the child. It has been seen that among the children with the learning disability, parents are totally ignorant and scold children for not learning. In some other cases where there are broken families, children are neglected. In such circumstances it is the responsibility of the school to observe the children, identify and assess their disabilities. School should also keep in touch with the family to get the facts about the child's history or apprise the family members about disability of the child. The schools can also organize small workshops for parents on the children's disabilities and how to deal with them.

9. *Holistic Approach*

The schools have to adopt a holistic approach and provide services to the children with disabilities who have special needs. Schools should have services for continual assessment of disabilities and needs of the child, medical facilities, guidance and counseling facilities, interaction with parents, provision for adaptation of school facilities, training of teachers, resource center, remedial teaching and so on. There may be a need for speech therapist, physiotherapist and or a medical doctor. Such facilities should be available with the school. The school may also have to have liaison with community resources including vocational training centers, employers, rehabilitation centers, sheltered workshops and NGOs so that children with special needs could be helped after they go out of the school system.

Role of Community

All children have to develop as responsible adults. Each and every child is a part of community whatever his or her disability may be. It is the responsibility of the community to provide a congenial atmosphere so that every child could get an equal opportunity to develop. Some of the steps a community can take in this direction are detailed below:

(i) *Mapping of Resources*

A resource mapping should be done at community level, which can be utilized for helping the disabled. These resources may be the special education teachers, special doctors, the physiotherapists, the hospitals, the education institutions, vocational training institutes and places where aids and appliances for disabled are available, financial institutions that may help the disabled, other institutional support such as sheltered workshops for mentally retarded or institutional homes for severely mentally challenged people, etc. The community should also know the counselling centers available at the nearby places. This information may be collected by either Residents Welfare Association of the community, by panchayat offficials, by some NGO or other residents of the community. Community should also have the information about types of disabled children in the community and their needs.

(ii) Dissemination of the Information

The information so collected by the community should be available for all the people. This can be disseminated through the notice board, through the pamphlets, inviting the residents for a meeting, etc. The community should help the families where there is a disabled child.

(iii) Awareness Generation

Awareness generation programmes should also be organized at community level so that not only parents could understand their disabled child but also some level of acceptance is generated in the community for acceptance of disabled.

(*iv*) *Integration of Disabled in the Community*

A variety of efforts are made by various communities to integrate the disabled child in the mainstream. There are instances where communities celebrate various festivals together or competitions are organized at community level where disabled children also participate. Such activities help in removing the misconceptions about the disabilities.

(*v*) *Volunteer Services*

Community can help in providing volunteer service to the community-disabled children. For example, a blind student may need the help of a writer during the examination. A volunteer from the community may help him for this purpose. Volunteers may also work for motivating the disabled in participating in community activity. Community workers may also help integration of the child in the school.

(*vi*) *Attitudinal Change*

As has been discussed elsewhere, positive attitudes are important for normal growth of the disabled child. Favourable attitudes facilitate positive personality development. The attitude change may come from the awareness about the disability and removal of stereotype prejudices against disabled. For this purpose, film shows may be organized at community level. Talks from experts, from doctors, etc. may also help in attitudinal changes. Sometimes community people have a lot of queries about disabilities. In such a situation it is necessary that community meetings are organized where a doctor or a specialist may be invited to interact with the people. Some success stories where disabled people could do things as normal children do may also help in attitudinal change of the people.

Summary Table

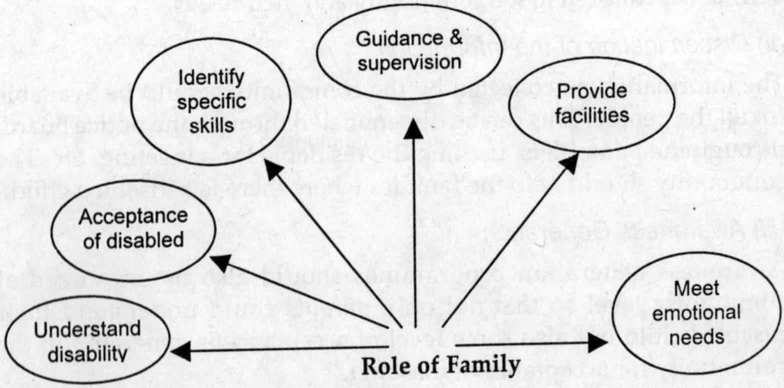

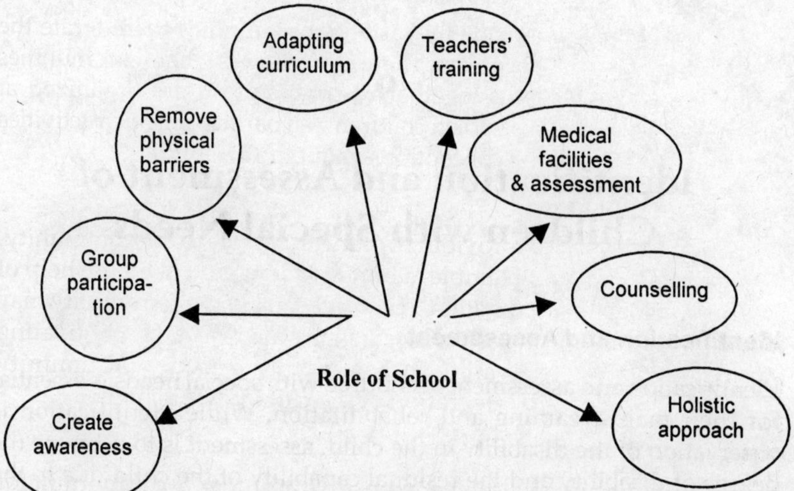
Adapting curriculum
Teachers' training
Remove physical barriers
Medical facilities & assessment
Group participation
Counselling
Role of School
Create awareness
Holistic approach

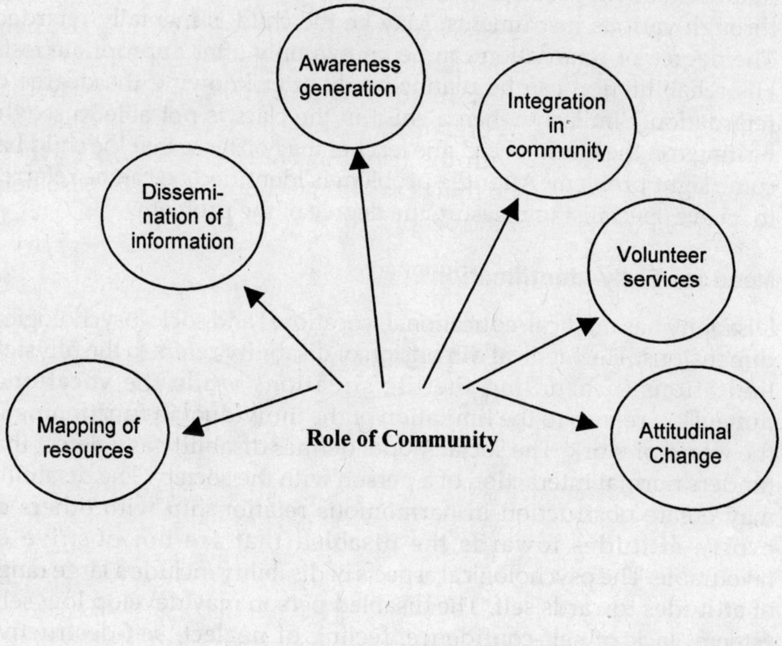
Awareness generation
Integration in community
Dissemination of information
Volunteer services
Mapping of resources
Role of Community
Attitudinal Change

9

Identification and Assessment of Children with Special Needs

Identification and Assessment

Identification and assessment of children with special needs is essential for their mainstreaming and rehabilitation. While identification is observation of the disability in the child, assessment is to estimate the degree of disability and the residual capability of the child due to the specific disability. Identification of the disability is the first step and once the disability is identified, the child can be taken to the appropriate place for assessment. For example, if a child is not able to perform well in the school, his problem in learning, when detected, can be measured through various instruments. May be the child is mentally retarded. The degree of retardation can be known only after appropriate tests. His rehabilitation can be planned only after knowing the degree of retardation. Similarly when a child in the class is not able to see the writings on the black- board, the teacher may observe that the child has some sight problem. After the problem is identified he can be referred to an eye specialist to measure the degree of the problem.

Need for Early identification

Disability has medical, educational, vocational and socio-psychological dimensions. The medical dimension of disability refers to the physical limitations in handling the life situations while the vocational dimension relates to the limitation of the individual in functioning in the world of work. The social model defines disability as a defect that hinders normal interaction of a person with the society. The disability may create obstruction in harmonious relationship with others or evolve attitudes towards the disabled that are not positive or favourable. The psychological aspects of disability include a large range of attitudes towards self. The disabled person may develop low self-esteem, lack of self-confidence, feeling of neglect, self-destructive behaviour. All these hamper normal personality development.

Due to the aversive and apathetic attitudes towards disabled, capacities of the person remain unutilized or under-utulized, which is a loss both to the disabled as well as to the society. The neglect of the child by the family and the society keeps the child off from the accessibility to medical care and support, leading to further aggravation of the problems. Early identification and assessment of the disability is, thus, essential. It can help the child in following manner:

- With the early identification of the disability, child can get timely medical help.
- The residual functioning capabilities of the child can be measured and accordingly educational-vocational support can be provided
- Early identification leads to the early acceptance of the disability on the part of the child, family and community.
- Training can be provided to the child to lead a normal life along with his disability.
- Preventive measures can be adopted to curtail the severity of the problem.
- One disability may lead to other. If properly detected adequate measures can be taken to prevent its multiplication.

After the disability has been identified its assessment is essential. Assessment is required to be done at proper intervals. Assessment of specific disabilities has been discussed in the chapters on individual types of disabilities such as visual impairment, hearing handicap, learning disabilities etc. In this chapter some general aspects relating to assessment of disabilities and techniques that could be adopted would be elaborated. There are specific medical and psychological tests and equipments with which the degree of disability can be measured. Some other non-testing techniques are there that are used for identification of handicaps.

Process and Basis of Identification and Assessment

The process of identification starts soon after the birth – whether the child can see, can hear, can move his limbs, whether he is reacting to gestures, his responses to various stimuli, etc. When the handicap is not severe as, for example, when the child can see but vision is not very clear, or responses of the child are not sharp or a hearing impaired child does not react to the sounds the way he should do, it is somewhat difficult to identify the handicap. The basis of identification is the child's behaviour. If the child's behavour is different from that of other students of the class, it can serve as a useful indicator for identification of the problem. Another basis can be the family and peer group. If parents report some specific observation about the abnormality of the child, the school authorities should take it seriously and further investigations should be made. The opinion of the peer group can also be a basis for identification of the problem of the child. The school performance in general or in specific subject can also provide some clue about the problem of the child. The participation of the child in various activities of the school, his interactions with teachers, peers, past medical record, information on the Cumulative Record Card all are useful in the identification of the problem of the child.

The following techniques can be adopted to identify the handicap of the child. These techniques are also termed as informal techniques of assessment.

1. *Observation*

The child has to be watched regularly and his behaviour observed carefully. The child who is suffering from vision problems may show specific characteristics like rubbing his eyes, watery eyes, not keeping proper distance while reading, watching T.V. from very close distance, etc. Similarly a child with hearing difficulty may come near when some thing is said to him, or may not respond properly. Children with learning difficulties and educable mental retardation should be observed continuously to see their progress in school as well as at home. The behaviours of children, such as their interaction with other children, teachers, parents, and reactions to learning situations, their frequent aggression and frustration to various situations are indications that child is not growing normally and is suffering from some disability. Observations thus made should be recorded. If certain observations are repeated continuously, the child must be helped. The school can have a team of doctor, speech therapist, physiotherapist, school counsellor and teachers to assess the disability of the child on the basis of the record of observations. There are medical equipments available that can assess physical disability. Observation technique can be used in natural environment. Another way of using this technique is a structured way in which a child is asked to act in a certain way. Structured observations involve following methods.

(i) *Anecdotal Record*: Randall has defined Anecdotal Record as "A record of some significant item of conduct, a record of an episode in the life of the student, a word picture of the student in action… a word snapshot at the moment of the incident: any narration of events in which the student takes such a part as to reveal something which may be significant about his personality".

Anecdotal record is a useful instrument where the behaviour of a student is observed during some specific incident in which the student was also a party. It is also called a word picture because the person who observes the behaviour of the student describes the incident to show the real picture of his behaviour. The teacher may provide such records to the school to understand the student better. The reporting person should be very clear and free from prejudices. He should not confuse between the facts and his own feelings. The purpose of anecdotal record is to narrate the behaviour of the student during the incident. Anecdotal records are used in combination of various other techniques. Moreover, there should be a series of anecdotes at different timings. Only one incident cannot describe the behaviour of a person. Anecdotal reports may be prepared in a format given below.

Format of Anecdotal Report—a sample

1. Name of the Student
2. Class
3. Observation made by whom, with date
4. Place where observation was made
5. Narration of the Incident
6. Situational details and settings
7. Observations of the observer
8. Comments from the observer
9. Recommendations

Such records about the individual should be maintained and collated for integration and necessary actions. This kind of behaviour observation may provide clues about the individual's relationship with peer group, with teachers, his aspirations and motivations, his problems etc.

It is not possible to record anecdotes for each and every student. It has to be considered carefully as to who should be studied and why. At primary level for example, a teacher can identify a child who does not speak. Anecdotes may be written about those children who are difficult to understand during normal interactions.

Example

Name	: Vanita
Class	: IV
Observation made by	: Mrs. Smita Gupta, Mathematics teacher

With date : on 10.9.05
Place where observation made: Class
Narration of the incident and situational details : While attending the class, she wascoming near the blackboard from her seat. Another girl Nina was unable to see the board as Vanita was standing between Nina and Board. Nina commented 'What's wrong with you'? On this Vanita started crying.

Triggers identified:

(a) Vanita was not able to read the board from the seat she was sitting in.

(b) Comment of Nina hurt her and triggered her mental state.

Observation and Commets

Vanita is good in studies.

She is always cooperative and helping. She remains smiling.

Recommendation:

Doctor should check eyes of Vanita and help.

(*ii*) The (Problem) Checklist

Checklist method in observation is used when the purpose of the teacher is to identify certain specific problems of a child. The list of problems is provided to the observer and he has to tick the problem, which he observes the individual to have. For example, the problems can be slow learning, lack of response in the class, lack of communication skills etc.

Example—

Problem:

A girl has mental ability. She is studying in IX standard. Her academic achievement is not up to mark.

Checklist—

- Concentrates in the class
- Takes notes
- Brings the books and note books to the class
- Answers questions in the class
- Does homework regularly
- Irritable or calm
- Aggressive
- Talks with classmates during the class

- Writes something in the class
- She is hardworking
- Attentive to the lectures
- Takes interest in the subjects.
- Cannot write
- Cannot speak
- Cannot do some specific activities etc.

The above checklist would provide information about learning disabilities of the child

(*iii*) *Rating Scales*

Rating scales may also be used as instruments for observation. Rating scales provide comparability of observations. These scales may be designed according to the purpose. Observations on a particular characteristic can be rated on 5 or 7 point scale.

Example –

Purpose: To observe maladjustment of the child with the peer group who has lost his both legs.

Items:	*Never*	*Rarely*	*Sometimes*	*Often*	*Always*
• Talks with other classmates					
• Shares his things with others					
• Talks with the classmate sitting next to him					
• During lunch time eats food all alone					
• During recess plays with Others					
• Other students talk with him					

While Anecdotal Records are 'observer descriptions', the Rating Scales are `observer evaluations'. The Rating Scales also provide information about the degree of the characteristics.

How to prepare Rating Scales: For preparing a Rating Scale, one should list out the characteristics that are to be rated. These could be self-confidence in the student, self-dependence, industriousness, cheerfulness, helping attitude. Each characteristic should be well defined and be understood by the Rater. Moreover, only such characteristics should be chosen that are relevant and observable in the given situation. In a school situation where teachers are supposed to rate a disabled student, 'love for siblings' would not be an observable characteristic.

A few things should be kept in mind before making a Rating Scale.

(a) It should be free from prejudices and subjectivity. This difficulty may be overcome by choosing more than one Rater.

(b) Some observers have a tendency to rate a person at one point on all the characteristics. This is known as 'halo effect'. For example, the Rater may rate a student as excellent on all the characteristics. This does not give the real picture about the person. In such cases, more than one student may be rated on one characteristic, then on another, and so on.

The problems of rating scales may be lessened if the Rater is also asked to support his Ratings with justifications.

(iv) Systematic Case Study

Under this method, the major activity is to collate all the information collected from various sources and techniques. This can be the information from the school record, from achievement record of the student, the psychological tests, or information collected by teachers. All these collected bits of information may be systematically reviewed and analyzed and prepared in the form of the case study.

For preparing the case study, some order of reporting may be prescribed, say, introduction, scores on achievement test, school progress, teacher's observations, learning defects, family history, social background, health background, scores on psychological tests, personal problems, pupil groups observations and the interpretation.

Case studies are important records in situations where individual counseling is required by a disabled child. They can serve as successful cases to be referred to other students. Case study record also indicates the gaps in information.

Example: How to prepare Case Study:

Problem: Child belongs to educable mental retarded category and has problems in adjustment in the school.

Case Record:

1. Name	:	Smriti Kumari
2. Class	:	V
3. Age	:	14 years
4. Family Background	:	Smriti's parents are illiterate and are landless labourers. She is the eldest child in the family. She has two younger sisters
5. Economic Background of the family	:	Being landless labourers, the family lives hand to mouth. They hardly get two meals a day. The family migrated from a remote village of Bihar to the town area where they work on someone else's farms or sometimes are engaged by some transporter for loading- unloading work.
6. Social background of the family	:	The family belonged to Scheduled Tribe category. The village they were living belonged to high castes. The family was working in the village on the farm of the Head of the Panchayat. They were paid a very meager wage or sometimes no wage at all. So they moved out of the village.
7. Educational background of the family	:	The family is illiterate. No body in the family got any education through generations. After migration from the remote village to a small town, they started to send their eldest child to school. Her younger sister who was 11 years' old looked after the other sibling while parents were at work.
8. Problem stated by the teacher	:	The teacher stated that the girl was unable to concentrate in the class and referred the case to Resource teacher. It was stated that the girl does not complete her home work. She forgets to bring the note book or the pencil or the text book to the school. She does not understand

		fully what is taught in the class. Even after scolding the child, no improvement has taken place.
9. Interview with the child & her problem	:	During the interviews with the child it was understood that the parents were sending the child to school for 'mid-day meal' scheme, as they were not able to feed all their children. She was unable to understand the study material along with other students of the class as she was educable retarded. This fact was understood only when she was administered Psychological tests. There was nobody to help her at home as parents were illiterate. She used to get more tensed when scolded by the teacher in the presence of the other girls of her class. The other girls also teased her. She didn't want to continue with the school.
10. Interaction with Parents	:	In this case, interactions were had by counsellor with the parents, who told him that they were unable to meet the demands of the school to buy things for preparing charts, or raw-material for preparing models etc.
11. Counselor's Observations	:	• Neither the parents nor the child knew the importance of education. • Financial problems of the child. • Teacher was not able to understand the adjustment problems of the child and was unable to handle her with sensitivity. • Child required remedial teaching.
12. Counselling and Outcome Summary	:	Counselor discussed the case with the teacher and suggested as to how to be sensitive towards the child's problems. Remedial classes to help the child in doing homework etc. were arranged. Parents were counseled to understand the importance of education. Financial support for education was arranged

		from school's fund meant for poor children. Group activities were arranged so that the child could be friendly with other classmates.
13. Follow up	:	Follow up was done after 15 days. Teacher reported a little improvement in the child. The child also reported better adjustment with the school environment.

(v) *Curriculum-based Measurement*

Of recent some new techniques have been evolved for assessing the children's problems. In Western countries use of curriculum-based measurements (CBM) is very popular specially for assessing learning disabled and mentally retarded children. Under this technique various samples of performance of the child are collected. These samples are based on general, local level curriculum or what the teacher has taught in the class. Performance relate to general skills such as reading, writing or mathematical ability. These small samples of performance are also known as "probes" which are measured against criteria of frequency. Frequency means – how many words the child has read or written. The mathematical problems solved correctly and correct sequencing done are also counted. These frequencies are measured against a norm of average score of the students of that level. Curriculum-based measurement is useful in monitoring child's progress and planning the educational curriculum and strategy.

(vi) Criterion—Reference Tests

Under this technique the present performance of the child is measured on the basis of his past performance. This indicates the child's progress in a subject. For example, if the child knew five alphabets earlier, and after a week can write seven alphabets, it shows his/her progress. Criterion reference tests do not compare the child with others in the group as is being done in the curriculum based measurement.

Formal Assessment

Formal assessment involves medical and psychological measurement of the child. A child with a vision problem should be taken to an eye-specialist so that his eyesight etc. could be checked up. Similarly, for hearing-impaired child medical tests are there which can diagnose the extent of the problem. In case of orthopaedic handicapped residual capacity of the child can be measured. For learning disabled and in cases of mental retardation a number of psychological tests are available that can measure the intelligence level of the child and can identify his problems. It should be kept in mind that the child should be taken to an authorized psychologist or a doctor. Many hospitals have facilities for such testing and measurement.

Some tests available for Formal Assessment are:

General Ability Measurement Tests

- *Battelle Developmental Inventory*: The Riverside Publishing Company. This test is designed for children birth through age eight. It tests in several different developmental domains such as cognition, motor, self-help, language, and social skills
- *Bayley Scales of Infant Development*: The Psychological Corporation. This is for children ages one month through 42 months. The test assesses areas of mental, motor and behaviour development.
- *Stanford-Binet Intelligence Scale (Fourth Edition)*: The Riverside Publishing Company. The Stanford-Binet tests individuals ages 2-23. The test measures general intelligence. It focuses on the areas of verbal reasoning, quantitative reasoning, abstract/ visual reasoning, and short-term memory.
- *Wechsler Preschool and Primary Scale of Intelligence-Revised (WPPSI-R)*: The Psychological Corporation. A standardized test for children ages 4½ to 6. It assesses areas of language and perception.
- *McCarthy Scales of Children's Abilities*: The Psychological Corporation. The McCarthy tests children ages 2 ½-8 ½. The purpose of the test is to evaluate the general intelligence level of children. It also identifies strengths and weaknesses in several ability areas. These areas include: verbal, perceptual-performance, quantitative, memory, motor, and general cognitive skills.
- *Transdisciplinary Play-Based Assessment (TBA)*: Paul H. Brookes Publishing Company. This informal assessment is for children birth through 6. Through play children can be assessed in areas of cognition, social-emotional, communication and language and sensorimotor skills.

Language/Communication Measurement

- *Sequenced Inventory for Communication Development-Revised (SICD)*: Slosson Educational Publications. The SICD assesses children ages 4 months to 4 years. The test assesses areas of expressive and receptive language skills.

- *Preschool Language Scale – 3 (PLS-3):* The Psychological Corporation. This test is designed for children aged birth through 6. The test assesses areas of language including auditory comprehension and expressive communication.
- *Clinical Evaluation of Language Fundamental-Preschool*: Charles E. Merrill Publishing Company. The assessment identified nature and degree of language disabilities in the language areas of processing, production, and speech sounds.
- *Peabody Picture Vocabulary Test (PPVT-R):* American Guidance Service. The Peabody tests ages 2 ½ to age 40. The purpose of the test is to measure vocabulary in English and non-verbal receptive (hearing). The test uses picture recognition for single word vocabulary.
- *Test of Early Language Development (TELD):* The TELD assesses children ages three through seven on language development.
- *Transdisciplinary Play-Based Assessment (TBA):* Paul H. Brookes Publishing Company. This informal assessment is for children birth through 6. Through play children can be assessed in areas of cognition, social-emotional, communication and language and sensorimotor.

Motor

- *Peabody Developmental Motor Scales:* The Riverside Publishing Company. The Peabody assesses children ages birth to seven years. The test measures gross-motor and fine-motor development skills.
- *Bayley Scales of Infant Development:* The Psychological Corporation. The Bayley is designed for children ages one month through 42 months. The test assesses areas of mental, motor and behavior development.
- *Transdisciplinary Play-Based Assessment (TBA):* Paul H. Brookes Publishing Company. This informal assessment is for children birth through 6. Through play children can be assessed in areas of cognition, social-emotional, communication and language and sensorimotor.

Measurement for Social/emotional behaviour

- *Child Behavior Checklist (CBCL),* this behavior rating scale assesses behaviors associated with learning disabilities. The checklist is designed for children ages 2 through 18. It contains a parent and a teacher checklist.
- *Vineland Adaptive Behavior Scale (VABS):* The Vineland tests

infants to children ages 18 and 11 months. The purpose of the test is to assess social competence. The areas of assessment include: communication, daily living, socialization, and motor skills.

- *California Preschool Social Competency Scale:* This test assesses children ages 3-6 on self-help and social development.
- *Burks' Behavior Rating Scales:* The rating scale is designed for children ages 3-6, which assesses the social area of development.
- *Transdisciplinary Play-Based Assessment (TBA):* Paul H. Brookes Publishing Company. This informal assessment is for children birth through 6. Through play children can be assessed in areas of cognition, social-emotional, communication and language and sensorimotor.

Self-help/Adaptive Behaviour Measurement

- *Battelle Developmental Inventory:* The Riverside Publishing Company. This test is designed for children birth though age eight. It tests in several different developmental domains such as self-help, motor, cognition, language, and social skills.
- *Vineland Adaptive Behavior Scale (VABS):* The Vineland tests infants to children ages 18 and 11 months. The purpose of the test is to assess social competence. The areas of assessment include: communication, daily living, socialization, and motor skills.
- *Hawaii Early Learning Profile (HELP) This* test is for children ages birth through age three. The HELP is a criterion-referenced tests which assesses children in the developmental areas of self-help, motor, cognition, language, speech, and social development.

Role of Teachers in Identification and Assessment

The teachers can play an important role in identification and assessment of a disabled child. It is detailed below:

- In case parents at home do not observe a disability, teacher can observe the behaviour of the child and find out why a child is behaving in a certain manner. If a low vision child sitting at the back of the classroom is not able to see the writing on the board and comes to the front often, the teacher can observe this behaviour. Similarly observations can be made for other disabilities such as learning disabilities, hard of hearing etc.

- Teacher can refer the child to the doctor, therapist or to other referral services.
- Teaching methodology and strategy has to be designed according to the disability of the child.
- Teacher's role is to make the disabled child familiar with the school environment.
- Teacher should make the child familiar about the resources available for him in the school and outside.
- Teachers can provide help in using and maintenance of appliances/equipments used by handicapped children.
- Information about the disabilities of the children is necessary to facilitate their integration in the class.
- Teacher can interact with parents in the assessment process of disability and their acceptance.
- After identification and assessment of disability children can be referred to referral services if required

10

Teaching Learning Strategies and Social Educational Provisions

Education is a Fundamental Right under the Constitution. The Sarva Shiksha Abhiyan started by the government has a goal of educating each and every child without any kind of discrimination. Therefore, children with special needs also have a right to education irrespective of the type of their disability, its degree, category etc. The schools have to provide a congenial environment for all types of children including children with special needs. A 'Zero Rejection' policy has been accepted under Sarva Shiksha Abhiyan. The educational policy of the country talks about the integrated education for the disabled children, which indicates that children with the disabilities are to be placed in the normal schools along with the other children. Various approaches and methods have been adopted for educating the children with special needs which includes the formal and non-formal education, open school system, home based education, remedial teaching, vocational education, arrangement for resource teachers, curriculum adjustment, etc. Teaching learning strategies and social education provisions with reference to the children with disabilities include a number of components such as curriculum adjustment and adaptation, classroom management, mapping of community resources, teaching strategies etc.

(A) Curriculum Adjustment and Adaptation

Let us observe a situation. In a class where there are children with learning disabilities, a teacher comes to the class, teaches the topic for the day, gives some home work to be done and leaves the class after the time for the topic is over. Next day, the teacher asks for the homework done by the students, some students do not submit their workbooks. Teacher scolds them for not doing the work. The basic reason for not doing the work is that these children had not been able to understand the lesson, which was taught by the teacher, as these children were suffering from learning disabilities. In this case, the curriculum adjustment and adaptation becomes essential. In case of disabled children the curriculum has to be adapted in a manner, which is close to the real life situation than teaching the topic with a theoretical perspective. The curriculum has to have a practical orientation combined with functions. A theoretical approach to teach a lesson would be to tell about the things, while a functional approach would be to show the objects to the children, which they may face or interact with in their lives. For example, in a theoretical method, the teacher may tell about the various vegetables, while in a practical orientation the teacher may bring the specimens of those vegetables, which a student is familiar with at home. Another way can be that teacher takes the children to the market and asks them to identify the vegetables. In other words, the subject has to be taught to the children in relation to its functional utility.

Different categories of disabilities have been discussed in the earlier chapters and curriculum adjustment has to be done according to the specific disabilities. The general considerations for curriculum modifications would be as follows:

1. *Identification of Needs of the Children*

The first step for curriculum adjustment is to identify the needs of the children with various disabilities. Their residual capacities are to be assessed and their interacting behaviours are to be mapped. According to the levels of abilities and residuals capacities, curriculum has to be modified and adapted. For example, in case of visually impaired who have a very low vision, the study material should be presented in large prints while in case of totally blind the text books are to be adapted in Braille system, and maps and charts etc. are to be presented before these children in embossed manner. In case of learning disabled children, the curriculum has to be divided into a small and sequenced set of activities. In the case of blind students, written material (in Braille) has to be followed up by verbal instructions, while in the case of children with hearing disability there has to be more use of visuals. Disability-specific safety measures are to be adopted in the laboratories. For example, the apparatuses are to be labeled in Braille system for blinds while for hearing impaired some flash light system has to be installed to alert them against any danger.

2. Holistic Approach to Curriculum

Education in general focuses upon the overall development of children but curriculum has to be very specific in case of disabled children according to their specific needs of development and adjustments. The curriculum should include topics like self-care, safety measures, use of aids and appliances and their maintenance, mobility training, development of coping strategies for their problems, community and school resources available to them, peer interaction, development of positive self-image and overall personality development. The curriculum has to be so devised that the children who suffer from disability may not have feeling of neglect or self-derogation.

3. Curriculum and Group Interactions

A school curriculum is not restricted to teach a topic only. The curriculum should provide ample opportunities for group interaction and participation. There are cases where at the time of group exercises, the teacher not fully aware about the disability, may ask the disabled child to just observe what is happening in the group and not to participate. Sometimes some teachers make a remark like 'this child cannot do'. These develop a sense of negative self in the child. All children should be integrated to participate and interact among each other without any discrimination. The support services, which are necessary for such participation, should be made available to the children in need.

4. Curriculum and Functional Orientation

Curriculum should be related to day-to-day lives of the children. It is more important in case of disabled children. Children would be able to identify better with the things they are familiar with in their day-to-day living. Teaching through these objects/material is easier than quoting the examples of unknown things and material. For example, it is easy for a blind child to touch a potato because he is eating it and when he is taught about it he can learn it easily. Things become more difficult for him if the teacher explains the concept of vegetables in abstract manner giving the examples of some vegetables the child has not experienced. More and more visits for outside experience, motivating the other senses should be included in the curriculum for the disabled children. The functional orientation of curriculum involves setting the objectives that would facilitate the functioning of the individual as an independent person. To develop a disabled child as an independent functioning person, specific objectives in terms of skills to be developed should be identified and listed. These skills are to be linked to various tasks in various settings in which the child has to live. These settings are family, school, employment, the community and the society.

General Objectives → Specific Objectives → Skills to be Developed → Tasks to be Identified

5. *Adapting Published Material*

According to the varying needs of the children with disabilities, the curriculum should be divided into various topics, topics into various concepts and concepts into various skills to be developed in the child. For developing these skills various activities may be planned in the class according to the residual capacities of the children. Here, while adapting the published material it should be kept in mind that one skill at a time should be developed. If the concept of colour is being taught to learning disabled child, at the first step he should try to learn about one or two colours. Then he should learn about more colours and their differentiations as a next step, their identification from various colours at the later stage etc. in a sequenced manner. Practice of the same concept is necessary for retention.

Adapting a published material involves the following steps:

1. The total curriculum has to be divided into various topics
2. Each topic must be divided into various concepts
3. Each concept should be divided into skills to be developed in the child.
4. Tasks are to be identified according to the skills to be developed. It must be remembered that one skill at a time must be developed.

Special needs of the disabled children

Sl.No.	*Types of needs*	*Curriculum adaptation*
1.	Academic needs	Reading, writing, learning of specific subjects like language, mathematics
2.	Social needs	Interaction with others, understanding of disability, adjustment with the environment
3.	Communication needs	Speech, written communication, learning grammar and usage of sentence, how to develop communication skills, use of equipment, training in lip reading, etc.
4.	Mobility needs	To be able to move by self, familiarity with environment structure to facilitate mobility, training in obstacles identification.
5.	Living needs	Training in living independently and doing the daily routine tasks like bathing, wearing clothes, eating, managing home
6.	Vocational needs	Vocational needs of disabled children to be identified according to residual capacities. vocational training in schools with linkages of children with vocational training centers. Training for interviews, guidance for skills while meeting with employers.
7.	Safety needs	Use of apparatus, equipments and their maintenance, precautions for injuries
8.	Leisure needs	Identification of specific interests, aptitudes and abilities to be developed as leisure time activity like music, painting, crafts, playing, dramas, games, etc.
9.	Psychological needs	Understand and accept the child with his/her disability by self and others.

Components of Curriculum Adaptation

Curriculum adaptation has following components:

1. What to teach: The matter
2. How to teach – the process and methodology

3. Establishing Learning environment
4. Evaluation of teaching

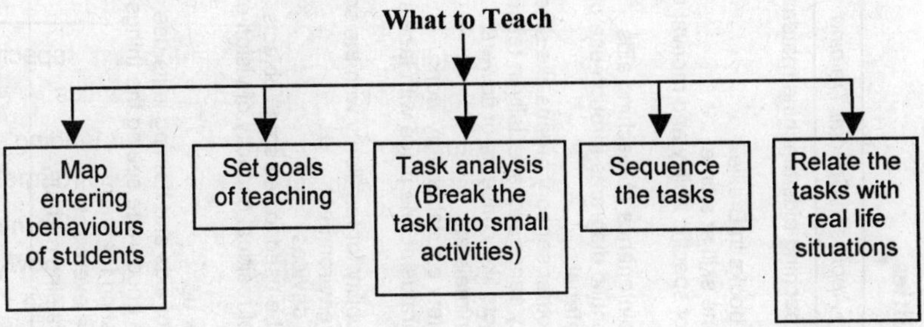

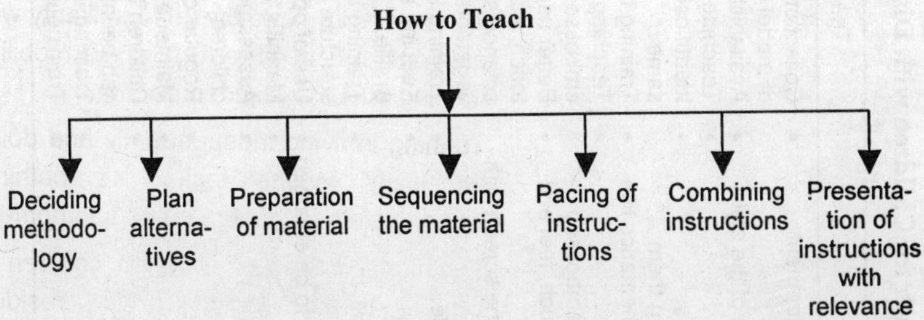

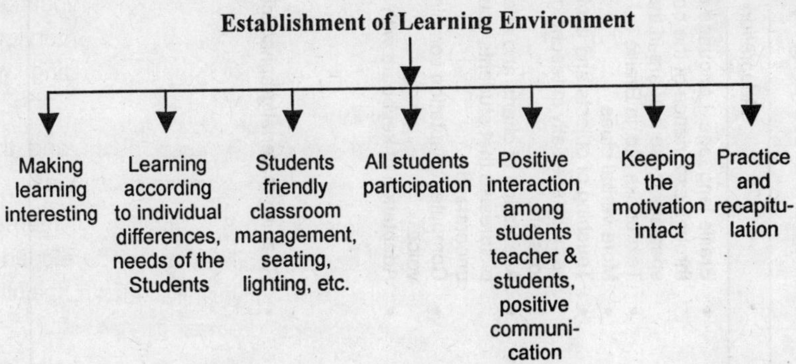

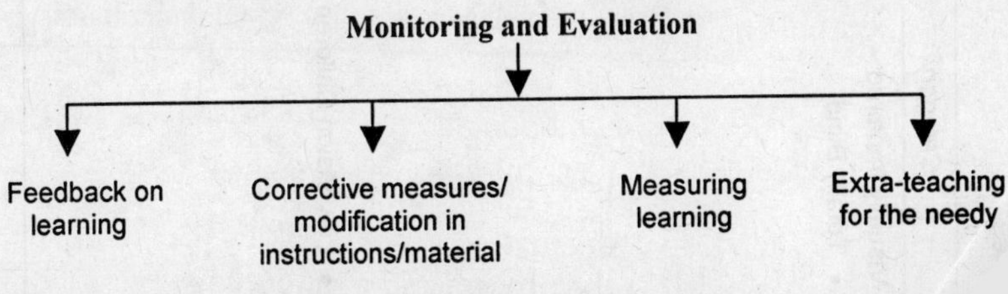

Curriculum and Teaching Approach for Children with Disabilities

Category	*Adaptation*	*Teaching Approach/Special Training*
1. Visually Impaired • Totally Blind	• Braille language. Language development through experience of the objects specially those that are in the use of the child • Text books etc. in Braille • More verbal clues • Touching of objects and explaining them verbally specially in teaching mathematics like toys etc. • Adaptation of charts and atlas in embossed pictures so that students could touch, feel and understand. • Computer adaptation combining the screen with voice. • Adaptation of keyboard with Braille.	• Collection of teaching aids/teaching material/use of model etc. • Availability of books in Braille • Teaching of one skill at a time • Identification of specific ability and motivating the same • Training in maintenance of teaching aids • Teaching scientific diagrams through use of embossed material. • Better use of other sensory organs like smell, touch, auditory sense etc. specially in teaching science subjects like concepts of flowers, vegetables, animals etc. • Training in safety e.g. laboratory work. • Keeping apparatus at one place with labels in Braille. • Training in mobility for familiarity with the school structure and environment
• Low Vision Children	• Reading material/graphs/pictures to be enlarged	• Use of optical devices • Magnifiers to be used to see small objects • Assessment of residual capacity of vision of children. • Regular check up • Maintenance of aids and training in its use • Children to be encourage seeing the things that can be interesting for them. • Training in eye exercises • Training in retaining memory

(*Contd.*)

(*Contd.*)

		• Practice in seeing objects and discriminating amongst them. • Arrangements for special classes and remedial teaching • Teacher should give verbal instructions along with showing pictures or graphs. • Children may use recording system • Volunteers who can read for visually impaired
2. Children with Hearing Disability	• Curriculum to have more visuals • Assessment of needs of children with hearing disability, curriculum according to the category and degree of deafness and pre or post language deafness.	• Use of hearing aids • Use of sign language • Training in lip reading • Help from Resource teacher Interpreter as per need of the child. • Teaching in regular class with special individual classes wherever required. • If the child is familiar with lip reading, teacher should always speak facing the child. Also he should use non-verbal communication. • Written Instructions to be circulated along with verbal instructions. • Use signboards, visual alarms or flashlights for safety measures especially in laboratories. • Teacher should have clarity of speech and he should be slow in speaking.

Mental Retardation	Curriculum adaptability	Teaching Strategy/Training
1. Educable mentally retarded	• Repetitive kinds of activities • Use of material with progressive difficulty and its sequencing • Behaviour modification • Aggression control • Use of daily routine examples in teaching • Avoidance of abstract concept • Identify specific capability of the child & develop it • Focus on development of functional skills • Frequent evaluation of the child on his performance and repetition of class/extra class • Lesson to be divided in very small parts • Vocational training along with educational curriculum as educable mentally retarded are not able to go to higher classes • Vocational training in repetitive kinds of activities • Curriculum according to assets of the child not according to deficiencies • Parents participation and acceptance.	• Holding the interest of the child • Use of such material in teaching the child is familiar with • Teach one part of lesson at a time, take feed back, repeat if necessary • Before going to next part, recapitulate the part the child has already learnt • Training in managing himself • Training in maintaining the hygiene • Multi-sensory approach in teaching • Flexible approach in teaching • Training to keep physical stamina and use of limbs • Training in communication skills • With proper training a retarded child can learn many things • Positive re-inforcement to the child • Teaching in slow pace • Don't force him learn something specific • Training in safety • Field trips can facilitate learning • Modification in tests to evaluate the performance of the child. • Adaptation of instructions to the daily routine so that learning could be used, recalled and practiced. • Use of games, computers • Training in sharing.
2. Other Categories mentally retarded children	• Children who are not educable retarded have more serious problems. They may be confined to wheel chairs may have more than one handicap. Such children require institutional help. Even those who are not confined to wheelchairs may have communication difficulties, problems in walking, balancing, doing routine activities. Such children need help of occupational therapist, speech therapist, physiotherapist, etc. They can be trained in slow pace to communicate with fingers, eye-movements.	• Teaching & training to such children required lot of patience. A trained teacher is required. • Learning is gradual in small parts • Training in learning about body parts and their use. • Coordination of limbs training • Balancing skills • One small activity at a time like training in walking – train taking one step with full support; step with holding a railing on both side; support on one side and take a step; leaving support; more than one step.

(Contd.)

(*Contd.*)

		Gradually they can develop some skills to be independent. Some children can be trained to work in sheltered workshops and doing repetitive kinds of activities. • Continuous support may be required in certain severe retardation cases. • When placed with normal schools, children with severe disabilities should be taken for participation in various activities of the school like outings, music – art classes, gardening, parties, etc.	• Training in handling objects and how to take safety measures • Training in eating • Adjustment with work demands • Training in language skills – one word and its repetition many times. • Training in home living and community living, self-care and mobility. These are major functional areas where training is essential. • Close liaison with special schools and normal schools for mainstreaming of such children.
3.	Learning Disabled	• Direct instruction material • Assignment preparation for practice of the topic • Use of examples • Simple content • Evaluation techniques to be modified • Identify the learning disability and curriculum adaptation accordingly • Training in time management • Training in peer interaction and relationship	• Direct instructions, extra instructions in skills where the child is weak • Repeated readings/writings • Use of calculators and other devices • Questions in simple language • Simple sentences • One task at a time • Make learning interesting • The length of the task should be reduced.
4.	Orthopedically Handicapped	• Curriculum should include health care • School environment free from architectural barriers • Orientation to school environment • Resources available for the handicapped in the school • Functional curriculum • Projects that the child could do • Planning of activities suitable for the child • Physical adaptation of the classroom if necessary	• Acceptance of the child by the teacher and class • Training in using the artificial limbs and their maintenance • Giving awareness about the problem to the fellow students • Choice of activity and use of material that the child can do with his residual capacity and does not harm him. • Modifications in practicals and exercises • Participation of handicapped child in group activities • Seating arrangement suitable for the child • Caring attitude

(B) Classroom Management

The school and the classroom should be free from architectural barriers as far as possible. Educational institutions must provide ramps etc. in the buildings to facilitate the movement of the disabled. The management of the classroom involves the identification of appropriate places for seating the disabled children, the arrangement of lighting system, ensuring adequate visibility of directions, locating apparatus and equipment at a proper place, etc. The disabled children should be given a seat where they can feel comfortable in seeing written material on the board (for visually impaired and for hearing impaired) and do not get restricted from outside noise. A seat in the front of the class may be given so that they may not have to move much. The place of equipment and apparatus in the class should not be changed as such changes might affect the mobility of disabled. For visually impaired child it is necessary to see that the glare of the light does not come on his or her eyes. Lights should come from behind and adequate light should be available for deaf children who read from lip movement. Their seating should be such that they could watch the teacher talking. The peer group should be motivated to volunteer to help the disabled, for example, reading for the blind children. The other children of the class should also be made aware of the various disabilities so that they could interact with the children with disabilities in a normal manner.

Wherever needed interaction with parents should be made and they should be made partners in the development of the children. In Indian situations, parents and community are not much aware of various disabilities and their coping strategies, and people are illiterate and biased about disabilities. In such situations it is more important that the school keeps the parents involved in the education process of the disabled child and apprise them of the problem and progress of these children. Behaviour management is another aspect of class management. The desired behaviours should be developed through encouragement. Teacher should be sensitive to the problems of the disabled and should not pass derogatory comments. The teacher should also understand how and where to use the reinforcement for encouraging desired behaviours. He or she should consider ignoring undesired behaviours to the extent reasonable, and if such behaviours are not to be ignored should understand how to correct them by providing adequate directions.

(C) Peer Tutoring

In earlier days academic non-achievement was considered as the responsibility of the child but now, in modern times, the focus of blame for failure is shifting from student to classroom, learning environment and the manner in which interaction between teacher and student and among students takes place. Various researches on classroom environment show that if good opportunities are created through proper learning atmosphere in the class, incidence of failures would be reduced. To create good learning environment in the class various techniques have been adopted, one of which being peer tutoring. In this technique, a student plays the role of a teacher and teaches the other student of his class or a student who is in the lower class. The teacher supervises such types of teaching. The student teacher learns the techniques of teaching, chooses a topic, prepares a lesson and then teaches other students. Such arrangement may be made while planning the weekly programme of teaching. Periods can be allotted to 'Peer Tutoring'.

Peer tutoring can be for one student or for a group of students or for the whole class. The student teacher may take practice classes or teach the topics in which students face some difficulties to understand.

Peer tutoring helps in a number of ways:

- The student teacher develops self-confidence and a sense of responsibility.
- Before teaching the peers, he clears his own concepts for the topic he has to teach.
- Interaction among students develops, harmonious relations develop and disabled children are accepted in the class through this technique.
- Understanding with each other grows.
- The students who are finding difficulties in learning may ask about their difficulties freely from the student teacher, which they may not like to do in the regular class.
- Once better learning atmosphere is created through better interaction among students, undesirable behaviors from the students can be modified.

(D) Teaching Strategies

Thomas Becker and Armstrong said that "a teacher can modify and control the behaviour of her students by controlling her under response". In other words, a teacher can play a vital role in teaching of the disabled, if she can devise the proper strategies of teaching. All children cannot be taught through one strategy or through one teaching module. The abilities of children vary, some learn fast while some are slow in understanding things. The understanding of various subjects also varies from student to student. Some children can understand the concepts of mathematics much faster than their counterparts while others may be good in language skills. These variations may be more acute in case of disabled children while in the same class there may be children with learning disabilities, mental retardation, the blind, the deaf, etc. The teacher has to have a flexible approach to teaching. The teacher's role is not only to teach the subject but also to provide other training such as mobility training, self-care training, preparation of teaching material according to the needs of the disabled children, training in use and maintenance of aids and so on. Teaching strategies in respect of specific disabilities have been indicated in the table above.

(E) Teaching and Social Perception Skills

One of the objectives of teaching is modifying behaviours and motivating the child to learn new behaviours. The strategies of teaching should be adopted in such a manner that could lead to meet this objective of teaching. Behaviours are to be learned that are viewed favourably in the society and are according to the accepted societal norms. Such behaviours are developed through developing social skills. These skills are to be developed in the school so as to make a child good and respectable citizen of the society. Some of these social skills are:

- *Social Competence Skills:* These can help the disabled in dealing with others, making friends, respecting elderly, treating the needy with concern, making a place and acceptance in the society, showing desired behaviours etc.
- *Social Maintenance Skills:* These skills relate to helping other people in the society, accepting others with their problems, cooperate with others, learning to live with each other in the society and maintaining a social system.
- *Conflict Resolution Skills*: Third category of social skills is conflict resolution skills. Conflicts take place in the society. How to deal with them? Teacher has to develop conflict resolution skills among the students. They are to be taught how to compromise and persuade others for conflict resolution. Good communication techniques help in conflict management.

The above skills are to be developed in each child attending the school but for disabled children development of such skills is extremely necessary as they are to be taught to accept their disability also.

The social skills can be developed using various methods. These include:

(a) *Direct intervention*: Teacher can point out the behaviours that are not desirable.

(b) *Direct teaching*: Teacher can prepare direct instruction material to teach social skills.

(c) *Indirect methods* like demonstration, role-play, and modeling or showing films indicating desired behaviours.

An Appropriate Teaching Strategy

(a) *Choice of Instructional Material*: Instructional material and methodology should be selected which is culturally and traditionally appropriate and the child could relate himself to. For example, children in Rajasthan may identify with puppets. Whenever new material is chosen, child should be made fully familiar with it.

(b) *Management in the Class*: The teacher has to perform the management functions in the class that involve planning, organising, controlling and motivating. For all these four functions, communication is extremely important. A teacher can plan the activities in the class, can organize according to the time schedule, control the class and motivate the students in learning if he knows the proper communication techniques. The teacher has to be positive, empathetic and patient. Verbal communications should follow the non-verbal communications. For example, if the teacher wants to appreciate a child it should also be reflected with the tone and pitch of the speech, the facial expressions and other body gestures. The teacher should be able to develop team spirit in the class and gaps between normal and disabled children should be reduced. Teacher should also have a flexible approach in dealing with disabled students. If a methodology of instruction is not giving the desired outcome, it should immediately be modified. Variety should also be introduced to make the teaching interesting.

In a classroom, in managing the behaviours of the students, alternative activities should be introduced. For example, if a student is hyper-active and trying to disturb the class, he may be given some constructive activity to be engaged in like writing an assignment or making a drawing or making a model with the clay. Such alternative activities can be introduced according to the need and topic of the period.

Disabled students should be encouraged to participate in the activities of the class. Assistance may be provided to facilitate their participation. In case the child has not picked up the activity correctly, he should be guided on how to do, through demonstration.

Class management also involves providing feedback on the behaviours and learning of the children and giving reinforcements. Teacher should be able to decide when and how to provide such feedback. In case of disabled children feedback should be given immediately. If the child is doing right, he should be encouraged, if he needs corrections, he should be stopped so that he may not practice a task in the wrong manner.

(c) *Parents Participation:* Home is the first place where child interacts. Parents first observe the behaviours of a child and have first hand knowledge about the child. They know what interests the child, how he can be motivated, what are the triggers that make him aggressive or frustrated, what material or toys have been used to make him learn various activities. Thus, parents can play a very positive role in the development of the child if they share the information with the teacher in the school and other authorities. School should plan regular interaction with the parents. In such meetings, progress of the child, the problem areas, the difficulties etc. should be discussed. In certain cases, parents should be apprised of the methods of dealing with their child. Parents may have to be provided training in dealing with their disabled child.

(d) *Community Resource Mapping:* Community resources are helpful in the development of a disabled child. They can also help the child in learning his daily activities and also provide mobility training and develop functional skills. For example, if the disabled child is taken to a fruit shop, he can be trained how to pick up fruits, how the fruits are kept in the shop, how and where to pay and how to carry the purchased fruits back. Similarly, the child can be taken to various places depending upon what is to be learnt. He can, thus, be taught the use of stairs, elevators, use of parking places, use of other technological equipments, and familiarity with the area he has to live in. He can be taught how to keep himself safe and secure.

Resources in the Communities

For a disabled child, the following can be the resources:

1. Medical facilities like doctors, hospitals, and dispensaries.
2. Places of availability of equipments for the disabled.
3. Sheltered workshops

4. Physiotherapists, speech therapists etc.
5. Hobby clubs, gyms, youth clubs, playgrounds
6. The counsellors
7. The rehabilitation centers
8. Market and other places of interests and functional areas like parks, museums.
9. Banks
10. Libraries and computer centres
11. Religious places
12. Employment Exchange, placement agencies and employers
13. NGOs that can help the disabled
14. Other services available for the disabled like vocational training available at various places.

Schools should map these resources of the community a child lives in.

11

Integrated and Inclusive Education for the Disabled

Integrated Education

Children with disability suffer due to misconception and unfavourable attitudes of the society towards them. In many cases, societies are reluctant to accept the child with a disability and even parents in some cases try to hide that they had a disabled child in the house. Sometimes, mentally retarded children are referred to as 'mad' children. The normal children and people see the disabled with great curiosity; some times pass undesirable remarks or laugh at them. Of late, the attention of the world has been drawn towards the problems of disabled, their needs and necessity for their acceptance in the society like other human beings. The ideas of equality, liberty and fraternity under the French revolution led to reforms in the attitudes towards disabled. India also witnessed such a change.

A number of alternatives for disabled children have been tried and modified to make the disabled a part of the society. Separate institutions to look into the needs of disabled children of various categories have been established, the first being the School for the Deaf which was established in 1883 in Bombay.

Initiatives have also been taken for the education of children with disabilities. Initially, special schools and residential schools were established to educate such children. More than 3,000 such schools for various categories of disabled children have been established across the country. The efforts made in this direction achieved limited success due to various problems. The first problem was that the schools are not able to reach to all the disabled as these schools were mostly set up in the urban areas of the country. Moreover, the goal of accepting the disabled in the society along with the other human beings could not be fulfilled as they were segregated from the other children and they could not mix up with the other normal children. Nor the other children could accept them as their own. A different community of disabled grew in the society aloof and alone. It had socio- psychological implications. To overcome this, the concept of integrated education came into being to mainstream these children. Kautman, Cottlieb, Agard and Kukic have defined mainstreaming in these terms: "mainstreaming refers to the temporal, instructional and social integration of eligible exceptional children with normal peers based on on-going, individually determinant educational planning and programming process and requires classification of responsibility among regular and special education, administrative, instructional and supportive personnel." The definition shows that mainstreaming of disabled involves integration of these children with other normal children; educational planning and programming i.e. the support system to be developed for disabled; and classification of responsibilities to deal with disabilities is required such as provision of counseling, a resource teacher, etc.

Here integrated education does not mean that special schools would be closed. But it envisages that when the disabled children would be educated along with the normal children many problems that emerge with the special schools may be tackled and the accessibility of education to disabled children would increase. In case of acute disabilities, children may need special schools. Ministry of Human Resource Development introduced integrated education in India through Integrated Education of Disabled Children (IEDC) Scheme in collaboration with UNICEF in 1987 where Project Integrated Education for the disabled was started. The approach was based on area project instead of an individual school approach. All the disabled children in a cluster were identified and put in all the schools of that area. Under this approach, a mechanism of implementation of the programmes, specific objectives and specific arrangements in the schools are required including the teacher training programmes, removal of architectural barriers in the schools, etc.

Inclusive Education

The concept of inclusive education is a very new concept, which originated from the phenomenon of respect for an inherent dignity of all human beings. Under the inherent dignity of all human beings concept, the active participation of all the people in the society irrespective of their characteristics is emphasized. Inclusive education refers to "To all learners, young people—with or without disabilities being able to learn together in ordinary pre-school provisions, schools and community educational setting with appropriate network of support services." In this, it is believed that if a child is not able to learn it is not due to the disability of the child but due to the school system. It is the responsibility of the school to manage teaching in such a way that the needs of all the children are met.

The Central Advisory Board of Education reconstituted in 2004 in its report stated that implementation of an inclusive system of education for all assumes greater significance of systematic reforms specially in the context of disability since in the core of their exclusive and marginalisation is inadequacy of the basic education system and processes that have failed to guarantee equal access and full participation. In order to make inclusive education a reality, in addition to the provision of aids and appliances, a flexible, broad and balanced curriculum that can meet the needs of all children is a necessity. An inclusive curriculum recognizes the need for the schools to be organized with the individual differences of students in mind and adopt flexibility to enable all students to achieve their goals. Implementation of an inclusive curriculum would require a number of changes in the present day teaching practices, curriculum content, evaluation procedures and available resources at the school level without which the goal of providing quality education would remain elusive. It is also important to mobilize support from parents, the community, and special schools. It recommended that all schools be made inclusive by:

- Enforcing without exception the neighborhood school policy
- Removing physical barriers
- Reviewing barriers created by admission procedures (screening, identification, parental interaction, selection and evaluation including private schools
- Building capacity of teachers to function in an inclusive setting
- Making the curriculum flexible and appropriate to accommodate the diversity of school children including those with disability in both cognitive and non-cognitive areas
- Making support services available in the form of technology (inclusive ICT), teaching-learning materials and specialists.
- Involving parents, family, and community at all stages of education.
- Gear all teacher education programmes (both pre-service and in-service to develop pedagogical skills required in inclusive classroom
- Mobilise special schools as resource centers for providing support to inclusive schools.

The concept of inclusive education has been introduced in District Primary Education Programme (DPEP), which recognized that there is a need for community mobilisation and early detection of disability, training for teachers, mapping of resources, support services, provision of educational aids and appliances and removal of architectural barriers.

Specific Considerations in Mainstreaming of the Disabled: (A Plan of Action)

Organisation of Classes According to the Needs of Disabled

There is a need to organize special classes in the school for disabled children according to their needs. All the disabled may not require the same kind of special teaching. The retarded child has to be given an opportunity to develop at his own pace. The curriculum has to be modified. Similarly, a modification of the syllabus tailored to the cognitive abilities of the profoundly deaf child may be necessary. No doubt, these children can participate in other regular activities of the school like physical education, social studies when taught through audio-visual methods, arts and crafts, co-curricular activities etc.

Periodic assessment of every handicapped child should be made and areas should be identified in which he could be integrated with other children. Where ever needed arrangements should be made for special or remedial classes

Resource Room Facility

Many disabled children can participate in the regular classroom activities and teaching. But there may be a need for a specially trained teacher who can teach use of special equipment or maintaining the same. Resource teachers may also help in guiding the disabled about safety measures. A blind or partially sighted child may need to be brought in the resource room to learn Braille, a partially hearing child may have to be brought to the resource room where hearing aids are available. Schools should be equipped with such resource rooms. Number of resource rooms can be established according to the types of disabled children, their number and their needs for such facilities. The responsibility of the resource room should be given to the teacher who has special training and is familiar with maintaining the equipments.

The Trained Teacher (Itinerant)

Trained teachers are required to deal with disabled. Sometimes schools find it difficult to appoint special teachers if the number of students is less in a certain kind of disability. In such scenario a trained teacher may be appointed for a cluster of schools and her itinerary to visit various schools may be fixed. Such arrangement is termed as itinerant programme.

Partial Integration

In certain cases it is not possible to integrate the disabled in the normal schools fully as the disabled may need constant supervision or support. For example, in the case of children with sensory limitations, learning disabilities, or multiple disabilities they may have to stay in a hostel provided by a special school. In such scenario, partial integration may be facilitated wherein they get their education in an ordinary school while getting other facilities from special school.

Structural Modifications

It is necessary for the school to remove architectural barriers to facilitate easy and comfortable mobility of the disabled for their integration. Other similar architectural arrangements like special toilets, wide doors for the movement of wheeled chairs etc. may be made where needed.

Teacher-pupil ratio

Successful integration of disabled in the normal schools also depends upon the teacher-pupil ratio. It has to be decided according to the types of disabled children and the degree of their disability. In case of learning disabled this ratio can be 1:10 while in case of orthopaedics this ratio may increase.

Vocational training

While vocational training is important for every child, it has special significance for a handicapped child. Adequate work experience and vocational training in the school for the disabled should be arranged. The work should be chosen according to the limitations of the child. The vocational exposure should vary according to the needs of the child. Every school generally has provision for such exposure in terms of work experience but in case of disabled, some new activities may have to be introduced or existing ones may have to be modified. In case some other nearby schools have some activities suitable for disabled, interactions can be had with such schools and possibilities can be explored to send some children to those schools for work experience exposure.

Counselling

It is important for every school to maintain a detailed profile of each child including his socio-economic background placed in an integrated programme so that appropriate counselling to parents and children could be provided. The provision of counselling should be available for disabled at least on an itinerant basis if the school cannot appoint a regular counselor.

Interaction

For disabled child it is essential that his/her integration with the normal school should have flexibility. Whenever required, the child should be sent to special school. There should be proper liaison between the special school and normal school.

Teachers for disabled

The success of every educational programme depends on the quality of the teachers and their attitudes. It is more important in case of disabled. Specialy trained teachers should be available for dealing with disabled. A teacher trained in dealing with blind children or the deaf can be appointed as a resource or an itinerant teacher. Similarly, a teacher trained in the education of the mentally retarded could be placed in charge of a special class of retarded children in an ordinary school.

A teacher of handicapped children should be familiar with normal teaching procedures. It is necessary for him to acquire additional qualifications to teach a particular category of children. If some subject teachers are interested, school may arrange for their training to deal with a certain category of disabled children. Special increments may be offered to such teachers for incentives. It can be done where schools cannot appoint special teachers.

The above points should be kept in mind before integrating the disabled children in the normal school. Integration is possible with greater awareness in the society about disabilities and inculcating positive attitudes towards disabilities. A family with four or five children or families, which follow, joint family system deal with persons of various age groups, abilities and attitudes at a time. Similarly a teacher can also deal with students of various abilities in her class. Integration is not imposible.

12

Policies and Programmes

Constitutional Obligations Universalisation of Elementary Education

In the Constitution of India, as it was originally enacted, right to education was not a Fundamental Right of the citizens. However, The Directive Principles of State Policy (Article 45, Part IV of the Constitution) laid down that "The State shall endeavor to provide within a period of ten years from the commencement of this Constitution for free and compulsory education for all children until they complete the age of fourteen years." This Constitutional goal, which was to be achieved by 1960, is still a distant goal.

In 2002, free and compulsory education of all children in the age group of six to fourteen years was made a Fundamental Right (under Article 21A) through the 86th Amendment to the Constitution. This Constitutional Amendment further provides that it shall be the fundamental duty of every citizen who is a parent or a guardian to provide opportunities for education to his child/ward in the age group six to fourteen years. Steps are currently being taken to enact a Right to Education Act to give a practical shape to guaranteeing this Fundamental Right.

The concepts of liberty, equality and justice are the pillars on which the Constitution of India stands. While the Constitution does not directly talk about the persons with disabilities, the principles of equality (in particular of opportunity) and justice (in particular, economic and social), enshrined in it demand that the Government pursues policies and programmes that ensure social justice and equality of opportunities for all the citizens, including those with disabilities. Further, while discussing the concept of equality as a Fundamental Right, the Constitution lays down that the State can make specific provisions for advancement of any socially and educationally backward classes of citizens. These constitutional directives have been governing the Indian Government's policies regarding the disabled persons.

Five Year Plans and the Disabled

In the earlier phases of planned development in India, the approach towards the disabled population was one of providing effective welfare services. The importance of providing social services to the disabled was recognized as early as in the First Five Year Plan and has continued to receive increasing attention over all the later Plans.

First Five Year Plan

The First Plan (1951-56) observed that "a certain number of welfare agencies are already working in this field, but little information about their resources and their ability to deal with the problem is at present available. ......The physically handicapped person, if he is not able to receive medical attention, or when such attention is found to be of no avail, has to depend upon his family for maintenance and shelter. Absence of family support leads to beggary, or dependence upon public charity. Inadequate medical treatment, absence of vocational training, and lack of opportunities for social adjustment of the persons to the environment has contributed to the sufferings of a large number of persons who ought to receive the intelligent assistance of the community, and if possible an effective assistance from the State. Physically handicapped persons are classified as (i) those lacking in one or more physical senses, i.e., blindness and deafness, or combinations; (2) those suffering from movement difficulties; i.e., orthopedic, malnutrition and cardiacs; and (3) lepers, epileptics, rachitics, and dumb persons. The total number of afflicted persons in India has hardly ever been correctly estimated. This is due to defective enumeration, lack of definitions, and the desire of persons to avoid publicity to their handicaps. To obtain better estimates of afflicted persons, sample surveys in selected urban and rural areas are needed. Some provision for physically handicapped persons exists in several States. Voluntary associations which are already working the welfare programmes for this class of persons need to be encouraged and assisted."

Second Five Year Plan

The Second Five Year Plan (1956-61) was more focused on the education and training of the disabled. Referring to the National Advisory Council for the Education of the Handicapped set up in September, 1955 by the Ministry of Education the Plan remarked "The functions of this Council are to advise the Central Government on problems concerning the education, training, and employment and the provision of social and cultural amenities for the physically and mentally handicapped, to formulate new schemes and to provide liaison with voluntary organisations working in this field. It is proposed to undertake a survey of the problem of the physically and mentally handicapped. There are at present about 60 schools for the blind, 44 for the deaf-mutes, 9 for the crippled and diseased and 5 for the mentally handicapped. The majority of these are private institutions which are aided by Government. In the second plan provision has been made for providing additional facilities such as model schools for blind children and deaf children, a women's section in the training school for the adult blind, provision for scholarships etc. In the plans of a number of States also provision has been made for the welfare and education of physically and mentally handicapped persons. For the rehabilitation of persons suffering from incurable diseases provision has been made in the programmes of the Ministry of Health."

Third Five Year Plan

The Third Plan (1961-66) took notice of the progress achieved till then in developing special services and facilities for physically and mentally handicapped persons, specially those who are blind, deaf and dumb, and those who are orthopaedically handicapped and mentally deficient. It remarked that, "for each category, the primary object of the services provided for these groups should be to enable them to rehabilitate themselves through work. Since many persons in these groups come from rural areas, where traditionally the community readily provides a measure of help, it would be desirable to give a rural bias to the training and rehabilitation programmes for these groups. Facilities for enabling handicapped persons to find work have been provided at a few employment exchanges. Local bodies and voluntary organisations are already playing a significant role in serving handicapped persons. Their services should be further developed along the following lines:

(a) teaching handicapped persons in their homes;
(b) providing work in the homes or in the neighbourhood for those not able to move;
(c) providing recreational facilities for the handicapped, the aged and the infirm; and
(d) providing assistance by way of special aids.

During the period of training for new employment, there should be provision for financial assistance, stipends, etc."

Fourth Five Year Plan

The Fourth Plan (1969-74) recognized that in providing social services to the handicapped and the destitute, the government could only "attempt limited tasks to try and ensure optimal benefits from both State and voluntary effort. Such tasks will include various types of assistance—monetary, technical and administrative—to voluntary organisations. Government can undertake demonstration of pilot projects. They can legislate where necessary, regulate and administer welfare organisations and coordinate the relevant activities of education, health and social welfare".

The Plan proposed to expand and improve the services in the National Centre for the Blind at Dehra Dun which already had a model school, a training centre, a workshop for the manufacture of Braille appliances for education, a central Braille press, and a national library for the blind. It also proposed to start a school for partially sighted children. The training centre for the adult deaf which offered facilities to boys of 16 - 25 years of age in engineering and non-engineering occupations would be expanded and a school for the partially deaf started. The model school for mentally retarded children in Delhi for boys and girls between 6 to 15 years in age with I. Q. ranging from 50 to 75 would be expanded and workshop facilities provided. The Plan also proposed to make a beginning with a national centre for the physically handicapped to serve as a demonstration project for the development of services for the orthopaedically handicapped in different parts of the country and to provide the necessary training facilities. As a first step it is proposed to start a school for the cerebral palsied children and a vocational training centre for the severely crippled.

The Plan proposed to continue with the means-cum merit tested scholarships for the physically handicapped already provided. A significant proposal contained in the Fourth Plan was to initiate some pilot schemes for the integrated education of the blind, the partially blind and the partially deaf. Training facilities for the teachers of the handicapped were proposed to be expanded and improved. Grant-in-aid would continue to be given to voluntary organisations for purchase of equipment and improvement of standards of services. Institutions in the State for the education and training of the physically handicapped would be expanded and the services improved. To facilitate the employment of the handicapped, the Plan advised the special employment exchanges to make efforts to convince the employers that in many occupations the physically handicapped are as efficient and productive as normal workers and convey to the training institutions the requirements of employers so that training can be progressively improved.

Fifth Five Year Plan

The Fifth Plan continued with programmes such as improvement of existing national institutes for the blind, the deaf, the mentally retarded and the orthopaedically handicapped, research on aids and appliances for the handicapped, scholarships for the disabled, sheltered workshops and assistance to voluntary agencies in the field of welfare and development of the disabled. However, from the Fifth Plan (1974-79), there had been a significant change in approach. Up to the close of the Fourth Plan, most of the programmes were curative or related to easing the difficulties. From the Fifth Plan onwards, emphasis has been on the promotion of preventive and developmental services.

The Sixth Plan (1980-85) aimed at encouraging the physically handicapped to integrate with the normal stream of life. Their education, training and employment had to be promoted to facilitate such integration. Prevention and early detection of physical handicaps was given importance.

Sixth Five Year Plan

The Sixth Plan called for a comprehensive primary health care, distribution of Vitamin 'A' to prevent blindness among children and intensive educational programme for the prevention of accidents on a high priority. "Medical and para-medical health services for pre- and postnatal care and immunisation would be expanded in order to prevent several types of deformities. Legal frame-work for the prevention and treatment of accidents as also insurance against them would be suitably provided. Safety regulations would be devised for various categories of occupations and strictly enforced."

The Sixth Plan aimed at creation of opportunities for integrated education, vocational training and economic rehabilitation in order to integrate the disabled with the main stream of socio-economic life. It envisaged that the scheme of integrated education (which aims at placing the disabled children in ordinary schools with the help of special teachers, aids and resources, trained teachers, special equipment and books, resource and assessment facility) would be revised and expanded so that the varying needs of different types of handicapped children might be met effectively. Designs of buildings may be suitably modified to facilitate mobility of the handicapped along with the normal persons. Special schools would be discouraged except for severely handicapped, who could not be educated with normal children. The scheme of scholarships, both at the Centre and the States, would be expanded further to offer financial support to the students pursuing educational and vocational pursuits. The existing facilities for the production of text books and literature would be augmented to meet the requirements of expanded educational facilities. The Apprenticeship Training Scheme would be extended to all categories of disabled to substantially expand and develop in-plant training. The Sixth Plan also proposed that the scope of Vocational Rehabilitation Centres (VRCs), then undertaking only evaluation and adjustment training for the rehabilitation of the physically handicapped, primarily for the orthopaedically handicapped, be expanded by imparting 'Skill training' to the physically handicapped and 'providing job oriented experience in close collaboration with local industry to promote employability of the disabled. Towards this end, 'skill training' workshops and training-cum-production centres were proposed to be added to the VRCs.

Besides educational and vocational training, the Plan recognized that the functional ability of the disabled would be improved by equipping them with proper aids and appliances. Provision of these aids would enable them to participate in the educational and economic activities in a better way. Simple, durable and inexpensive equipment will be made available to them. For this purpose, the Artificial Limbs Manufacturing Corporation would widen its activities to cover all categories of the handicapped and will develop the required aids and appliances. The National Institute of Prosthetic and Orthotic Training would take lead in the development of rehabilitative techniques and equipment in this field. Training of medical and paramedical staff in rehabilitation techniques would be provided for. Community health volunteers and teachers would be given training in early detection of handicaps.

Employment Opportunities for the handicapped would be increased substantially. Schemes linked with vocational training for self-employment would be strengthened and expanded. The reservation of one per cent of vacancies each for the blind, deaf and orthopaedically handicapped in Group 'C' and 'D' 'posts in Central services and in comparable posts in public sector undertakings made by the Government in 1977 would be followed by strengthening the arrangements for monitoring at the Central and State levels, possibilities for reservation of jobs, stalls and counters at Cinema house's, railway stations and other public places as well as other avenues for open competitive employment, self-employment of various types, would be fully explored to provide larger scope for their absorption. Voluntary organisations would be aided for setting up sheltered workshops for the 'severely handicapped to supplement these efforts.

The Sixth Plan proposed that mass media be utilised to give widest publicity to the promotion of preventive, medical, vocational, educational and rehabilitative aspects of various schemes intended for the benefit of the handicapped.

At the time of formulating the Sixth Plan, there were at that time four National Institutes for the Handicapped i.e. one each for the visually handicapped, deaf and dumb orthopaedically handicapped and mentally handicapped. The Plan called for strengthening and expansion of these institutes so that they could fulfill the tasks envisaged, particularly research and training at the national level. In addition, the national associations and research organizations would be encouraged to undertake research into the problems relating to the identification of techniques and adaptations for rehabilitation of various categories of the disabled, training of teachers, development of technical and prosthetic aids and other areas.

Seventh Five Year Plan

The Seventh Plan (1985-90) continued with the approach of the earlier Plan and stressed that education and training played a vital role in the socio-economic rehabilitation of the physically handicapped. The Plan, accordingly proposed that the handicapped persons would be encouraged to pursue education and vocational training through scholarships and other promotional aids in order to draw them closer to the normal stream of life. Prevention of disabilities through early detection and treatment of the physically handicapped would be given relatively high priority compared to purely curative services. Observing that a large number of disabilities are preventable, if timely measures were taken in the areas of health and nutrition and accident prevention, the Seventh Plan proposed strengthening the activities of immunisation/ prophylaxis against diphtheria, whooping cough and tetanus, nutritional anemia and blindness due to Vitamin 'A' deficiency, vaccination against polio and typhoid and the provision of nutritional supplements, education in health and nutrition, suitable measures to prevent and control disabilities caused by accidents and an intesified programme of mass education for early identification of disabilities and the symptoms causing them.

The Seventh Plan envisaged educational incentives like scholarships/stipends, book-grants, uniforms etc., to improve the enrollment ratio of physically handicapped children at the primary and middle levels. The Plan proposed to strengthen and expand training institutions to make them perform the roles expected of them at the national level. Special attention to be given to the development of multi-disciplinary services, both in identification and treatment of the handicapped. Facilities for fitting of aids and appliances, particularly in the remote and backward areas, to be expanded in order to enable the beneficiaries to participate in economic and cultural activities to the fullest possible extent. The schemes of orthotic and prosthetic aids to physically handicapped persons had to be expanded further with adequate facilities of fitting centres. It stated that the National Institute for Rehabilitation, Training and Research (NIRTR), earlier known as National Institute of Prosthetic and Orthotic Training (NIPOT), would continue to conduct training courses for prosthetic and orthotic technicians, multi-rehabilitation assistance, doctors and other professionals. Training schemes would be so devised as to impart adequate vocational skills leading to employment in the open market or to self-employment. Sheltered workshops for the severely handicapped would seek to supplement those efforts. Suitable arrangements were envisaged for organising supply of raw materials and for marketing their products. Employment officers specialising in placement of handicapped persons were proposed to be added in all employment exchanges with registration of 150 or more handicapped persons. Incentives would continue to encourage disabled workers to improve their standard of performance to persuade employers to accept physically handicapped persons. The scheme of District Rehabilitation Centres (DRC), which aimed at providing comprehensive and integrated care services to the handicapped individual from early childhood till he is rehabilitated in the community, was taken up on a pilot basis.

Eighth Five Year Plan

The Eighth Five Year Plan (1992-97) recognized that a coordinated approach was needed in providing services for the disabled, which covered the entire range of aspects from prevention of handicaps to rehabilitation. The main thrust of the policy was to enable the disabled to become self-dependent and productive members of the society through opportunities for education, vocational training and employment. The Plan also recognized that the services, as far as possible, be community based.

The specific programmes in the Eighth Plan in the area of prevention of disabilities included continuation and strengthening of the universal immunization, streamlining of the nutrition services and safety measures to prevent occupational and other accidents through better enforcement of the laws and generation of awareness in the families and community. Among the curative measures included were expansion of therapeutic and fitment services and research and development in these areas to render the disabled self-reliant. Recognizing that education and training had an important role in the economic rehabilitation of the disabled, the Plan called for strengthening of the programme for integrated education of the disabled and expanding the network of special schools. Other important programmes included in the Eighth Plan were expansion of the scheme of scholarships, particularly in the rural and backward areas, diversification of vocational training in tune with the market demand, financial and other assistance to the disabled to pursue self-employment activities, strengthening of the national institutes for various types of disabilities and involving them more actively in the design and implementation of alternative service models and in raising the standards of service. It emphasized continued involvement of and assistance to voluntary agencies to take up activities providing services to the disabled.

Ninth Five Year Plan

The Ninth Five Year Plan (1997-2002) marked another paradigm shift in approach to the issue of the disabled, from one of welfare to one of rights. It emphasized the process of empowerment of the disabled and called for

- Every possible effort towards effective enforcement of the Persons with Disabilities Act (PDA), 1995
- 'Reaching the rural disabled' – those who have been neglected so far will receive special attention
- Continuing efforts to converge of the existing services in welfare —specific and other welfare—related sectors to gain the optimum benefit
- Creation of an enabling environment for persons with disabilities to exercise their rights for equal opportunities and full participation will be put into action through joint efforts of both Governmental and Non-Governmental Organisations
- Adoption of a special strategy of family / Community-Based Rehabilitation (CBR) by pooling the resources of both financial and manpower, of all the concerned
- Special efforts to prevent disabilities through supplementary nutritional feeding for both children and expectant / nursing mothers, early detection and timely intervention
- Strengthening / expansion of special schools and vocational training programmes with barrier-free environment

- Positive discrimination through earmarking not less than 3% of benefits under various employment cum poverty alleviation programmes like IRDP, JRY, NRY, PMRY, EAP, DWCRA etc.
- Strengthening and expansion of existing National Institutes for the persons with disabilities
- Special efforts to equip the persons with disabilities with most suitable, simple, durable and inexpensive Aids and Appliances
- Setting up of a National Trust to ensure total care and custodianship of those with Mental Retardation and Cerebral Palsy.

The Ninth Plan reaffirms the earlier commitment of making disabled active, self-reliant and productive contributors to the national economy. Accordingly, it lays special emphasis on adopting an integrated approach to empowering the disabled and mainstream them. To this effect, the Plan called for systematic efforts to converge the existing services under the welfare-related sectors of health, nutrition, education, science and technology, rural development, urban development, women and child development, information and broadcasting etc. In these efforts, the rural disabled, who have been neglected all through, should receive special attention. Efforts should be made to reach the services to the rural disabled right up to the district level and with perspectives to extend up to the village level in a phased way starting from the Ninth Plan, through a comprehensive National Programme for Rehabilitation of Persons with Disablities.

Noting that empowerment of the persons with disabilities would be a continuous process wherein the joint efforts of both governmental and non-governmental organisations would be required to create an enabling environment for the disabled to exercise their rights for equal opportunities and full participation with the strength and support of the recently enacted Persons with Disabilities(PD) Act, 1995, the Plan called for every effort towards effective enforcement of the Act on a priority basis.

The Ninth Five Year Plan further proposed:

Implementation of the strategy of Community Based Rehabilitation for pooling the efforts of the persons with disabilties, their families and the communities, as well as that of the concerned Ministries/ Departments in a coordinated way. To fill the existing void in the rural areas, efforts would be made to promote the CBR through voluntary organisations.

Special efforts to strengthen the preventive measures as the incidence of the disability can be prevented through early detection and timely intervention. Such efforts include the on-going supplementary nutrition feeding programmes including prophylaxis against Vitamin A, anaemia and Iodine deficiency, universalization of immunization, safety measures for prevention of accidents on roads and at work- places and education and awareness generation to the family and the community

Encouragement to more and more children with disabilities to join the Integrated Schools by extending special incentives like free books, uniforms, transport and aids and appliances etc. so that the disabled children would be able to complete their school education in these Integrated Schools, which are equipped with infrastructural facilities, support services and barrier-free environment. Besides, the ongoing scheme of the Integrated Education for the Disabled Children (IEDC) would be further expanded during the Ninth Plan to meet the growing demand for these types of schools, especially in the context of enacting the P.W.D. Act, 1995, ensuring equal opportunities for the disabled. In this regard, special attention will be paid to those districts which have poor, or no, educational facilities of Integrated Education.

Substantial expansion of vocational training programmes for the persons with disabilities, which are employment-oriented by activating the existing Industrial Training Institutes (ITIs), Craft Training Centres (CTCs) and Vocational Rehabilitation Centres (VRCs). Simultaneously, efforts would also be made to set up Training-cum-Production Centres and Sheltered Workshops to ensure that the trained persons with disabilities are kept gainfully engaged either on wage or self-employment. While planning for the training programmes for the disabled, every effort would be made to diversify the trades, besides giving priority to the up-coming trades, keeping in view the trends and the demands in the employment market.

Earmarking of certain percentage of benefits for the disabled under various poverty alleviation programmes like IRDP, DWCRA, JRY, EAP etc.

Continuous monitoring of the implementation of the policy of 3 per cent reservation of vacancies for the blind, deaf and orthopaedically disabled in Group 'A', 'B', 'C' and 'D' posts in Central Services and in the Public Sector Undertakings

Conducting a needs assessment survey to assess the status of women and girls with disabilities.

Support to voluntary organisations, who have been playing an important role in the delivery of services for the persons with disabilities, to widen their operations so as to reach the unreached, viz. the rural disabled. They would be involved in sensitizing the rural population towards prevention, early detection, timely intervention, appropriate referral and follow-up services, rehabilitation etc.

Setting up of a National Trust to ensure total care and custodianship of those with mental retardation and cerebral palsy. For the welfare and care of the Spastics, special service centres would be set up to cater to the urban slums and backward rural areas, undertake large-scale manpower development programmes, and evolve new approaches to information dissemination and community awareness. Rehabilitative services, like appropriate treatment, psychological support, day-care centres and specialised training for manpower development, especially in the area of cerebral palsy and mental retardation, would be expanded

Setting up an exclusive National Institute for Multiple Disabilities, in addition to the existing National Institutes which will be devising practical strategies to extend services to the disabled living in the backward rural and remote tribal areas.

Special endeavour to equip the persons with disabilities with simple, suitable, durable and inexpensive aids and appliances so as to improve their functional ability and enable them to take up various income generation activities to become economically independent and self-reliant.

Tenth Five Year Plan

The Tenth Plan (2002-07) found the strategy of 'Empowering the Disabled' adopted during the Ninth Plan to be effective in achieving the goals set, and has, therefore, chosen to continue with the same approach. The Plan aimed to strengthen the process by adopting a multi-sectoral approach to attend to the needs of the disabled and achieving convergence of the existing services in all the welfare-related sectors, so that the required services of preventive, curative, rehabilitative, welfare and development can be extended. The Tenth Plan observed that the PWD Act of 1995 had already generated a lot of awareness among the disabled to make them conscious of their rights, besides raising their expectations towards a better future, and that the government would need to take steps to fulfill these expectations through effective policies and programmes. The Tenth Plan's commitment was, therefore, to create an enabling environment in which persons with disabilities can exercise their rights, enjoying equal opportunities and full participation with the strength and support of the PWD Act of 1995. To ensure adequate financial support to the programmes envisaged to achieve this goal, Tenth Plan advocated the introduction of a 'Component Plan for the Disabled' in the budget of all the concerned Ministries/Departments.

The Tenth Plan also proposed to accord special priority to the rural disabled who continue to be the neglected lot. Efforts had to be made to remove the existing lacuna of limiting the coverage only to urban areas under various programmes. The Plan stated that action would be initiated to enhance the outreach and extension services to the rural areas by tailoring the programmes to suit the local requirements through Area-specific Action Plans. It emphasized that these facilities are extended right up to the district level and ultimately to the village level in a phased manner through the on-going 'National Programme for the Rehabilitation of Persons with Disabilities'.

The Tenth Plan, thus, aims at following:

- Effective enforcement of the PWD Act, 1995 .
- Reaching the Un-reached in rural and remote areas through the specially launched 'National Programme for the Rehabilitation of Persons with Disabilities'.
- Introduction of a 'Component Plan for the Disabled' to promote the flow of funds/benefits to the disabled from all the concerned Ministries/Departments.
- Motivating the Disabled to organise themselves into Self-Help Groups through the special strategy of Community-Based Rehabilitation and encouraging family members, especially the women, to be the primary care-givers to the disabled.
- Strengthen the National Institutes, Indian Spinal Injuries Centre and other Regional/Composite Rehabilitation Centres and outreach their services to the needy groups and areas.
- Prevent disabilities through early detection, timely immunisation, dietary corrections, supplement both macro and micro nutrients to children and expectant and nursing mothers; and ensure safety on both roads and at work places with a special watch on the increasing and emerging variants of disabilities.
- Integrate disabled children into mainstream education through universalisation of education with a barrier-free environment.
- Provide various options of schooling systems to disabled children like Inclusive Education, Integrated Schools, Special Schools, Non-Formal Education etc. to suit their specific needs/ requirements.
- Expand Special Schools and Vocational Training opportunities

in the up-coming trades for the disabled, especially for the disabled women and adolescent girls.

- Equip the disabled with suitable, simple, durable inexpensive Aids and Appliances, including specially designed gender-specific assistive devices.
- Earmark not less than 3 per cent reservation of benefits in all the Poverty Alleviation Programmes in action both in rural and urban areas.
- Expand the existing and launch new programmes for generating more and more of employment opportunities, both wage and self-employment with 'forward' and 'backward' linkages to keep the disabled gainfully employed.
- Increase employment opportunities for the disabled in the service sector through effective identification and filling up of reserved posts up to 3 per cent of the vacancies in the Government and Public Sector Undertakings through Special Employment Exchanges/ Special Cells in the Regular Employment Exchanges.
- Provide special thrust to the welfare and rehabilitation of mentally disabled through specific services like special education, sheltered workshops, day care centres and long term stay institutions etc under the aegis of the National Trust for the Welfare of Persons with Autism, Cerebral Palsy, Mental Retardation and Multiple Disabilities.

Policies for Education of Persons with Disabilities

For quite some years after Independence, policies in relation to persons with disabilities focused on their economic rehabilitation. The emphasis was mainly on development of vocational skills among the disabled to enable them earn their livelihood and on their medical rehabilitation through provision of aids and appliances. In so far education of the disabled children was concerned, setting up of special schools, mainly by the non-government agencies, was encouraged. There were attempts to move away from the model of special education towards that of integrated education during the seventies, and the shifting emphasis was well reflected in the New Education Policy adopted in 1986.

National Policy on Education (NPE), 1986

The National Policy on Education, 1986, which provided for a comprehensive policy framework for the development of education in India. This policy pronouncement and the Programme of Action that followed in the same year, assigned specific responsibilities for organising, implementing and financing the educational activities. The Policy placed "special emphasis on the removal of disparities and to equalize educational opportunity by attending to the specific needs of those who have been denied equality so far". In so far as the children with disabilities are concerned, NPE stated that the objective of education should be to integrate the physically and mentally disabled with the general community as equal partners and to prepare them to face life with courage and confidence. It also suggested proper orientation and pre-service training for general teachers on disability management and provision of vocational training.

The specific measures suggested are:

(i) wherever feasible, the education of children with major handicaps, and other mild handicaps, will be common with that of others;

(ii) Special schools with hostels will be provided, as far as possible, at district headquarters, for the severely handicapped children;

(iii) Adequate arrangements will be made to give vocational training to the disabled;

(iv) Teacher's training programmes will be reoriented, in particular for teachers of primary classes, to deal with the special difficulties of the handicapped children; and

(v) Voluntary effort for the education of the disabled, will be encouraged in every possible manner.

The National Educational Policy was revised further in 1992. While there were no changes in the specific measures for the education of the disabled indicated above, there were certain measures included for promotion of equality of educational opportunity in general. These included comprehensive programmes of post-literacy and continuing education through establishment of continuing education centers of diverse kind to enable adults to continue their education of their choice; workers' education through employers, trade unions and government; wider promotion of books, libraries and reading rooms; use of radio, TV and films as mass as well as group learning media; creation of learners' groups and organizations; and programmes of distance learning.

National Policy for Persons with Disabilities, 2006

In keeping with the international trends, there has been a change in the perception about the disabled in recent years. There is a growing realization that the quality of lives of persons with disabilities can be raised by providing them opportunities and appropriate facilities. The disabled have equal rights with other members of the society to enjoy the fruits of development. The National Policy for Persons with Disabilities announced by the Government of India in 2006 reflects this new emphasis on bringing persons with disabilities into the mainstream of the society. It recognises that "persons with disabilities are valuable human resource for the country". It seeks to create an environment that provides them equal opportunities, protection of their rights and full participation in society.

The focus of the National Policy is on:

(a) *preventions of disabilities* and
(b) *rehabilitation measures.*

In so far as prevention is concerned, the National Policy seeks to prevent the incidence of disabilities through programmes for prevention of diseases that bring about disabilities and for creation of awareness about measures for prevention of disabilities.

The rehabilitation measures include

(i) physical rehabilitation (through early detection, counselling and medical interventions, provision of aids and appliances and development of rehabilitation personnel),
(ii) educational rehabilitation (through promotion of education and development of vocational skills) and
(iii) economic rehabilitation (through provision of opportunities and for employment in government, wage employment in private sector and self-employment.

The Policy also stresses on the special needs of women and children with disabilities, importance of creating barrier-free environment and social security, and the important role that can be played by the non-government organizations in services to the persons with disabilities.

Recognising that education is the most effective vehicle of social and economic empowerment, the National Policy emphasizes the need for mainstreaming of the persons with disabilities in the general education system through Inclusive Education. The role of the existing programmes of Sarva Shiksha Abhiyan (SSA) and the Integrated Education for Disabled Children (IEDC) Scheme are highlighted by the National Policy. Identification of children with disabilities through regular surveys and their enrolment in appropriate schools, right kind of learning material, trained and sensitized teachers, disabled-friendly schools, development of facilities for technical and vocational education suitable for productive economic activities, and access to universities, technical institutions and institutions of higher learning are some of the aspects finding mention in the National Policy. The objective is to ensure that every child with disability has access to appropriate pre-school, primary and secondary level education by 2020.

Some of the specific interventions proposed in the National Policy for educational development of the disabled are:

- Make schools (building, approaches, toilets, playgrounds, laboratories, libraries etc.) barrier free and accessible for all types of disability.
- Medium and method of teaching will be suitably adapted to the requirements of most disability conditions.
- Technical/ supplementary/ specialized system of teaching/ learning will be made available within the school or at a common center easily accessible to a cluster of schools.
- Teaching/learning tools and aids such as educational toys, Braille/talking books, appropriate software etc. will be made available. Incentives will be given to expand facilities for setting up of general libraries, e-libraries, Braille-libraries and talking books libraries, resource rooms etc.
- National Open School and distance learning programmes will be popularized and extended to other parts in the country.
- Sign language, Alternative and Augmentative Communications (AAC) and other modes as a viable medium in inter personal communication will be recognized, standardized and popularized.
- Schools will be located within easy traveling distance. Alternatively, viable travel arrangements will be made with the assistance of the community, State and NGOs.
- Parent-Teacher counseling and grievance redressal system will be set up in the schools.
- There will be separate mechanism to review annually the intake and retention of the girl child with disability at primary, secondary and higher levels of education.
- Many children with disabilities, who cannot join inclusive education system, would continue to get educational services from special schools. Special schools shall be appropriately re-modeled and re-oriented based on technological development. These schools will also help prepare children with disabilities to join mainstream inclusive education.

- In some cases due to the nature of disability (its type and degree), personal circumstances and preferences, home-based education will be provided.
- Course curriculum and evaluation system for children with various disabilities shall be developed keeping in view their capabilities. Examination system will be modified to make it disabled friendly by exemptions such as learning mathematics, learning only one language, etc. Further, facilities like extra time, use of calculators, use of Clarke's tables, scribes etc would be provided based on the requirement.
- Model Schools of Inclusive Education will be set up in each State/ U.T to promote education of persons with disabilities.
- In the era of knowledge society, computers play very important role. Efforts will be made so that every child with disability gets suitably exposed to the use of computers.
- Children with disabilities up to the age of 6 years will be identified and necessary interventions made so that they are capable of joining inclusive education.
- Educational facilities will be provided in psychosocial rehabilitation centres for mentally ill persons.
- Many schools discourage enrollment of students with disability due to lack of awareness about the capabilities of disabled persons. Programmes will be taken for sensitization of teachers, principals and other staff members in all schools.
- Special Schools presently being supported by the Ministry of Social Justice & Empowerment will incrementally become resource centres for inclusive education. Ministry of Human Resource Development shall open new special schools depending upon the requirement.
- Adult learning/ leisure centers for adults with severe learning difficulties will be promoted.
- Three percent reservation for persons with disabilities in admission to higher educational institutions shall be enforced. Universities, colleges and professional institutions will be provided financial support to establish Disability Center to take care of educational needs of students with disabilities. They will also be encouraged to make classrooms, hostels, cafeterias and other facilities in the campus accessible to students with disabilities.
- A module will be included in induction and in-service training programmes of teachers on issues relating to management of children with disabilities.

The full text of the National Policy for the Persons with Disabilities is given at Annexure II.

The Persons with Disabilities Act, 1995 (PWD Act)

The Persons with Disabilities (Equal Opportunities, Protection of Rights and Full Participation) Act, 1995, as its title implies, is a legislation to ensure equal opportunities for people with disabilities and their full participation in national development. It provides, among others, for prevention and early detection of disabilities, education, vocational training, employment and social security of the persons with disabilities, non-discrimination and grievance redressal, making available aids and appliances, allotment of land at concessional rates and other affirmative action, and research and manpower development.

Regarding education of persons with disabilities, the Act has the following specific provisions:

- Every child with disability shall have the right to free education until the age of 18 years in integrated schools or special schools;
- Appropriate transportation, removal of architectural barriers and restructuring of curriculum and modifications in the examination system shall be ensured for the benefit of children with disabilities;
- Children with disabilities shall have the right to free books, scholarships, uniforms and other learning material;
- Special schools for children with disabilities shall be equipped with vocational training facilities;
- Non-formal education shall be promoted for children with disabilities;
- Teacher's Training institutions shall be established to develop requisite work force;
- Parents may move to appropriate forums for the redressal of grievances regarding the placement of their children with disabilities.

Integrated Education

Concept and Need

The traditional approach to education of children with exceptional needs is that of 'special education' by segregating the children with exceptional needs in a totally different learning environment in special educational institutions, like the schools for the blind, for the deaf, for the mentally retarded, etc. The curricula adopted and the teachers and the teaching methods followed in these special institutions are specific to the disability concerned and are different from those in the normal schools. Even though the number of such special institutions has increased over the years, they have been able to take care of only a small fraction of the disabled persons. The progress was far too slow and could not have helped much in reaching the goal of universal education. While educational opportunities have expanded substantially since Independence, the disabled children have not benefited to any significant extent through the traditional approach of special schools. This approach has also been considered unacceptable by social activists on the grounds that a) the long-term exclusion of the children with disabilities from the mainstream is socially and educationally harmful to both groups, b) segregation in the childhood eventually leads to segregation in the adult life violating human rights, c) the breaking of relationships, which is an inevitable result of segregation, is the most serious form of social deprivation that further damages the children's ability to learn, and d) 'special needs' is not another term for the needs of the disabled but signify needs which are currently unmet in the mainstream education.

An alternative to the segregated education is the system of integrated education, which gained popularity from the early years of the second half of twentieth century. This system seeks to integrate the disabled children with the normal school system.

Scheme of Integrated Education for Disabled Children (IEDC)

The Scheme of Integrated Education for Disabled Children (IEDC) was launched in December 1974 with the following objectives:

- To provide educational opportunities for the disabled children in general schools and to facilitate their retention in the school system
- To facilitate integration of children in special schools into general schools once they acquire the communication and daily living skills at the functional level.

The Scheme is implemented through the State Governments, autonomous organizations and voluntary agencies with experience in the field of education of the disabled. The Central Government provides 100 per cent financial assistance to these implementing agencies for creating various facilities like special teachers, books and stationery, uniforms, transport, readers' allowances for visually disabled, hostel allowance, equipment cost, removal/modification of architectural barriers in schools, purchase/development of instructional material, training of general teachers and equipment for Resource Rooms.

IEDC Scheme extends equal opportunities for children with mild and moderate disabilities which are appropriate to their special needs, in a least restrictive environment along with other normal children. Mild and moderate disability groups who are in the regular schools system will be addressed with the help of IEDC.

The scope of IEDC includes pre-school training for the disabled children and counseling for the parents, as a preparatory step to enable the children to come into the regular school system. This includes, among other things, special training for those with hearing disabilities, mobility and orientation training for those with visual disabilities, daily living and communication skills training for children with other disabilities, parent counseling and training in home management of these children. The education of children with disabilities under this Scheme continues up to the senior secondary school level and includes vocational courses equivalent to that level. Thus, the benefits under IEDC are generally available for children with disabilities in the age group 6 to 18 years.

Disabled children in blocks/districts are to be identified through a survey to be conducted by teachers in the area, for which the teachers have to be given orientation training. It is envisaged that a three-member Assessment Team comprising a doctor, a psychologist and a special educator would make a comprehensive assessment of these children to facilitate their educational programming by providing a profile of what the child can or cannot do during testing situations. The report would also indicate whether the child can be put directly into general school or should receive preparation in special school/ special preparatory class in an Early Childhood Education Centre specially equipped for the purpose.

In general, disabled children covered under IEDC may be given the following benefits:

- Actual expenses on books and stationery up to Rs. 400 per annum
- Actual expenses on uniform up to Rs. 200 per annum
- Transport allowance up to Rs. 50 per month, except when the child is admitted to hostel
- Reader allowance of Rs. 50 per month in case of blind children after Class V
- Escort allowance of Rs. 75 per month for severely disabled with lower extremity disability

- Actual cost of equipment up to a maximum of Rs. 2,000 per student for a period of 5 years.

Resource Rooms

The IEDC Scheme envisages that properly equipped Resource Rooms be set up for a cluster of schools implementing the Scheme. The Resource Rooms should have all the essential equipment, learning aids and materials. A Handbook prepared by NCERT indicates, inter alia, the type of facilities that have to be provided in the Resource Room. The average cost of such equipment is estimated Rs. 30,000. The need for equipment would depend upon the disability types of the students enrolled in the schools covered by the Resource Room. The aids and appliances that have to be provided for different types of disabilities are shown in Table 3.1 (on next page).

The Resource Room should be set up preferably in an existing accommodation in one of the schools. A new room may be built only when satisfactory accommodation is not available, for which a grant of Rs. 50,000 can be provided. Non-Government Organisations dealing with the disabled and special schools for the disabled, if available in the area, should be used as resource centres for the Integrated Education programme in the general schools.

Sarva Shiksha Abhiyan (*SSA*)

Sarva Shiksha Abhiyan (SSA) is a comprehensive and integrated programme of Government of India to attain Universal Elementary Education (UEE) in the country. SSA aims to provide useful and relevant education to all children in the age group of 6-14 age by 2010 and improve the quality of education. The main objectives of the project are as follows:

- All children complete five years of primary schooling by 2007
- All children complete eight years of elementary schooling by 2010
- To increase the quality of education of all elementary school students so that learning will be improved and transition rates from primary education to upper primary education will increase.
- To bridge the existing gender and social gaps. Bridge at primary stage by 2007 and at elementary education level by 2010 so that enrolment of girls will be near parity with boys, enrolment of children of Scheduled Castes and Scheduled Tribes will be near parity with that of other groups; and enrolment of children with disability will increase.
- Universal retention in schools by 2010

Table 3.1: Aids and Equipments in Resource Rooms

	Aids and Equipments			
Disability	Individuals	Sharing within school	Sharing amongst schools	Instructional material
Orthopaedic	Adjustable furniture, special writing, thick pen	Adjustable furniture, provision for development of improvised prosthetics		
Visually impaired Blind	Braille slate and stylus Abacus, Taylor frame, mobility canes	Brailler, Abacus, Taylor frame Cassette and talking books, maps, recreational materials	Braille sheets, thermoform machine, Indu Brailon maintenance services for Brailler, embossed recreational materials	Braille textbooks, material on cassette and talking
Partially sighted and low vision children	Special adaptive equipment like hand magnifiers to be used with spectacles, portable reading lamps	Specially designed desks with adjustable magnifiers, white boards in place of lack boards	Special arrangements for producing large print materials	Large print materials
Hearing impaired	Individual hearing aids	Voice trainer, mirror in size of 3'X6' for speech therapy, big mirrors 10'X6' in each classroom, group hearing aids, cells for hearing aids	Audiometer, voice trainer maintenance facilities for hearing aids	Special learning materials like flash charts, educational games, handouts of classroom activities
Mentally retarded		Sensory apparatus and kits prepared on the lines of Maria Montessori kits or produced by NCERT for Early Childhood Education Programme		Material written on a lower reading level than average

Its key objective is Universalization of Elementary Education (UEE). It implies access, enrolment and retention of all children in 6-14 years of age in the educational system. Constitutional (86th Amendment) Act, has made free and compulsory elementary education a Fundamental Right for all the children in the age group of 6-14 years which has given a new thrust to the education of children with special needs, as without their inclusion, the objective of UEE cannot be achieved.

SSA envisages to ensure that every child with special needs, irrespective of the kind, category and degree of disability, is provided education in the appropriate environment. It adopts a 'zero rejection' policy so that no child is left out of the education system. This means that no child having special needs should be deprived of the right to education and should be taught in an environment, which is best suited to his/her learning needs.

Experience has shown that such a goal of inclusive education is best achieved by taking into account the individual needs of the child. Most children with special needs can be enrolled and retained in regular schools if adequate resource support is provided to them, whereas there are others who might have to be provided some kind of pre-integration programmes, before they can be mainstreamed in a classroom. There might also be still some with severe profound disabilities, who would require an educational programme and intensive specialized support completely beyond the purview and scope of a formal school in the current situation.

Under SSA, a continuum of educational options, learning tools and aids, mobility assistance, support services are made available to students with disabilities. This includes education through an open learning system and open schools, alternative schooling, distance learning, special schools, home based education where necessary, itinerant teacher model, remedial teaching, part-time classes, community based rehabilitation and vocational education. Thus, SSA has adopted a more expansive and a broad-based understanding of the concept of inclusion, wherein a multi-option model of educating children with special needs is being implemented.

The ultimate objective of all these interventions is to successfully mainstream children with special needs into the fabric of formal elementary schooling. Thus, the objective is a) to bring more children with special needs under the umbrella of SSA and b) to provide to such children appropriate need-based skills, be it vocational, functional literacy or simply activities of daily living, in the most appropriate learning environment.

The interventions under SSA for inclusive education are identification of children with special needs, functional and formal assessment, appropriate educational placement, preparation of Individualized Educational Plan, provision of aids and appliances, teacher training, resource support, removal of architectural barriers, research, monitoring and valuation and a special focus on girls with special needs.

Under SSA, there is a provision of financial assistance of Rs.1200/- per child to institutions that are helping the inclusion of disabled children, as per specific proposal, per year. District plan for children with special needs is formulated within the Rs.1200/- per child norm. Financial assistance is also provided for assistive devices and barrier free access, both of which aim enhancement of the functional capacity/mobility of children with disabilities.

Individual States have adopted different approaches and strategies to identify and enroll children with disabilities. Andhra Pradesh, Rajasthan and Uttar Pradesh, have conducted residential bridge courses for such children with the main objective of preparing them for regular schools. Many States have adopted the home-based education for children with severe-profound disabilities with the objective of either preparing them for schools or for life by imparting to them basic living skills. Again States have adopted different ways to provide such home-based support. States like Himachal Pradesh and Uttaranchal are using NGOs for this purpose, whereas States like Haryana and Kerala have appointed resource teachers who visit the homes of children with special needs to provide them basic functional skills. Still other States like Tamilnadu are using special schools as resource centers to provide short-time or part-time help to individual children with special needs and their parents. Parental counseling and vocational training are two important aspects of the entire home-based instruction programme. Haryana have opened model inclusive schools in every block and equipped them with all possible facilities (like transport, equipment for physio- therapy, occupational therapy, resource teachers etc.) mainly to provide all kinds of support services, including remedial teaching to CWSN.

Special Institutions for the Disabled

Rehabilitation Council of India

Rehabilitation Council of India (RCI) was initially established by the Government of India as a registered body in 1986 for standardization and monitoring of training programmes for personnel in the field of rehabilitation of the disabled all over the country. Subsequently, the Rehabilitation Council of India Act, 1992, was enacted converting RCI into a statutory body from 1993. The objectives of RCI are:

- To regulate the training policies and programmes in the field of rehabilitation of persons with disabilities
- To prescribe minimum standards of education and training for various categories of professionals dealing with persons with disabilities
- To regulate these standards in all training institutions to bring about uniformity throughout the country
- To recognize/derecognize institutions and courses in the field of rehabilitation of the disabled
- To recognize foreign degrees/diplomas/certificates
- To maintain Central Rehabilitation Register of persons possessing recognized qualifications
- To encourage continuing rehabilitation education
- To promote research in rehabilitation and special education

The categories of professionals under the purview of RCI are Audiologists and Speech Therapists; Clinical Psychologists; Hearing and Ear Mould Technicians; Rehabilitation Engineers and Technicians; Special Teachers for Education and Training of the Handicapped; Vocational Counsellors, Employment Officers and Placement Officers dealing with Handicapped; Multi-purpose Rehabilitation Therapists and Technicians; Speech Pathologists; Rehabilitation Psychologists; Rehabilitation Social Workers; Rehabilitation Practitioners in Mental Retardation; Orientation and Mobility Specialists; Community Based Rehabilitation Professionals; rehabilitation Counsellors/ Administrators; Prosthetists and Orthotists; Rehabilitation Workshop Managers; and any other category of professionals notified from time to time under the RCI Act.

The Council has over 25,000 professionals/personnel in the field of rehabilitation registered on its Central Rehabilitation Register. It has recognized nearly 184 institutions conducting educational programmes at Certificate to Master's degree level.

National Institutes

The Government of India have set up six National Level institutions, one in each major area of disability, to deal with various aspects of rehabilitation of different types of disabled population.

Table 3.2: National Level Institutes in the Field of Rehabilitation of the Disabled

Institute	*Nature of Disability handled*	*Location*	*Year of Setting Up/Registration as Autonomous Body*
1. National Institute for Mentally Handicapped	Mental disabilities	Secunderabad, Andhra Pradesh	1984
2. National Institute for the Orthopaedically Handicapped	Orthopaedical disabilities	Kolkata, West Bengal	1982
3. Ali Yavar Jung National Institute for Hearing Handicapped	Hearing disabilities	Mumbai Mahartashtra	1983
4. National Institute for the Visually Handicapped	Visual disabilities	Dehradun, Uttaranchal	Set up in 1979 Registered in 1982
5. Institute for Physically Handicapped	Physical handicaps	New Delhi Delhi	1976
6. National Institute of Rehabilitation Training and Research.	Training & Research	Olatpur, Cuttack Orissa	1984

These National Institutes, staffed with talented professionals and equipped with modern equipment, develop appropriate models of care and rehabilitation services relevant to their specific field of specialization. Their main functions include

- Training of manpower for delivery of quality services
- Undertake and coordinate research on different aspects of rehabilitation
- Provide consultancy services to voluntary agencies
- Serve as documentation and information centres

As part of their activities in the field of development of manpower, the Institutes conduct various special courses to train professionals such as Degree courses in Physiotherapy, Occupational /therapy, Prosthetic and Orthotic Engineering, Degree courses in Mental Retardation, Diploma in Special Education (Mental Retardation), Diploma in Vocational Training and Employment (Mental Retardation), Bachelor's and Master's Degree courses in Education (Hearing Impaired), and in Hearing, Language and Speech, Bachelor's and Master's Degree in Audiology and Speech Rehabilitation, Primary and Secondary level Teachers' Training Programme for Visually Handicapped and Training Course for Orientation and Mobility Instructors for Visually Handicapped.

National Trust for Welfare of Persons with Autism, Cerebral Palsy, Mental Retardation and Multiple Disabilities

The National Trust for Welfare of Persons with Autism, Cerebral Palsy, Mental Retardation and Multiple Disabilities Act, 1999 came into force from 30th December, 1999. The National Trust supports programmes which promote independence, facilitate guardianship where necessary and address the concerns of those special persons who do not have their family support. The Trust also seeks to strengthen families and protect the interest of persons with autism, cerebral palsy, mental retardation and multiple disabilities after the death of their parents. The Trust is empowered to receive grants, donations, benefactions, bequests and transfers of funds.

District Rehabilitation Centres

The Government of India launched the District Rehabilitation Centre Scheme in early 1995, to provide comprehensive rehabilitation services to the rural disabled right at their door steps. The scheme, at present, is operational at 11 different districts of the 10 States of the country. These are:

Bhubaneshwar (Orissa), Bilaspur (Madhya Pradesh), Kharagpur (West Bengal), Mysore (Karnataka), Chengalpattu (Tamil Nadu), Sitapur (Uttar Pradesh), Vijaywada (Andhra Pradesh), Bhiwani (Haryana), Kota (Rajasthan), Virar (Maharashtra) and Jagdishpur (Uttar Pradesh)

The services provided in the scheme include:

- Prevention and Early Detection
- Medical Intervention and Surgical Correction
- Fitment of Artificial Limbs, Aids and Appliances
- Therapeutic Services
- Training for acquiring Vocational Training, Job Placement etc.

Regional Rehabilitation Training Centres

Four Regional Rehabilitation Training Centres (RRTCs), have also been set up at Chennai, Cuttack, Lucknow and Mumbai for training and manpower development in the field of rehabilitation, particularly for the District Rehabilitation Centres. The RRTCs have been conducting training programmes for communities, parents and even for persons with disabilities themselves.

Composite Regional Centres for Persons with Disabilities

Composite Regional Centres (CRCs) are set up to provide composite services for different kinds of disabilities and function as the Outreach Centres of National /Apex Institutes to facilitate the process of capacity building at local levels, in regions in which these are being set up. The objectives of CRCs are:

- Provide the infrastructure for training and manpower development, research and delivery of rehabilitation services in regions where such infrastructure is lacking at present
- To serve as Resource Centre for rehabilitation and special education of persons with disabilities. To start with, short term and orientation courses are to be taken up.
- To establish linkages with existing medical, educational and employment services, following the principles of community-based rehabilitation and offer extension services in the rural areas.
- To develop strategies for delivery of rehabilitation services suitable to the socio-cultural background of the region.
- To undertake designing, fabrication and fitment of aids and appliances.
- To undertake services of education and skill development leading to enhancement of opportunities for employment, rehabilitation, mobility communication, recreation and integration in society.

The scheme envisages five such CRCs, one each in Uttar Pradesh, Madhya Pradesh, Himachal Pradesh, Assam and Jammu & Kashmir. Of these, two have so far been set up in Lucknow and Srinagar.

Vocational Rehabilitation Centres

The Ministry of Labour have been implementing from 1968 a scheme for setting up of Vocational Rehabilitation Centres (VRCs) for the Handicapped.

Twenty VRCs are functioning (in 2006) in the country—one each at Ahmedabad, Mumbai, Bhubaneswar, Bangalore, Kolkata, Delhi, Jaipur, Hyderabad, Jabalpur, Guwahati, Kanpur, Ludhiana, Chennai, Thiruvananthapuram, Vadodara, Agartala, Patna, Una, Pondicherry and Jammu. Out of these, Vocational Rehabilitation Centre at Vadodara has been set up exclusively for handicapped women.

These Centres evaluate the residual capacities of the handicapped and provide them adjustment training, facilitating their early economic rehabilitation. Effort is also made to assist them in obtaining other suitable rehabilitation services, such as job placement, training for self-employment and in plant training.

In order to facilitate speedy rehabilitation of the handicapped, seven Skill Training Workshops (STWs) have been set up at the VRCs in Mumbai, Ahmedabad, Bangalore, Chennai, Thiruvananthapuram, Hyderabad and Kanpur. Non-formal job-oriented skill training is provided at these Centres.

Rehabilitation Services are also extended to the handicapped living in rural areas through mobile camps and Rural Rehabilitation Extension Centres. Rural Rehabilitation Extension Centres have been setup in 11 Blocks under five VRCs viz, Mumbai, Kolkata, Kanpur, Ludhiana and Chennai.

Persons with Locomotor disabilities, visual impairment, hearing impairment, mild mental retardation (whose IQ is between 51 and 70) and cured leprosy are eligible for registration at the VRC. People with disabilities between 15 to 45 years of age are eligible for registration. Educational qualifications are not prescribed. However, rehabilitation assistance would commensurate with education and skill level of the person. On the basis of findings of the different tests, the VRC will help the disabled to choose a vocation and also assist in admission to regular training institutes such as Industrial Training Institutes, Polytechnics and other professional institutes, if the person has adequate educational qualifications for admission to these. In case the qualifications are not adequate the VRC provides non-formal skill training in the selected trade either at VRC itself or other workshops or institutions.

The VRCs regularly organize pre-examination training programs for competitive examinations conducted by Staff Selection Commission etc. They also organize entrepreneurship development programs to guide in establishing self-employment ventures. The VRCs also register the disabled persons' names for sponsoring against notified vacancies of the government sector. The officers of the VRC solicit vacancies with small, medium and large industries and establishments for vacancies and sponsor the candidates as per their requirement. Further, the VRCs assist in formulating schemes for self-employment, identifying the financial institutions and help in forwarding and follow up of the applications. Respective financial institutions provide the loans. The loan amount would depend on the project and skills. The VRCs also assist in procuring ability aids through NGOs, service clubs and other schemes.

Facilities for the Education of the Disabled

CBSE Relaxation for Disabled Children

The main facilities extended by the Central Board of Secondary

Education to the disabled candidates (Dyslexic, Blind, Spastic and Candidate with Visual Impairment) are:

1. The persons with disabilities (Dyslexic, Blind, Spastic and Candidate with Visual Impairment) have the option of studying one compulsory language as against two. The language opted by them should be in consonance with the overall spirit of the Three Language Formula prescribed by the Board. Besides one language they can offer any four of the following subjects: Mathematics, Science and Technology, Social Science, Another Language, Music, Painting, Home Science and Introductory Information Technology.
2. Alternate questions in lieu of questions requiring special skills based on visual inputs have been provided in Mathematics and Science for Secondary School Examination (Class X).
3. Blind, Physically Handicapped and Dyslexic Students are permitted to use amanuensis. The amanuensis must be a student of a class lower than the one for which the candidate is taking the examination. Amanuensis is paid @ Rs. 100/- per day/paper daily by the Centre Superintendent from the centre charges amount
4. Disabled candidates are allowed additional one hour (60 minutes) for each paper of external examination.
5. Exemption from examination in the Third Language is given to the disabled.
6. Physiotherapic exercises are considered as equivalent to Physical and Health Education course of the Board.
7. Separate question papers in Science & Mathematics at Secondary (Class X) level have been provided for blind students.

Scheme of the University Grants Commission

The UGC had started the scheme of assistance to universities/colleges to facilitate Teacher Preparation in Special Education (TEPSE) and Higher Education for Persons with Special Needs (Differently-abled Persons) (HEPSN) during the Ninth Five-Year Plan, keeping in view the need to provide special education programmes as well as infrastructure to differently-abled persons. The infrastructure needs to be designed in a manner to enable them to easily access classrooms, laboratories, toilets, etc.

The main objectives of the scheme are:

- To encourage universities/colleges of education in the country to promote teacher preparation programmes in the field of special education.

- To provide equal educational opportunities to disabled persons in higher education institutions.
- To create awareness among the functionaries of higher education about the specific educational needs of persons with disabilities.
- To equip higher education institutions with the facilities to provide access to disabled persons.
- To provide appropriate financial assistance to disabled individuals to increase their sustainability in higher education.
- To explore suitable placement opportunities for educated disabled graduates in public as well as private sector enterprises.
- To monitor the implementation of all existing and future legislations and policies pertaining to higher education of persons with disabilities.

This scheme is aimed particularly at:

- providing assistance to universities/colleges of education to start teacher preparation courses in special education at the B.Ed./M.Ed. level; and
- Creating appropriate facilities for persons with special needs in higher education.

Colleges/university departments offering special education course at B.Ed. and/or M.Ed. level, having the approval of the Rehabilitation Council of India, and satisfying certain conditions are given financial assistance subject to certain conditions for: (a) establishment of Special Units for Differently-abled Persons in Universities/Colleges to develop awareness about the needs of the differently-abled persons in the higher education system, (b) providing access to persons with disabilities and (c) providing special equipment to augment educational services for disabled.

Special Employment Exchange for Physically Handicapped

There are 23 Special Employment Exchanges across the country exclusively for Handicapped. These Exchanges are functioning at Hyderabad, Ahemdabad, Delhi, Bangalore, Mumbai, Chandigarh, (Punjab), Chennai, Kolkata, Kanpur, Jabalpur, Thiruvananthapuram, Patna, Chandigarh (Haryana), Jaipur, Guwahati, Agartala, Shimla, Bhubneshwar, Surat, Vadodra, Rajkot, Vishakhapatnam, and Imphal.

ANNEXURE-I

State-Wise Disabled Population by Type of Disability, 2001

S. No.	*State/UT*	*Visual disability*	*Speech disability*	*Hearing disability*	*Locomotor disability*	*Mental disability*	*All Disabilities*
(1)	(2)	(3)	(4)	(5)	(6)	(7)	(8)
1.	Jammu & Kashmir	208,713	16956	14,157	37,965	24,879	302,670
2.	Himachal Pradesh	64,122	12,762	15,239	46,512	17,315	155,950
3.	Punjab	170,853	22,756	17,348	149,758	63,808	424,523
4.	Chandigarh	8,422	882	607	3,828	1,799	15,538
5.	Uttaranchal	85,668	16,749	15,990	56,474	19,888	194,769
6.	Haryana	201,358	24,920	27,682	151,485	49,595	455,040
7.	Delhi	120,712	15,505	8,741	64,885	26,043	235,886
8.	Rajasthan	753,962	73,147	75,235	400,577	109,058	1,411,979
9.	Uttar Pradesh	1,852,071	255,951	128,303	930,580	286,464	3,453,369
10.	Bihar	1,005,605	130,471	73,970	512,246	165,319	1,887,611
11.	Sikkim	10,790	3,174	3,432	2,172	799	20,367
12.	Arunachal Pradesh	23,079	2,429	3,072	3,474	1,261	33,315
13.	Nagaland	9,968	4,398	5,245	4,258	2,630	26,499
14.	Manipur	11,713	2,769	2,994	6,177	4,723	28,376
15.	Mizoram	6,257	2,006	2,421	2,476	2,851	16,011
16.	Tripura	27,505	5,105	5,699	13,970	6,661	58,940
17.	Meghalaya	13,381	3,431	3,668	5,127	3,196	28,803
18.	Assam	282,056	56,974	51,825	91,970	47,475	530,300
19.	West Bengal	862,073	170,022	131,579	412,658	270,842	1,847,174
20.	Jharkhand	186,216	39,683	28,233	138,323	55,922	448,377
21.	Orissa	514,104	68,673	84,115	250,851	103,592	1,021,335
22.	Chhattisgarh	160,131	30,438	34,093	151,611	43,614	419,887
23.	Gujarat	494,624	66,534	70,321	310,765	103,221	1,045,465
24.	Daman & Diu	1,898	189	120	690	274	3,171

(Contd.)

(*Contd.*)

(1)	(2)	(3)	(4)	(5)	(6)	(7)	(8)
25.	Dadra & Nagar Haveli	2,346	295	337	795	275	4,048
26.	Maharashtra	580,930	113,043	92,390	569,945	213,274	1,569,582
27.	Madhya Pradesh	636,214	75,825	85,354	495,878	115,257	1,408,528
28.	Andhra Pradesh	581,587	138,974	73,373	415,848	155,199	1,364,981
29.	Karnataka	440,875	90,717	49,861	266,559	92,631	940,643
30.	Goa	4,393	1,868	1,000	4,910	3,578	15,749
31.	Lakshadweep	603	207	147	505	216	1,678
32.	Kerala	334,622	67,066	79,713	237,707	141,686	860,794
33.	Tamil Nadu	964,063	124,479	72,636	353,798	127,521	1,642,497
34.	Pondicherry	10,646	1,818	2,277	8,830	2,286	25,857
35.	Andman & Nicobar	3,321	652	545	1,870	669	7,057
	India						21,906,769

Sources: Census, 2001

National Policy for Persons with Disabilities

Introduction

The Constitution of India ensures equality, freedom, justice and dignity of all individuals and implicitly mandates an inclusive society for all including persons with disabilities. In the recent years, there have been vast and positive changes in the perception of the society towards persons with disabilities. It has been realized that a majority of persons with disabilities can lead a better quality of life if they have equal opportunities and effective access to rehabilitation measures.

(2) According to the Census 2001, there are 2.19 crore persons with disabilities in India who constitute 2.13 percent of the total population. This includes persons with visual, hearing, speech, locomotor and mental disabilities. Seventy five per cent of persons with disabilities live in rural areas, 49 per cent of disabled population is literate and only 34 per cent are employed. The earlier emphasis on medical rehabilitation has now been replaced by an emphasis on social rehabilitation. There has been an increasing recognition of abilities of persons with disabilities and emphasis on mainstreaming them in the society based on their capabilities. The Government of India has enacted three legislations for persons with disabilities viz.

(i) Persons with Disability (Equal Opportunities, Protection of Rights and Full Participation) Act, 1995, which provides for education, employment, creation of barrier free environment, social security, etc.

(ii) National Trust for Welfare of Persons with Autism, Cerebral Palsy, Mental Retardation and Multiple Disability Act, 1999 has provisions for legal guardianship of the four categories and creation of enabling environment for as much independent living as possible.

(iii) Rehabilitation Council of India Act, 1992 deals with the development of manpower for providing rehabilitation services.

(3) In addition to the legal framework, extensive infrastructure has been developed. The following seven national Institutes are working for development of manpower in different areas, namely,

- Institute for the Physically Handicapped, New Delhi.
- National Institute of Visually Handicapped, Dehradun
- National Institute for Orthopaedically Handicapped, Kolkata
- National Institute for Mentally Handicapped, Secunderabad.
- National Institute for Hearing Handicapped, Mumbai
- National Institute of Rehabilitation Training & Research, Cuttack.
- National Institute for Empowerment of Persons with Multiple Disabilities, Chennai.

4. There are five Composite Rehabilitation Centres, four Regional Rehabilitation Centres and 120 District Disability Rehabilitation Centres (DDRCs) providing various kinds of rehabilitation services to persons with disabilities. There are also several national institutions under the Ministry of Health & Family Welfare working in the field of rehabilitation, like National Institute of Mental Health and Neuro Sciences, Bangalore; All India Institute of Physical Medicine and Rehabilitation, Mumbai; All India Institute of Speech and Hearing, Mysore; Central Institute of Psychiatry, Ranchi, etc. In addition, certain State Government institutions also provide rehabilitation services. Besides, 250 private institutions conduct training courses for rehabilitation professionals.
5. National Handicapped and Finance Development Corporation (NHFDC) has been providing loans on concessional terms for undertaking self-employment ventures by the persons with disabilities through State Channelizing Agencies.
6. Panchayati Raj Institutions at Village level, Intermediary level and District level have been entrusted with the welfare of persons with disabilities.
7. India is a signatory to the Declaration on the Full Participation and Equality of People with Disabilities in the Asia Pacific Region. India is also a signatory to the Biwako Millennium Framework for action towards an inclusive, barrier free and rights based society. India is currently participating in the negotiations on the UN Convention on Protection and Promotion of the Rights and Dignity of Persons with Disabilities.

National Policy Statement

8. The National Policy recognizes that Persons with Disabilities are valuable human resource for the country and seeks to create an environment that provides them equal opportunities, protection of their rights and full participation in society. The focus of the policy shall be on the following:

I. *Prevention of Disabilities*

9. Since disability, in a large number of cases, is preventable, there will be strong emphasis on prevention of disabilities. Programme for prevention of diseases, which result in disability and the creation of awareness regarding measures to be taken for prevention of disabilities during the period of pregnancy and thereafter will be intensified and their coverage expanded.

II. *Rehabilitation Measures*

10. Rehabilitation measures can be classified into three distinct groups: (i) physical rehabilitation, which includes early detection and intervention, counseling & medical interventions and provision of aids & appliances. It will also include the development of rehabilitation professionals. (ii) educational rehabilitation including vocational education and (iii) economic rehabilitation for a dignified life in society.

IIA. *Physical Rehabilitation Strategies*

(a) *Early Detection and Intervention*

11. Early detection of disability and intervention through drug or non-drug therapies helps in minimization of impact of disability. Therefore, there will be emphasis on early detection and early intervention, and necessary facilities will be created towards this end. Government will take measures to disseminate information regarding availability of such facilities to the people especially in rural areas.

(b) *Counseling and Medical Rehabilitation*

12. Physical rehabilitation measures including counseling, strengthening capacities of persons with disabilities and their families, physiotherapy, occupational therapy, psychotherapy, surgical correction and intervention, vision assessment, vision stimulation, speech therapy, audiological rehabilitation and

special education shall be extended to cover all the districts in the country by active involvement and participation of State Governments, local level institutions, NGOs including associations of parents and persons with disabilities.

13. Currently, rehabilitation services are largely available in and around urban areas. Since seventy five percent persons with disabilities live in rural areas, the services run by professionals will be extended to cover uncovered and un-served areas. Privately owned rehabilitation service centres shall be regulated for maintenance of minimum standards which shall be laid down. 14. To expand coverage in rural and unserved areas, new district Disability Rehabilitation Centres (DDRCs) will be set up with support from the State Government.
15. The National Rural Health Mission through Accredited Social Health Activist (ASHA) addresses the health needs of rural population, especially the vulnerable sections of society. The ASHA inter-alia will take care of the comprehensive services to the persons with disabilities at the grass root level.

(c) *Assistive Devices*

16. The Government of India has been assisting persons with disabilities in procuring durable and scientifically manufactured, modern aids and appliances of ISI standard that can promote their physical, social and psychological independence by reducing the effect of disabilities.
17. Every year through National Institutes, State Governments, DDRCs and NGOs, persons with disabilities are provided with devices such as prostheses and orthoses, tricycles, wheel chair, surgical footwear and devices for activities of daily living, learning equipments (Braille writing equipments, Dictaphone, CD player/ tape recorder), low vision aids, special mobility aids like canes for blind, hearing aids, educational kits, communication aids, assistive & alerting devices and devices suitable for the persons with mental disabilities. The availability of devices will be expanded to cover uncovered and under-serviced areas.
18. Private, public and joint sector enterprises involved in the manufacture of high tech assistive devices for persons with disabilities will be provided financial support by the public sector banks.

(d) *Development of Rehabilitation Professionals*

19. Human resource requirements for rehabilitation of persons with disabilities will be assessed and development plan will be prepared so that the rehabilitation strategies do not suffer from lack of manpower.

II. B. *Education for Persons with Disabilities*

20. Education is the most effective vehicle of social and economic empowerment. In keeping with the spirit of the Article 21A of the Constitution guaranteeing education as a fundamental right and Section 26 of the Persons with Disabilities Act, 1995, free and compulsory education has to be provided to all children with disabilities up to the minimum age of 18 years. According to the Census, 2001, fifty-one percent persons with disabilities are illiterate. This is a very large percentage. There is a need for mainstreaming of the persons with disabilities in the general education system through Inclusive education.
21. Sarva Shiksha Abhiyan (SSA) launched by the Government has the goal of eight years of elementary schooling for all children including children with disabilities in the age group of 6-14 years by 2010. Children with disabilities in the age group of 15-18 years are provided free education under Integrated Education for Disabled Children (IEDC) Scheme.
22. Under SSA, a continuum of educational options, learning aids and tools, mobility assistance, support services etc. are being made available to students with disabilities. This includes education through an open learning system and open schools, alternative schooling, distance education, special schools, wherever necessary home based education, itinerant teacher model, remedial teaching, part time classes, Community Based Rehabilitation (CBR) and vocational education.
23. IEDC Scheme implemented through the State Governments, Autonomous Bodies and Voluntary Organizations provides hundred percent financial assistance for various facilities like special teachers, books and stationery, uniform, transport, readers allowance for the visually handicapped, hostel allowance, equipment cost, removal/ modification of architectural barriers, financial assistance for purchase/ production of instructional material, training of general teachers and equipment for resource rooms.
24. There will be concerted effort on the part of the Government to improve identification of children with disabilities through

regular surveys, their enrollment in appropriate schools and their continuation till they successfully complete their education. The Government will endeavor to provide right kind of learning material and books to the children with disabilities, suitably trained and sensitized teachers and schools which are accessible and disabled friendly.

25. Government of India is providing scholarships to students with disabilities for pursuing studies at post school level. Government will continue to support the scholarships and expand its coverage.
26. Facilities for technical and vocational education designed to inculcate and bolster skill development suited to various types of productive activities by adaptation of the existing institutes or accelerated setting up of institutes in un-served/ underserved areas will be encouraged. NGOs will also be encouraged to provide vocational training.
27. Persons with disabilities will be provided access to the Universities, technical institutions and other institutions of higher learning to pursue higher and professional courses.

II.C. *Economic Rehabilitation of Persons with Disabilities*

28. Economic rehabilitation of Persons with disabilities comprise of both wage employment in organized sector and self-employment. Supporting structure of services by way of vocational rehabilitation centres and vocational training centres will be developed to ensure that disabled persons in both urban and rural areas have increased opportunities for productive and gainful employment. Strategies for economic empowerment of persons with disabilities would be the following.

(i) *Employment in Government Establishments*

The PWD Act, 1995 provides for 3% reservation in employment in the establishments of Government of India and Public Sector Undertakings (PSUs) against identified posts. The status of reservation for Government in various Ministries/ Departments against identified posts in Group A, B, C & D is 3.07%, 4.41%, 3.76% and 3.18% respectively. In PSUs, the reservation status in Group A, B, C & D is.78%, 8.54%, 5.04% and 6.75%, respectively. Government will ensure reservation in identified posts in the Government sector including public sector undertakings in accordance with the provisions of the PWD Act, 1995. The list of identified posts, which was notified in 2001, will be reviewed and updated.

(ii) *Wage Employment in Private Sector*

Development of appropriate skills in persons with disabilities will be encouraged for their employability in private sector. Vocational rehabilitation and training Centres engaged in developing appropriate skills amongst persons with disabilities keeping in view their potential and abilities will be encouraged to expand their services. Considering rapid growth of employment opportunities in service sector, persons with disabilities will be encouraged to undertake skill training suitable to the market requirement. Pro-active measures like incentives, awards, tax exemptions etc. will be taken to encourage the employment of persons with disabilities in the private sector.

(iii) *Self-Employment*

Considering slow pace of growth in employment opportunities in the organized sector, self-employment of persons with disabilities will be promoted. This will be done through vocational education and management training. Further, the existing system of providing loans at softer terms from the NHFDC will be improved to make it easily accessible with transparent and efficient procedures of processing. The Government will also encourage self-employment by providing incentives, tax concessions, exemptions from duties, preferential treatment for procurement of goods and services by the Government from the enterprises of persons with disabilities, etc. Priority in financial support will be given to Self Help Groups formed by the persons with disabilities.

III. *Women with Disabilities*

29. According to Census-2001, there are 93.01 lakh women with disabilities, which constitute 42.46 percent of total disabled population. Women with disabilities require protection against exploitation and abuse. Special programmes will be developed for education, employment and providing of other rehabilitation services to women with disabilities keeping in view their special needs. Special educational and vocation training facilities will be setup. Programmes will be undertaken to rehabilitate abandoned disabled women/ girls by encouraging their adoption in families, support to house them and impart them training for gainful employment skills. The Government will encourage the projects where representation of women with disabilities is ensured at least to the extent of twenty five percent of total beneficiaries.

30. Steps shall be taken to provide short duration stay homes for women with disabilities, hostels for working disabled women, and homes for aged disabled women.
31. It has been noted that women with disabilities have serious difficulty in looking after their children. The Government will take up a programme to provide financial support to women with disabilities so that they may hire services to look after their children. Such support will be limited to two children for a period not exceeding two years.

IV. *Children with Disabilities*

32. Children with disabilities are the most vulnerable group and need special attention. The Government would strive to: -
    (a) Ensure right to care, protection and security for children with disabilities;
    (b) Ensure the right to development with dignity and equality creating an enabling environment where children can exercise their rights, enjoy equal opportunities and full participation in accordance with various statutes.
    (c) Ensure inclusion and effective access to education, health, vocational training along with specialized rehabilitation services to children with disabilities.
    (d) Ensure the right to development as well as recognition of special needs and of care, and protection of children with severe disabilities.

V. *Barrier-Free Environment*

33. Barrier-free environment enables people with disabilities to move about safely and freely, and use the facilities within the built environment. The goal of barrier free design is to provide an environment that supports the independent functioning of individuals so that they can participate without assistance, in every day activities. Therefore, to the maximum extent possible, buildings/ places/transportation systems for public use will be made barrier free.

VI. *Issue of Disability Certificates*

34. The Government of India has notified guidelines for evaluation of the disabilities and procedure for certification. The Government will ensure that the persons with disabilities obtain the disability certificates without any difficulty in the

shortest possible time by adoption of simple, transparent and client-friendly procedures.

VII. *Social Security*

35. Disabled persons, their families and care givers incur substantial additional expenditure for facilitating activities of daily living, medical care, transportation, assistive devices, etc. Therefore, there is a need to provide them social security by various means. Central Government has been providing tax relief to persons with disabilities and their guardians. The State Governments/ U.T. Administrations have been providing unemployment allowance or disability pension. The State Governments will be encouraged to develop a comprehensive social security policy for persons with disabilities.
36. Parents of severely disabled persons with autism, cerebral palsy, mental retardation and multiple disabilities feel a sense of insecurity regarding the welfare of their wards after their death. National Trust for persons with autism, cerebral palsy, mental retardation and multiple disabilities has been providing legal guardians through Local Level Committee. They are also implementing the Supported Guardianship Scheme to provide financial security to persons with the above-mentioned severe disabilities who are destitute and abandoned by supporting the cost of guardianship. This scheme, which is presently implemented in a few districts, shall be expanded to over other areas in a phased manner.

VIII. *Promotion of Non-Governmental Organizations (NGOs)*

37. The National Policy recognizes the NGO sector as a very important institutional mechanism to provide affordable services to complement the endeavors of the Government. The NGO sector is a vibrant and growing one. It has played a significant role in the provisions of services for persons with disabilities. Some of the NGOs are also undertaking human resource development and research activities. Government has also been actively involving them in policy formulation, planning, implementation, monitoring and has been seeking their advice on various issues relating to persons with disabilities. Interaction with NGOs will be enhanced on various disability issues regarding planning, policy formulation and implementation. Networking, exchange of

information and sharing of good practices amongst NGOs will be encouraged and facilitated. The following programmes will be undertaken:

(i) A Directory of NGOs working in the field of disability will be prepared properly mapping them by geographic regions along with their major activities. For NGOs supported by the Central/State Governments, their resource position, both financial and manpower will also be reported. Disabled persons organizations, family associations and advocacy groups of parents of disabled persons shall also be covered in the directory identifying them separately.

(ii) There are regional/State imbalances in the development of the NGO movement. Steps will be taken to encourage and accord preference to NGOs working in the underserved and inaccessible areas. Reputed NGOs shall also be encouraged to take up projects in such areas.

(iii) NGOs will be encouraged to develop and adopt minimum standards, codes of conduct and ethics.

(iv) NGOs will be provided opportunities for orientation and training of their human resource. Training in management skill which is already being provided, will be strengthened. Transparency, accountability, procedural simplification etc. will be guiding factors for improvement in the NGO-Government partnership.

(v) The NGOs shall be encouraged to mobilize their own resources to reduce the dependence on grants-in-aid from the Government and also to improve the availability of funds in the sector. Tapering of assistance in a schematic manner will also be considered so that the number of NGOs to be helped within the available resources could be maximized. Towards this end, NGOs will be trained in resource mobilization.

IX. *Collection of Regular Information on Persons with Disabilities*

38. There is a need for regular collection, compilation and analysis of data relating to socio-economic conditions of persons with disabilities. The National Sample Survey Organization has been collecting information on Socio-economic conditions of persons with disabilities on regular basis once in ten years since 1981. The Census has also started collection of information on persons with disabilities from the Census-2001.

The National Sample Survey Organization will have to collect the information on persons with disabilities at least once in five years. The differences in the definitions adopted by the two agencies will be reconciled.

39. A comprehensive web site for persons with disability will be created under the Ministry of Social Justice & Empowerment. Organizations both in public and private sector will be encouraged to make their web sites accessible to the visually impaired using Screen Reading Technologies.

X. *Research*

40. For improving the quality of life of persons with disabilities, research will be supported on their socio-economic and cultural context, cause of disabilities, early childhood education methodologies, development of user-friendly aids and appliances and all matters connected with disabilities which will significantly alter the quality of their life and civil society's ability to respond to their concerns. Wherever persons with disabilities are subjected to research interventions, their or their family member or caregiver's consent is mandatory.

XI. *Sports, Recreation and Cultural life*

41. The contribution of sports for its therapeutic and community spirit is undeniable. Persons with disabilities have right to access sports, recreation and cultural facilities. The Government will take necessary steps to provide them opportunity for participation in various sports, recreation and cultural activities.

XII. *Amendments to Existing Acts Dealing with the Persons with Disabilities*

42. Ten years have passed since the Persons with Disabilities (Equal Opportunities, Protection of Rights and Full Participation) Act, 1995 came into operation. With the experience gained in the implementation of the Act and developments in the disability sector, certain amendments to the Act have become necessary. These amendments will be carried out in consultation with the stakeholders. RCI and National Trust Acts will also be reviewed and if necessary, required amendments would be made.

Principal Areas of Intervention

I. *Prevention, Early Detection and Intervention*

43. In order to ensure prevention and early detection of disabilities, the following action will be taken:

(i) National, regional and local programmes of immunization (for children as well as expectant mothers), public health and sanitation will be expanded.

(ii) Medical and paramedical personnel will be adequately trained and equipped for early detection of disability amongst children.

(iii) Training modules and facilities in disability prevention, early detection and intervention will be developed for medical and paramedical health functionaries and Anganwadi workers.

(iv) Training programmes of postgraduate, undergraduate degree and diploma in medical education will include modules on disability prevention, early detection and interventions.

(v) Disability specific manuals for families having persons with disabilities will also be developed and provided free of cost.

(vi) Human resource development institutions will ensure that the personnel needed to provide support services such as special education, clinical psychology, physiotherapy, occupational therapy, audiology, speech pathology, vocational counseling & training and social work are available in adequate numbers.

(vii) The latest research findings in the field of genetics will be utilized appropriately to minimize congenital disability including mental illness.

(viii) Appropriate plan of action for limiting effects of disability and prevention of secondary disabilities within the existing health delivery system will be evolved.

(ix) Attention will be paid towards improving awareness of nutrition, health care and sanitation amongst adolescent girls, expectant mothers and women in the reproductive period. Awareness programmes for prevention will be built in at the school level and at the level of teacher's training courses.

(x) Programmes will be undertaken for screening of children to identify at risk cases.

II. *Programmes of Rehabilitation*

44. Medical, educational and social rehabilitation programmes will be developed with the assistance of medical and rehabilitation professionals and with the participation of persons with disabilities and their families, legal guardians and communities. Convergence of Government programmes will be ensured and the following specific measures will be taken:
    (i) State level centres for providing composite rehabilitation services including human resource development, research and long term specialized rehabilitation will be set up.
    (ii) Community based Rehabilitation programmes shall be encouraged. Self help groups of persons with disabilities and their family members/ caregivers shall be effectively involved in the process of rehabilitation.
    (iii) Setting up of mental health care homes for severely mental ill persons will be encouraged under district level Panchayati Raj institution with the involvement of NGOs. Alternatively, family support groups will be encouraged to setup Custodial Care Institutions for persons with mental disabilities without community and / or family support.
    (iv) Measures will also be taken to setup residential rehabilitation centres for providing vocational and social skills training for persons with mental disabilities.

III. *Human Resource Development*

45. The manpower will be developed in the following areas:
    (i) Training of primary level workers both in health care and in community development comprising of Anganwadi workers, AuxiliaryNurses (Midwifes) etc.
    (ii) Support for training and orientation of personnel of Government and NGOs providing services.
    (iii) Training and sensitization of community decision makers such as members of Panchayats, head of families etc.
    (iv) Training and orientation of family members as caregivers.
46. Human resources will be trained to meet the requirement of education for children with disabilities under inclusive education, special education, home-based education, pre-school education etc, The following training programmes of different specialization and levels shall be developed:

(i) Training modules for teachers for inclusive education.

(ii) Diploma, degree and high level programmes in special education

(iii) Training of caregivers for home-based education and care services for disabled adults/ senior citizens etc.

47. Rehabilitation Council of India shall be the nodal agency for preparation of plans for training of rehabilitation personnel. The role of the National Institutes in disability specific training will be clearly spelt out and a five-year Plan of Action will be drawn up.

IV. *Education of Persons with Disabilities*

48. It will be ensured that every child with disability has access to appropriate pre-school, primary and secondary level education by 2020. Special care will be taken to –

(i) Make schools (building, approaches, toilets, playgrounds, laboratories, libraries etc.) barrier free and accessible for all types of disability.

(ii) Medium and method of teaching will be suitably adapted to the requirements of most disability conditions.

(iii) Technical/ supplementary/ specialized system of teaching/ learning will be made available within the school or at a common center easily accessible to a cluster of schools.

(iv) Teaching/learning tools and aids such as educational toys, Braille/talking books, appropriate software etc. will be made available. Incentives will be given to expand facilities for setting up of general libraries, e-libraries, Braille-libraries and talking books libraries, resource rooms etc.

(v) National Open School and distance learning programmes will be popularized and extended to other parts in the country.

(vi) Sign language, Alternative and Augmentative Communications (AAC) and other modes as a viable medium in inter personal communication will be recognized, standardized and popularized.

(vii) Schools will be located within easy traveling distance. Alternatively, viable travel arrangements will be made with the assistance of the community, State and NGOs.

(viii) Parent-Teacher counseling and grievance redressal system will be set up in the schools.

(ix) There will be separate mechanism to review annually the intake and retention of the girl child with disability at primary, secondary and higher levels of education.

(x) Many children with disabilities, who cannot join inclusive education system, would continue to get educational services from special schools. Special schools shall be appropriately re-modeled and re-oriented based on technological development. These schools will also help prepare children with disabilities to join mainstream inclusive education.

(xi) In some cases due to the nature of disability (its type and degree), personal circumstances and preferences, home-based education will be provided.

(xii) Course curriculum and evaluation system for children with various disabilities shall be developed keeping in view their capabilities. Examination system will be modified to make it disabled friendly by exemptions such as learning mathematics, learning only one language, etc. Further, facilities like extra time, use of calculators, use of Clarke's tables, scribes etc would be provided based on the requirement.

(xiii) Model Schools of Inclusive Education will be set up in each State/ U.T to promote education of persons with disabilities.

(xiv) In the era of knowledge society, computers play very important role. Efforts will be made so that every child with disability gets suitably exposed to the use of computers.

(xv) Children with disabilities up to the age of 6 years will be identified and necessary interventions made so that they are capable of joining inclusive education.

(xvi) Educational facilities will be provided in psychosocial rehabilitation centres for mentally ill persons.

(xvii) Many schools discourage enrollment of students on account of their disability due to lack of awareness about the capabilities of disabled persons. Programmes will be taken for sensitization of teachers, principals and other staff members in all schools.

(xviii) Special Schools presently being supported by the Ministry of Social Justice & Empowerment will incrementally become resource centres for inclusive education. Ministry of Human Resource Development shall open new special schools depending upon the requirement.

(xix) Adult learning/ leisure centers for adults with severe learning difficulties will be promoted.

(xx) Three percent reservation for persons with disabilities in admission to higher educational institutions shall be enforced. Universities, colleges and professional institutions will be provided financial support to establish Disability Center to take care of educational needs of students with disabilities. They will also be encouraged to make classrooms, hostels, cafeterias and other facilities in the campus accessible to students with disabilities.

(xxi) Include a module in induction and in-service training programmes of teachers on issues relating to management of children with disabilities

49. The Ministry of Human Resource Development will be the nodal Ministry to coordinate all matters relating to the education of persons with disabilities.

V. *Employment*

50. The following steps will be taken for employment of persons with disabilities:

(i) The government shall initiate a dialogue with private sector organizations to help persons with disabilities in getting employment.

(ii) Develop appropriate home-based income generation programmes for the persons with disabilities especially for persons with severe and multiple disabilities, who opt for such programmes. The system of coaching for employment will also be encouraged for persons with disabilities and their caregivers.

(iii) Facilitate modifications in the design of machinery, workstation and work environment necessary for the disabled persons to operate without barriers in training centres/factories/industry/offices etc.

(iv) Provide assistance through appropriate agencies like Marketing Boards, District Rural Development Agencies (DRDAs), private agencies and Non Governmental Organizations in marketing of goods and services produced by persons with disabilities.

(v) Coverage of persons with disabilities in poverty alleviation programmes will be improved so that they get their due share of 3 percent as provided under statutory provisions.

VI. *Barrier-free Environment*

51. For creation of barrier-free environment, the following strategies will be adopted:

(i) Public buildings (functional or recreational), transport amenities including roads, sub-ways and pavements, railway platforms, bus stops/terminals, ports, airports, modes of transports (bus, train, plane and waterways), playgrounds, open space etc. will be made accessible.

(ii) Use of sign language in all public functions will be encouraged.

(iii) Modification of Curriculum of Architects and Civil engineers will be undertaken to include issues relating to construction of barrier-free buildings. In service training will be provided on these issues to the government architects and engineers.

(v) Full adoption of comprehensive building byelaws and space standards for barrier-free built environment shall be ensured. Effort will be made to ensure adoption of the byelaws and space standards by all the states, municipal bodies and Panchayati Raj institutions in the country. These authorities will ensure that all newly constructed buildings for public use are barrier-free.

(vi) State Transport Undertakings will ensure disabled friendly features in their vehicles. Railways will provide barrier-free coaches in a phased manner. They will also make the platforms-buildings, toilets and other facilities barrier-free.

(vii) The Government will ensure that Industrial establishments, offices, public utilities both in public and private sector provide disabled friendly work place for their employees. Safety standards will be developed and strictly enforced.

(viii) Proactive steps will be taken to ensure disability-friendly IT environment in the country.

(ix) All the buildings, which are for public use, will be audited for its accessibility to persons with disability. There may be a need to develop professionally recognized access auditors whose services would be utilized for the purpose.

(x) Banking system will be encouraged to meet the needs to the persons with disabilities.

(xi) Communication needs of the persons with disabilities will be met by making information service and public documents accessible. Braille, tape-service, large print and other appropriate technologies will be used to provide information for the persons with visual disability.

VII. *Social Protection*

52. The following steps will be taken to provide adequate Social Security to the persons with disabilities:-

(i) A system of regular review of the policies of tax relief granted to the persons with disabilities will be put in place so that necessary income tax and other tax relief remain available to persons with disabilities.

(ii) State Governments and UT Administrations will be encouraged to rationalize the amount of pension and unemployment allowance for persons with disabilities.

(iii) Life Insurance Corporation of India has been providing insurance cover to persons with specific type of disabilities. There is a need to encourage all insurance agencies to cover persons with disabilities without exception.

VIII. *Research*

53. Research for developing new technologies for persons with disabilities will be encouraged with international cooperation, wherever necessary. Results of research will be widely disseminated. It will be focused on the following aspects:-

(i) Socio-cultural aspects of disability, which inter alia include study of social attitude and behavioral patterns towards persons with disabilities.

(ii) Develop social indicators relating to the education of persons with disabilities so as to analyze the problems involved and take up programmes to improve access and opportunities

(iii) Generate statistics about the employment status of persons by type of disability especially for those who become disabled due to accidents and other disasters.

(iv) Study causes of different types and level of incidence of disabilities.

(v) Genetic research to minimize incidence of disability under the aegis of Indian Council of Medical Research

(vi) Adaptive technology research focusing on enhanced personal mobility, verbal/non-verbal communication, design changes in articles of every day usage etc. with a view to develop cost effective, user-friendly and durable aids & appliances with the help of premier technological institutes.

54. Ministry of Science & Technology shall set up Rehabilitation Technology Centre for coordinating and undertaking research and development, testing and certifying technologies, training etc Appropriate hardware and software suitable for persons with disabilities to ensure access to information technologies will be developed.

IX. *Sports, Recreation and Cultural Activities*

55. The following steps will be taken to ensure equal opportunities for sports, recreation and cultural activities: -

(i) Make places for recreation, cultural activities and sports, hotels, beaches, sports arenas, auditoriums, gym halls, etc. accessible.

(ii) Travel agencies, hotels, voluntary organizations and others involved in organizing recreational activities or travel opportunities should offer their services to all, taking into account the special needs of persons with disabilities.

(iii) Identification of talent amongst persons with disabilities in different sports shall be made with the assistance of local NGOs. (iv) Formation of Sports organizations and Cultural societies for persons with disabilities will be encouraged. There will be mechanism to support the participation of persons with disabilities in national and international events.

(v) A national award for excellence in sports for persons with disabilities shall be instituted.

Responsibility for Implementation

56. The Ministry of Social Justice & Empowerment will be the nodal Ministry to coordinate all matters relating to the implementation of the Policy.

57. An inter-ministerial body to coordinate matters relating to implementation of National Policy will be formed. All

stakeholders including prominent NGOs, Disabled Peoples Organizations, advocacy groups and family associations of parents/ guardians, experts and professionals will also be represented on this body. Similar arrangements will be encouraged at the State and Districts levels. Panchayati Raj Institutions and Urban Local Bodies will be associated in the functioning of the District Disability Rehabilitation Centres' District Level Committees to coordinate the matters relating to the implementation of the policy.

58. The Ministries of Home Affairs, Health & Family Welfare, Rural Development, Urban Development, Youth Affairs & Sports, Railways, Science & Technology, Statistics & Programme Implementation, Labour, Panchayati Raj and Departments of Elementary Education & Literacy, Secondary & Higher Education, Road Transport & Highways, Public Enterprises, Revenue, Women & Child Development, Information Technology and Personnel & Training will setup necessary mechanism for implementation of the policy. A five-year perspective Plan and annual plans setting targets and financial allocations will be prepared by each Ministry/ Department. The annual report of these Ministries/ Departments will indicate progress achieved during the year.

59. The Chief Commissioner for Disabilities at Central level and State Commissioners at the State level shall play key role in implementation of National Policy, apart from their statutory responsibilities.

60. Panchayati Raj Institutions will play a crucial role in the implementation of the National Policy to address local level issues and draw up suitable programmes, which will be integrated with the district and State plans. These institutions will include disability related components in their projects.

61. Infrastructure created during the course of implementation will be required to be maintained and effectively used for a long period. The community should take a leading role in generating resources with in themselves or through mobilization from private sector organizations to maintain the infrastructure and also to meet the running cost. This step will not only reduce the burden on state resources but will also create a greater sense of responsibility among the community and private entrepreneurs.

62. Every five years a comprehensive review will be done on the implementation of the National Policy. A document indicating status of implementation and a roadmap for five years shall be prepared based on the deliberations in a national level convention. State Governments and Union Territory administrations will be urged to take steps for drawing up State Policy and develop action plan.

ANNEXURE-III

Scheme of Integrated Education for the Disabled Children (As on 01.01.2004)

1. Introduction

The country has witnessed a phenomenal expansion of educational opportunities in the post-Independence period. The disabled children, however, have not benefitted substantially from this growth in educational facilities. The Government of India, therefore, has brought the education of this group of children for special attention to achieve the goal of education for all. The objective is to integrate the handicapped with the general community at all levels as equal partners, to prepare them for normal growth and to enable them to face life with courage and confidence.

2. Aims and Objectives

The Scheme of Integrated Education for the Disabled Children (IEDC) aims to provide educational opportunities for the disabled children in common schools, to facilitate their retention in the school system. The disabled children who are placed in special schools should also be integrated in common schools once they acquire the communication and daily living skills at the functional level.

3. Type of Scheme

This is a Centrally Sponsored Scheme under which the Central Government will assist the States/Union Territories in its implementation on the basis of the criteria laid down. Assistance for all the items covered in the scheme will be on 100 per cent basis but assistance for the programme would be conditional on provision of professionally qualified staff.

4. Implementing Agencies

The scheme shall be implemented through the State Governments/UT Administrations/Autonomous Organisations of stature having experience in the field of education and/or rehabilitation of the disabled. Because this scheme has to be implemented in schools, the Education Department would be the implementing agency. The State Governments may take the assistance of voluntary organisations also for this purpose as may be feasible.

5. Scope

5.1. It is proposed to provide educational facilities under this scheme for children with disabilities who can be integrated in general schools. While rehabilitation assistance will be made available to all children with disabilities, student benefits (para 10) will be extended on the recommendation by the Assessment Team.

5.2. The scope of the scheme includes pre-school training for the disabled children and counseling for the parents. This would be an activity preparatory to the child coming into the regular school system. It would include, among other things, special training for the hearing handicapped children, mobility and orientation training for the visually handicapped, daily living and communication skills training required by children with other disabilities, parent counselling and training in home management of these children.

5.3. The education of the disabled children under this scheme will continue up to the senior secondary school level and includes vocational courses equivalent to the senior secondary stage.

5.4. A disabled child in receipt of any scholarship/assistance under some other scheme relating to disability from State/Central Government will not be eligible for any of the benefits under this scheme unless he/she is willing to forego the other sources of assistance.

6. Procedure for Implementation

6.1. The implementing agency should set up an administrative cell under an officer not below the rank of Deputy Director to implement, monitor and evaluate the program. These officials will be chosen for their special qualifications in this field, or if they are not so qualified, will be trained in a course conducted by the National Council of Educational Research and Training (NCERT) or some other designated organization. This cell will identify the areas and institutions for implementing the scheme.

6.2. It is preferable that in order to properly plan and supervise the implementation of the scheme a number of developmental blocks should be selected for operation of the scheme, rather than scattering the schools under this scheme all over the State. Within the area of a selected block all the desired inputs should be provided to the schools covered.

6.3. To identify disabled children in the blocks/districts where the scheme is yet to be implemented, the first task should be to provide suitable orientation to all school teachers in the area for conducting a survey to identify disabled children in general schools. Teachers may be provided a small honorarium for conducting the survey. Each primary school may be provided Rs.100 (to be shared by teachers) for conducting this survey. The IEDC cell should provide printed survey forms for identification of these children. Assistance up to RS.10,000 may be provided to the IEDC cell for this purpose. These efforts should be supplemented by publicity through mass media.

6.4. The State-level cell will make arrangements for equipment, learning materials, staff, etc. in order to provide education to disabled children. The cell will also set up the machinery for assessment of the disabled children. Wherever survey has been conducted by any other agency it would be utilised and augmented with the survey of disabilities not covered by the earlier survey. Monitoring and evaluation of the scheme at the State level will be carried out by the cell. The cell will ensure that the information regarding the scheme is widely known.

7. Administrative Cell

The Administrative Cell to be set up by the State Education Department will have a Deputy Director (in the scale of pay applicable in the State Government), a Coordinator (who will be a psychologist) in the scale applicable to a university lecturer, a Special Educator in the pay scale applicable to a university lecturer, a Stenographer and a Lower Division Clerk in the pay scales applicable in the State/UT.

8. Assessment of the Disabled Children

8.1 The Coordinator of the programme will be responsible for arranging for the assessment of the children and monitoring their progress on ongoing basis. A three-member assessment team, comprising a doctor, a psychologist and a special educator will be formed. The State/UT assessment team would function under the Administrative Cell. Specialists will be drawn upon in consultation with the State Health Department. Wherever district rehabilitation centres have been established, its resources for assessment may be used. The non-government organisations (NGOs) with infrastructural facilities may also be used for assessment purposes.

8.2 The average cost of an assessment should not exceed Rs.150 per disabled child. It will be necessary to examine a large number of children to select those considered suitable for placement in an integrated programme. Members of the assessment team would be given TA and DA as per State Government/UT Administration rules.

8.3 The assessment report should be comprehensive enough for educational programming; a profile of what a particular child can or cannot do during testing situations should be adequately reported. The report should specifically indicate whether the child can be put directly into school or should receive preparation in special school/special preparatory class in the Early Childhood Education Centre specially equipped for this purpose. Functional assessment can be carried out by the teacher if formal assessment is to take a long time so that the educational programme can be started for these children.

9. Linkages

Integrated education of disabled children requires inputs from different Departments like Education, Health, Labour, Welfare, etc. For effective linkages between these Departments and NGOs, working in this area, coordination committees will be formed at State, regional, district and block levels.

10. Facilities for Disabled Children

I. A disabled child may be given the following kinds of facilities at the rates prevalent in the State/UT concerned. The facilities should, as far as possible, be given in kind. In case similar incentives are not being offered by the State Government/UT Administration under any other scheme, the following rates could be adopted.

(a) Actual expenses on books and stationery up to RS. 400 per annum.

(b) Actual expenses on uniform up to RS. 200 per annum.

(c) Transport allowance up to RS. 50 per month. If a disabled child admitted under the scheme resides in the school hostel within the school premises, no transportation charges would be admissible.

(d) Reader allowance of RS. 50 per month in case of blind children after Class V.

(e) Escort allowance for severely handicapped with lower extremity disability at the rate of RS. 75 per month.

(f) Actual cost of equipment subject to a maximum of RS. 2000 per student for a period of five years.

II. In the case of severely orthopaedically handicapped children, it may be necessary to allow one attendant for 10 children in a school. The attendant may be given the standard scale of pay prescribed for Class IV employees in the State/UT concerned.

III. Disabled children residing in school hostels within the same institution where they are studying may also be paid boarding and lodging charges as admissible under the State Government rules/schemes. Where there is no State scheme of scholarships to hostellers, the disabled children whose parental income does not exceed RS. 5000 per month may be paid actual boarding and lodging charges subject to a maximum of RS. 200 per month. However, disabled children should generally not be placed in hostels unless the required educational facilities are not available in the nearby schools.

IV. Severely orthopaedically handicapped children residing in school hostels may need the assistance of a helper or an ayah. A special pay of RS 50 per month is admissible to any employee of the hostel willing to extend such help to children in addition to his/her duties.

11. Special Teacher Support

Except for children with locomotor disabilities, special education teachers may be appointed in schools where the scheme is in operation to provide specific attention to the disabled children.

12. Appointment of Special Teachers

12.1 The teacher-pupil ratio for special education teachers envisaged under this scheme is 1:8. This ratio will be the same for normal classes as well as for preparatory pre-school classes. The same teachers will provide counselling to the parents. In accordance with this ratio the requisite number of special teachers may be appointed in schools (or for a cluster of schools) for children requiring special teacher support.

12.2. *Qualifications* : Special teachers so appointed should possess the following qualifications.

(a) *Primary*: Academic qualifications as prevalent in the States and Union Territories with one year course, preferably multi-category, in special education or with specialisation in teaching any type of disabled children depending upon the category of children enrolled in the IEDC Units. Such teachers can be oriented subsequently in the education of other categories of disability.

(b) *Secondary*: Graduates with B.Ed. (Special Education) or any other equivalent professional training in special education.

Prescribed qualifications should be adhered to. In case qualified special teachers are not available, teachers with short training course may be appointed with the condition that they will complete the full course within three years of appointment. Special allowance for these teachers will be admissible only after completion of the full course. Teachers with single disability professional courses will be encouraged to take courses in other disabilities to improve viability in rural areas.

Since teachers with experience in Non-Formal Education (NFE) and Adult Education (AE) are likely to have a better understanding of local environment and need, they could also be identified for training under the scheme and appointed as special teachers.

12.3 *Scales of Pay*: The same scales of pay as available to the teachers of the corresponding category in that State/UT will be given to special teachers. Considering the special type of duties, these teachers will be given a special pay of Rs 150 per month in urban areas and Rs 200 per month in rural areas. The State Education Department may recruit such teachers for this purpose following the normal recruitment procedures.

13. Training of Special Teachers

The facilities for the training of special teachers are readily available in the Regional Colleges of Education (RCEs), Regional Training Centres being run by the National Institute for the Handicapped, Special Education Departments in the universities and selected Colleges for Education. The training facilities are being further expanded. The State Government may prepare an estimate of the requirements of teachers under each category of disability and send it to the Regional Colleges Education/District Institutions of Education and Training (DIETs), National Institutes for the Handicapped and the University Grants Commission under intimation to the NCERT. Since the appointment of fully trained, full-time resource teachers is an essential input for the successful implementation of the scheme, the State-Government/UT Administration must ensure appointment of such teachers on priority basis.

Under the scheme, grant is available through UGC for instituting full-time training courses for special teachers. The university/training institutes are expected to utilise the existing infrastructural facilities and other resources to the extent possible. The cost of the additional aids/equipment/space, and the additional faculty members will be met from the funds under this scheme. DIETs should organise in-service training courses for general teachers and refresher courses for resource teachers.

14. Training of Other Staff

The successful implementation of the IED depends upon the responsiveness of the administrators and general teachers in the school. Short orientation courses for administrators, heads of the institutions and general teachers associated with the implementation of the scheme may be organised. Training of administrators/key persons will be organised by the NCERT. State Government/UT administration may organise orientation programmes of three days' duration for heads of the institutions and of five days' duration for general teachers of the institutions implementing the IED scheme with the help of RCEs, Regional raining Centres and DIETs for the handicapped. The modules for these orientation programmes will be provided by the NCERT. Expenditure on TA/DA of the participants will be borne by the State Government/UT Administrations concerned. The cost of honorarium and TA/DA of resource persons and contingencies, etc. will be met under this scheme. The average cost of a three-day orientation programme is estimated at Rs.4,500 and for a five-day programme at Rs.6,000.

15. Resource Room

A resource room having all the essential equipment, learning aids and materials may be provided for a cluster of schools implement ting the scheme of integrated education. The NCERT has prepared a handbook which also indicates the type of facilities which may be provided in the resource room. A list of equipments required for various disabilities is enclosed (APENDIX). The average cost of such equipment is estimated at Rs.30,000. The need for equipment would depend upon the disability types of the students enrolled in the associated schools. The resource room may be set up preferably in an existing room in the school. A new room may be built only where no accommodation is available to the satisfaction of the State Government. Grant shall be available for construction of a resource room in a school in such circumstances subject to a maximum of Rs.50,000. NGOs/special schools wherever available should be used as resource centres for the IED programme in general schools.

16. Removal of Architectural Barriers

It may be necessary to remove architectural barriers or to modify existing architectural facilities, so as to provide easier access to orthopaedically disabled children to the school premises. Grant shall be available for this purpose for the schools where such handicapped children are enrolled.

17. Instructional Materials

At present sufficient facilities for production of instructional material for children with different disabilities do not exist in the country. Availability of requisite teaching/learning material for the disabled is vital for successful implementation of the scheme. The requirement of such materials is bound to increase with the increased coverage of disabled children. Financial assistance under this scheme will be available for purchase/production of instructional materials for the disabled and also for purchase of equipment required there of. Wherever necessary the available material may be translated and produced in regional languages.

Visually and hearing impaired children should be allowed to take only one language as already recommended. Provision for alternative modes of examination for blind and other children with physical disabilities coming in the way of writing should be considered and provided by the Boards of Examination.

18. Regulations for Relaxation of Rules

State Government/UT Administrations/other implementing agencies should also frame regulations for relaxation of rules relating to admissions, minimum or maximum age limit for admissions, promotions, examination procedures, etc. for improving access of the disabled children to education. Provision for admission of disabled children older than the normal eligibility (up to 8-9 years instead of 6 years) is essential in the transitional phase at least till the target of universal primary education (UPE) is achieved.

19. Pre-School and ECCE Facilities

Preparation of disabled children for education being essential, preference should be given to the blocks where the schemes of Integrated Child Development (ICD) and Early Childhood Centres of Education (ECCE) exist while selecting blocks for implementation of the scheme. Support for services for disabled children will be available for instructional materials and training of teachers.

20. Procedure for Grants to State Governments/UT Administrations

The State Governments/UT Administrations should formulate their programmes, make assessment of their financial requirements and submit detailed proposals for the next financial year to the Ministry of Human Resource Development (Department of Education, Government of India) by the end of December every year. The proposals should contain full information on various items given in the format prescribed. The proposals should be accompanied by utilisation certificates for grants released in the previous year and implementation report in respect of the previous year indicating, inter alia, detailed information regarding areas covered, the number of disabled children covered school-wise, teachers' training programmes conducted etc. The proposal should specify clearly whether for the purpose of various allowances to the disabled children the State Government rates have been taken or in their absence the rates given in this scheme have been adopted. The proposals will be examined in the Ministry and 50% of the approved grant for the year will be released as the first installment. The remaining 50 per cent of the grant will be sanctioned as soon as the State/UT Administration reports utilisation of at least 75 per cent of the grant sanctioned earlier. The request for the release of the second installment should be accompanied by an implementation report and a detailed statement of expenditure.

21. Procedure for Grant to Voluntary Organisations

The voluntary organisations desirous of implementing the scheme should send their applications in the prescribed format through the concerned State Government/UT Administration (with a copy endorsed directly to the Ministry). The State Government should give its views within a period of three months regarding the organisations' eligibility, suitability, relevance of the proposal and the capacity of the agency to implement it. Comments should be sent by the State Government even if the proposal is not recommended giving reasons there of.

In order to be eligible for financial assistance under this scheme, voluntary organisations, public trusts and non-profit making companies should

(i) have proper constitution of articles of association;
(ii) have a properly constituted managing body with its powers and duties clearly defined in the constitution;
(iii) be in a position to secure the involvement, on voluntary basis, of knowledgeable persons for furtherance of their programmes;
(iv) not discriminate against any person or group of persons on ground of sex, religion, caste or creed;
(v) not be run for the profit of any individual or a body or individuals;
(vi) not directly function for the furtherance of the interests of any political party; and
(vii) not in any manner incite communal disharmony.

Only those eligible agencies which have been in existence for three years would be considered for assistance under this scheme. This requirement may be waived in respect of agencies with specially qualified workers or which can otherwise justify a special consideration.

If any agency is already receiving or expecting to receive grant from some other official source for a project for which application is made under this scheme, assistance under this scheme will be made after taking into consideration the grant received, or likely to be received from such other official source. It should also be ensured that an agency already in receipt of a grant from any other official source, Central or a State, should not transfer any part of that liability to a grant to be sanctioned under this scheme.

The proposals of the voluntary organisations with the recommendation of the State Government/UT Administration should be sent to the Ministry of Human Resource Development (Department of Education), Government of India by the end of December every year for the following financial year. The proposals will be examined in the Ministry and 50 per cent of the approved grant for a year will be released as the first installment and the remaining 50 per cent after the agency reports utilisation of at least 75 per cent of the grant sanctioned earlier. The request for release of the second installment should be accompanied by a progress report (in Proforma I and II) and statement of expenditure. The grant will be remitted to the agency directly by Demand Draft/Cheque drawn in its favour by the Ministry of Human Resource Development, Department of Education.

22. Conditions of Grant to Voluntary Organisations

(i) The grant-receiving agency will be required to execute a bond on a prescribed form. The bond should be supported by two sureties if the agency is not a legal entity.

(ii) An agency in receipt of financial assistance shall be open to inspection by an officer of the Union Ministry of Human Resource Development or the State Education Department.

(iii) The accounts of the project shall be maintained properly and separately and submitted as and when required. They should be open to check by an officer deputed by the Government of India or the State Government. They shall also be open to a test-check by the Comptroller and Auditor General of India at his discretion.

(iv) The audited accounts together with the utilisation certificate in the prescribed form duly countersigned by the Chartered Accountant are required to be furnished within six months in respect of a preceding year or after expiry of the duration for which grant is approved.

(v) The agency shall maintain a record of all assets acquired wholly or partially out of government grant and maintain a register of such assets in the prescribed proforma. Such assets shall not be disposed of, encumbered or utilised for the purposes other than those for which the grant was given, without prior sanction of the Government of India. Should the agency cease to exist at any time, such properties shall revert to the Government of India.

(vi) When the State Government/Government of India have reasons to believe that the sanctioned money is not being utilised for the approved purpose the payment of grant may be stopped and the earlier grants recovered.

(vii) The institution must exercise reasonable economy in the working of the approved project.

(viii) The grantee agency shall furnish to the Ministry of Human Resource Development reports as may be prescribed.

(ix) The decisions of the Secretary to the Government of India in the Ministry of Human Resource Development, Department of Education, on the question whether there has been breach of violation of any of the terms and conditions mentioned in the sanction letter shall be final and binding on the grantee.

23. Evaluation and Monitoring

23.1 State Governments/UT Administrations may identify institutions/agencies to take up concurrent evaluations of the programme in selected areas/schools. The cost of such evaluation studies would be reimbursable to the State Government under the scheme. The Central Government may also undertake a summative evaluation of implementation of the scheme through the NCERT (or other institutions) at the end of the Plan period.

23.2 Quarterly progress reports may also be furnished to the Ministry of Human Resource Development (Department of Education) with a copy to the NCERT.

Guidelines for Evaluation of Various Disabilities

1. Locomotor Disability

1.1 *Upper Limb*

1. The estimation of permanent impairment depends upon the measurement of functional impairment, and is not expression of a personal opinion.
2. The estimation and measurement must be made when the clinical condition is fixed and unchangeable.
3. The upper extremity is divided into two component parts the arm component and the hand component.
4. Measurement of the loss of function of arm component consists in measuring the loss of motion, muscle strength and co-ordinated activities.
5. Measurement of the loss of function of hand component consists in determining the Prehension, Sensation & Strength. For estimation of Prehension Oppostion, lateral pinch, cylindrical grasp, spherical grasp and hook grasp have to be assessed as shown in the column of "prehension component" in the proforma.
6. The impairment of the entire extremity depends on the combination of the functional impairment of both components.

Arm Component

Total value of arm component is 90%.

Principles of Evaluation of range of motion of joints:

1. The value of maximum R.O.M. in the arm component is 90%.
2. Each of the three joints of the arm is weighted equally (30%).

Example

A fracture of the right shoulder joint may affect range of motion so that active abduction is 90%. The left shoulder exhibits a range of active abduction of 180%. Hence there is loss of 50% of abduction movement of the right shoulder. The percentage loss of arm component in the shoulder is 50 x 0.30 or 15% loss of motion for the arm component.

If more than one joint is involved, same method is applied, and the losses in each of the affected joint are added. Say.

Loss of abduction of the shoulder = 60%
Loss of extension of the wrist = 40%
Then, Loss of range of motion for
the arm = (60 × 0.30) + (40 × 0.30)
= 30%

Principles of Evaluation of Strength of muscles

1. Strength of muscles can be tested by manual testing like 0-5 grading.
2. Manual muscle gradings be given percentages like
   0. : 100%
   1. : 80%
   2. : 60%]
   3. : 40%
   4. : 20%
   5. : 0%
3. The mean percentage of muscle strength loss is multiplied by 0.30.
4. If there has been a loss of muscle strength of more than one joint, the values are added as has been described for loss of range of motion.

Principles of Evaluation of co-ordinated activities

1. The total value for co-ordinated activities is 90%.
2. Ten different co-ordinated activities are to be tested as given in the Proforma.
3. Each activity has a value of 9%.

Combining values for the Arm Component

1. The value of loss of function of arm component is obtained by combining the values of range of movement, muscle strength & co-ordinated activities, using the combining formula.

$$a = \frac{b(90-a)}{90}$$

where a = higher value
& b = lower value

Example

Let us assume that an individual with a fracture of the right shoulder joint has in addition to 16.5% of motion his arm, 8.3% loss of strength of muscles, and 5% loss of coordination. We combine these values as:

Range of motion: 16.5%]
Strength of Muscles: 8.3%]

$$16.5 \qquad \frac{8.3(90–16.5)}{90}=23.3\%$$

$$\text{Co-ordination: } 5\% \qquad \frac{23.3+5(90-23.3)}{90}=90$$

So total value of arm component = 27.0%

Hand Component

Total value of hand component is 90%.

The functional impairment of hand is expressed as loss of prehension, loss of sensation, loss of strength.

Principles of Evaluation of Prehension

Total value of Prehension is 30%. It includes:

(A) Opposition (8%). Tested against
Index finger (2%), Middle finger (2%).
Ring finger (2%) & Little finger (2%).
(B) Lateral Pinch (5%). Tested by asking the patient to hold a key.
(C) Cylindrical Grasp (6%). Tested for
- (a) Large object of 4 inch size (3%)
- (b) Small object of 1 inch size (3%)

(D) Spherical Grasp (6%). Tested for
- (a) Large object 4 inch size (3%)
- (b) Small object of 1 inch size (3%).
- (E) Hook Grasp (5%). Tested by asking the patient to lift a bag.

Principal of Evaluation of Sensations

Total value of sensation is 30%. It includes:

1. Radial side of thumb (4.8%)
2. Ulnar side of thumb (1.2%).
3. Radial side of each finger (4.8%)
4. Ulnar side of each finger (1.2%)

Principles of Evaluation of Strength

Total value of strength is 30%. It includes:

1. Grip Strength (20%)
2. Pinch Strength (10%)

Strength will be tested with hand dynamo-meter or by clinical method (Grip Method).

10% additional weightage to be given to the following factors:

1. Infection
2. Deformity
3. Malalignment
4. Contractures
5. Abnormal Mobility
6. Dominant Extremity (4%)

Combining values of the hand component

The final value of loss of function of hand component is obtained by summing up values of loss of prehension, sensation and strength.

Combining Values for the Extremity

Values of impairment of arm component and impairment of hand component are combined by using the combining formula.

Example

Impairment of the arm = 27.0% 64 $\frac{27(90-67)}{90}$=71.8%

Impairment of the hand = 64%

Guidelines for Evaluation of Permanent Physical Impairment in Lower Limbs

The lower extremity is divided into two component and Stability component.

Mobility Component

Total value of mobility component is 90%. It includes range of movement and muscle strength.

Principles of Evaluation of Range of Movement

1. The value of maximum range of movement in the mobility component is 90%.
2. Each of the three joints i.e. hip, knee, foot-ankle component, is weighted equality – 0.30.

Example

A fracture of the right hip joint may affect range of motion so that active abduction is 27^0. The left hip exhibits a range of active abduction of 54^0. Hence, there is loss of 50% of abduction movement of the right hip. The percentage loss of mobility component in the hip is 50 x 0.30 or 15% loss of motion for the mobility component.

If more than one joint is involved. Same method is applied and the loses in each of the affected joints are added.

For example:

Loss of abduction of the hip	=	60%
Loss of extension of the knee	=	40%
Loss of range of motion for Mobility component	=	(60 x 0.30) + (40 x 0.30) = 30%

Principles of Evaluation of Muscle Strength

1. The value for maximum muscle strength in the leg is 90%.
2. Strength of muscles can be tested by manual testing like 0-5 grading.
3. Manual muscle gradings can be given percentages like
   Grade 0. - 100%
   Grade 1. - 80%
   Grade 2. - 60%]
   Grade 3. - 40%
   Grade 4. - 20%
   Grade 5. - 0%
4. Mean percentage of muscle strength loss is multiplied by 0.30.
5. If there has been a loss of muscle strength of more than one joint, the values are added as has been described for loss of range of motion.

Combining Values for the Mobility Component

Let us assume that the individual with a fracture of the right hip joint has in addition to 16% loss of strength of muscles.

Combining Values

Motion 16%

Strength 8% $\dfrac{16+8(90-16)}{90}=22.6\%$

Stability Component

1. Total value of stability component is 90%.
2. It is tested by 2 methods.
(i) Based on scale method.
(ii) Based on clinical method

Three different readings (in kilograms) are taken measuring the total body weight (W), Scale 'A" reading and scale 'B" read.

Guidelines for Evaluation of Permanent Physical Impairment of Trunk (Spine)

The local effects of lesions of spine can be divided into traumatic and non-traumatic lesions.

Traumatic Lesions

Cervical Spine Fracture
Percent Whole Body Permanent Physical
Impairment and Loss of Physical Function
To Whole Body

A.	Vertebral compression 25% one or two vertebral adjacent bodies, no fragmentation, no involvement of posterior elements, no nerve root involvement, moderate neck rigidity and persistent soreness.	*20*
B.	Posterior elements with X-ray evidence of moderate partial dislocation.	*15*
	(a) No nerve root involvement, healed	*25*
	(b) With persistent pain, with mild motor and sensory manifestations	*20*
	(c) With fusions, healed, no permanent motor or sensory manifestations	*25* *35*
C.	Severe dislocation, fair to good reduction with surgical fusion.	
	(a) No residual motor or sensory changes.	
	(b) Poor reduction with fusion, persistent redicular pain, motor involvement only slight weakness and numbness	
	(c) Same as (b) with partial paralysis, determine additional rating for loss of use of extremities and sphincters.	

	Cervical Interverterbral Disc	
1.	Operative, successful removal of disc, with relief of acute pain, no fusion, no neurologic residual.	10
2.	Same as (1) with neurological manifestations, persistent pain, numbness, weakness in fingers.	20

(Contd.)

(*Contd.*)

Thoracic and Dorsolumbar Spine Fracture
Percent Whole Body Permanent Physical
Impairment and Loss of Physical Functions
to Whole Body

A. Compression 25%, involving one or two vertebralbodies, mild, no fragmentation, healed, no neurological manifestations.	10
B. Compression 50%, with involvement posterior elements, healed, no neurologic manifestations, persistent pain, fusion, indicated.	20
C. Same as (B) with fusion, pain only on heavy use of back.	20
D. Total paraplegia	100
E. Posterior elements, partial paralysis with or without fusion, should be rated for loss of use of extremities and sphincters.	
Low Lumbar	
1. Fracture	
A. Vertebral compression 25%, one or two adjacement vertebral bodies, little or fragmentation, no definite pattern or neurologic changes.	15
B. Compression with fragmentation posterior elements, persistent pain. Weakness and stiffness, healed, no fusion, no lifting over 25 pounds.	40
C. Same as (B), healed with fusion, mild pain.	25
D. Same as (B), nerve root involvement to lower extremities, determine additional rating for loss of industrial function to extremities.	35
E. Same as (C), with fragmentation of posterior elements, with persistent pain after fusion, no neurologic findings.	
F. Same as (C) with, with nerve root involvement to lower extremities, rate with functional loss to extremities.	100
G. Total paraplegla.	
H. Posterior elements, partial paralysis with or without fusion, should be rated for loss of use of extremities and sphincters.	
2. Neurogenic Low Back Pain – Disc Injury	
A. Periodic acute episodes with acute pain and persistent body list, test, tests for sciatic pain positive, temporary recovery 5 to 8 weeks.	5
B. Surgical excision of disc. no fusion, good results, no persistent sciatic pain.	10
C. Surgical excision of disc. no fusion, moderate persistent pain and stiffness aggravated by heavy lifting with necessary modification of activities	20
D. Surgical excision of disc with fusion, activities of lifting moderately modified.	15
E. Surgical excision of disc with fusion, persistent pain and stiffness aggravated by heavy lifting, necessitating modification of all activities requiring heavy lifting.	25

Non – Traumatic Lesions

Scoliosis

The whole Spine has been given rating of 100% and region-wise the following percentages are given:

Doral Spine - 50%
Lumbar Spine - 30%
Cervical Spine - 20%

Kobb's method for measurement of angle of curve in standing position is to be used. The curves have been divided into three sub-groups.

	Cervical Spine	*Thoracle Spine*	*Lumbar Spine*
Less than 300	2%	5%	5%
310 - 600 (Moderate)	3%	15%	12%
Above 600 (Severe)	5%	25%	33%

In the curves ranging above 60^0, cardio-pulmonary complications are to be graded separately. The junctional curves are to be given that rating depending upon level of apex of curve. For example, if apex of dorso-lumbar curve falls in the dorsal spine the curve can be taken as a dorsal curve. When the scoliosis is adequately compensated, 5% reduction is to be given from final rating (for all assessment primary curves are considered for rating).

Kyphosis

The same total rating (100%) as that suggested for scoliosis is to be given for kyphosis. Region-wise percentages of physical impairment are:

Dorsal 50%
Cervical Spine 30%
Lumbar Spine 20%

For dorsal spine the following further grading are:

Less that 20^0 10%
21^0 - 40^0 15%
41^0 - 60^0 20%
Above 60^0 25%

For kyphosis of lumbar and cervical spine 5% and 7% respectively have been allocated. Paralysis of Flexors and Extensors of Dorsal and Lumbar Spine.

The motor power of these muscles to be grouped as follows:

Normal
Weak 5%
Paralysed 10%
Paralysis of Muscles of Cervical Spine

For cervical spine the rating of motor power is as follows:

	Normal	*Weak*	*Paralysed*
Flexors	0	5%	10%
Extensors	0	5%	10%
Rotators	0	5%	10%
Side bending	0	5%	10%

Miscellaneous

Those conditions of the spine which cause stiffness and pain etc., are rated as follows:

		% physical impairment
A.	Subjective symptoms of pain. No involuntary muscle spasm. Not substantiated by demonstrable structural pathology.	0%
B.	Pain, Persistent muscle spasm and stiffness of spine, substantiated by demonstrable mild radiological changes.	10%
C.	Same as B, with moderate radiological changes	15%
D.	Same as B, with severe radiological changes involving and one of the region of spine (cervical, dorsal or lumbar).	20%
E.	Same as D, involving whole spine.	30%

Guidelines for Evaluation of Permanent Physical Impairment in Amputees

Basic Guidelines

1. In case of multiple amputees, if the total sum of percentage permanent physical impairment is above 100%, it should be taken as 100%.
2. Amputation at any level with uncorrectable inability to wear and use prosthesis should be given 100% permanent physical impairment.
3. In case of amputation in more than one limb percentage of each limb is counted and another 10% will be added, but when only toes or fingers are involved only another 5% will be added.

4. Any complication in form of stiffness, neuroma, infection, etc. has to b given a total of 10% additional weightage.
5. Dominant upper limb has been given 4% extra percentage.

Upper Limb Amputations

In kypho-scoliosis, both curves to be assessed separately and then percentage of disability to be summed.

		Percent Permanent Physical Impairment and loss of physical functions of each limb
1.	Fore-quarter amputation	100%
2.	Shoulder Disarticulation	90%
3.	Above Elbow upto upper 1/3 of arm	85%
4.	Above Elbow upto lower 1/3 arm	80%
5.	Elbow disarticulation	75%
6.	Below Elbow upto upper 1/3 of forearm	70%
7.	Below Elbow upto lower 1/3 of forearm	65%
8.	Wrist disarticulation	60%
9.	Hand through carpal bones	55%
10.	Thumb through C.M. or through 1st MC Joint	30%
11.	Thumb disarticulation through metacarpephaiangeal Joint or through proximal phalanx	35%
12.	Thumb disarticulation through inter phalangeal joint or through distal phalanx	

		Index Finger (15%)	*Middle Finger (5%)*	*Ring Finger (3%)*	*Little Finger (2%)*
13.	Amputation through proximal phalanx or disarticulation through MP Joint	15%	5%	3%	2%
14.	Amputation through middle phalanx or disarticulation through PIP joint	10%	4%	2%	1%
15.	Amputation through distal phalanx or disarticulation through DIP joint	5%	2%	1%	1%

Lower Limb Amputations

1. Hind quarter	*100%*
2. Nip disarticulation	90%
3. Above knee upto upper 1/3 of thigh	85%
4. Above knee upto lower 1/3 of thigh	80%
5. Through knee	75%
6. B.K. upto 8 cm	70%
7. B.K. upto lower 1/3 of leg	60%
7. Through Ankle	55%
8. Syme's	50%
9. Upto mid-foot	40%
10. Upto fore-foot	30%
11. All toes	20%
12. Loss of first toe	10%
13. Loss of second toe	5%
14. Loss of third toe	4%
15. Loss of fourth toe	3%
16. Loss of fifth toe	2%

Guidelines for Assessment of Physical Impairment in Neurological Conditions

1. Assessment in neurological conditions is not the assessment of disease but it is the assessment of the effects, i.e. clinical manifestations.
2. Any neurological assessment has to be done after six months of onset.
3. These guidelines will only be used for Central and upper motor neurone lesions.
4. Proforma A & B will be utilized for assessment of lower motor neurone lesions, muscular disorders and other locomotor conditions.
5. Total percentage of physical impairment in neurological conditions will not exceed 100%.
6. In the mixed cases the highest score will be taken into consideration. The lower score will be added to it and calculations will be done by the formula.

$$a + \frac{b(100-a)}{100}$$

7. Additional rating of 4% will be given for dominant upper extremity.
8. Additional 10% has been given for sensation in each extremity, but the maximum total physical impairment will not exceed 100%.

Motor System Disability

	Disability Rate
Monoparests)	25%
Monoplegia)	50%
Hemiparesis)	
Paraparests	75%
Paraplegia	100%
Hemiplegia)	75%
Quardriparesis)	
Quadriplegia	100%

Sensory System Disability

	Disability Rate
Aneesthesia)	
Rypoeasthesia)	Each Limb 10%
Paraesthesia)	
For Involvement	
For involvement of hand/hands, foot/feet	25%

Guidelines for Assessment of Physical Impairment in Neurological Conditions

1. Assessment in neurological conditions is not the assessment of disease but it is the assessment of the effects, i.e. clinical manifestation.
2. Any neurological assessment has to be done after six months of on set.
3. These guidelines will only be used for Central and upper motor neurone lesions.
4. Proforma A&B will be utilized for assessment of lower motor neurone lesions, muscular disorders and other locomotor conditions.
5. Total percentage of physical impairment in neurological conditions will not exceed 100%.
6. In the mixed cases the highest score will be taken into consideration. The lower score will be added to it and calculations will be done by the formula

$$a + \frac{b(100 - a)}{100}$$

7. Additional rating of 4% will be given for dominant upper extremity.
8. Additional 10% has been given for sensation in each extremity, but the maximum total physical impairment will not exceed 100%.

Speech disability

	Disability Rate
Mild	25%
Moderate	50%
Severe	75%
Very Severe	100%

Tested by a 100 word text. Ability to read (in educated), comprehend when read out, answer questions on text clearly and ability to write a synopsis (in educated).

Guidelines for Evaluation of Physical Impairment due to Cardio Pulmonary Diseases

Basic Guidelines

1. Modified New York Heart Association subjective classification should be utilized to assess the functional disability.
2. The physician should be alert to the fact that patients who come for disability claims are likely to exaggerate their symptoms. In case of any doubt patients should be referred for detailed physiological evaluation.
3. Disability evaluation of cardiopulmonary patients should be done after full medical, surgical and rehabilitative treatment available, because most of these diseases are potentially treatable.
4. Assessment of a cardiopulmonary impairment should also be done in diseases which might have associated cardiopulmonary problems, e.g. amputees, myopathies etc.

The proposed modified classification is as follows:

Group 0: A patient with cardiopulmonary disease who is a symptomatic (i.e. has no symptoms of breath-lessness palpitation, fatigue or chest pain).

Group 1: A patient with cardiopulmonary disease who becomes symptomatic during his ordinary physical activity but has mild restriction (25%) of his ordinary physical activities.

Group 2: A patient with cardiopulmonary disease who becomes symptomatic during his ordinary physical activity and has 25-50% restriction of his ordinary physical activity.

Mental Disorders

Source: Glossary and guide to their classification. A publication by WHO.

"Mental Retardation": A condition of arrested or incomplete development of mind which is especially characterized by subnormality of intelligence. The coding should be made on the individual's current level of functioning without regard to its nature of causation—such as psychosis, cultural deprivation. Down's syndrome etc., where there is a specific cognitive handicap- such as in speech—the four digit coding should be based on assessments of cognition outside the area of specific handicap. The assessment of intellectual level should be based on whatever information is available, including clinical evidence, adaptive behaviour and psycho-metric findings. The IQ levels given are based on a test with a mean of 100 and a standard deviation of 15 – such as the Wechsle scales. They are provided only as a guide and should not be applied rigidly. Mental retardation often involves psychiatric disturbances and may often develop as a result of some physical disease or injury. In these cases, an additional code or codes should be used to identify and associated condition, psychiatric or physical. The impairment and Handicap codes should also be consulted.

(b) *Mild Mental Retardation*

Feeble-minded — Moron

High Grade defect — IQ 50-70

Mild mental subnormality

(c) *Other Specified Mental Retardation*

(i) *Moderate mental retardation* Imbecile IQ 35-49 — Moderate mental subnormality

(ii) *Severe mental retardation* IQ 20-34 — Severe mental subnormality

(iii) *Profound mental retardation* Idiocy IQ under 20

(d) *Unspecified Mental Retardatation*
Mental deficiency NIS Mental subnormality NOS.

Hearing impairment Categories

S. No.	Category	Type of Impairment	DB level and/or	Speech discrimination	Percentage of impairment
1.	I	Mild hearing impairment	26 to 40 dB in better ear	80 to 100% in better ear	Less than 40%
2.	II	Moderate hearing impairment	41 to 55 dB in better ear	50 to 80% in better ear	40% to 50%
3.	III	Severe hearing impairment	56 to 70 dB hearing impairment in better ear	40 to 50% in better ear	50% to 75%
4.	IV	(a) Total deafness	No hearing	No discrimination	100%
		(b) Near total	91 dB and above in better ear	-do-	100%
		(c) Profound hearing impairment	71 to 90 dB	Less that 40% in better ear	75% to 100%

(Pure tone average of hearing in 500, 1000 and 2000 Hz by air conduction should be taken as the basis for consideration as per test recommendations)

Visual impairment Categories

(All with corrections)

	Better eye	*Worse eye*	*Percentage impairment*
Category O	6/9 to 6/18	6/24 to 6/36	20%
Category I	6/18 to 6/36	6/60 to Nil	40%
Category II	6/60 to 4/60 <u>or</u> field of vision 110-20	3/60 to Nil	75%
Category III	3/60 to 1/60 <u>or</u> field of vision 100	F.C. at 1 ft. to Nil	100%
Category IV	F.C. at 1 ft. to Nil or field of vision 100	F.C. at 1 ft. to Nil or field of vision 100	100%
One-eyed Persons	6/6	F.C. at 1 ft. to Nil	30%

Source: Extracts from the Ministry of Welfare Notification No. 4-2/83-HW, III dated 6.8.86

ANNEXURE-V

Special Devices

Hearing Impaired

- Communication boards for those who cannot speak. Child indicates towards the symbol or letters written on the board: Electronic communication boards and voice synthesizers are available.
- Hearing Aid – amplifies sound. These aids can be used on the body or in the ear.
- Classroom Amplification System – A microphone is linked with teacher and student.
- Telecommunication Devices – This is for deaf students. Sounds are translated into written material.

Visually Impaired

- Braille.
- Computer Braille System – computer accepts written material in Braille and processes.
- Speaking computers – This is known as synthetic speech where computer converts printed material into speech.

For people with restricted mobility

- Animals that help: Blind people use guide dogs that help in mobility.
- Wheelchairs: Advanced wheelchairs are available for those who have limited mobility. Many advanced wheelchairs are equipped with communication devices, control systems and are suitable for various terrains.

Orthopedic Handicapped

Specially trained artisans known as orthotists and prosthetics make aids and appliances for these types of disabled persons. Aids and appliances are manufactured according to certain standards and scientific principles. Broadly, these aids and appliances can be classified into:

(a) Supportive aids and appliances.
(b) Substitutive aids and appliances.

(a) *Supportive aids and appliances:*

These are the appliances, which are being given as a support to the weak part of body. They cover a wide range of aids & appliances according to the disability and disease. For locomotor disability, these aids and appliances are:

1. Surgical shoes and boots
2. Molded shoe and boots
3. Various types of insoles
4. Splints: CTEV splint, Knuckle bender, Radial N. Splint, Triangular splint, VIC splint
5. Calipers: Below knee, Above knee, Calipers with pelvic belt
6. Spinal Braces - G.W. Brace, Taylor's Brace, Milwaukee Brace, Cervical Orthosis
6. Function – Assistive sticks
7. Crutches – Auxiliary Aluminum – Elbow) Wooden Walker

(b) *Substitutive aids & appliances:*

These are the aids and appliances which are given to disabled persons with complete loss of some part of body or complete loss of some function.

For locomotor disability, they include:

1. Different type of Prosthesis: PTB Prosthesis, A.K. Prosthesis, Cosmetic Prosthesis for upper limb, and Functional Prosthesis for upper limb.
2. Different types of function substitutive devices.

ANNEXURE-VI

List of Audio Book Production Centres in India

1. The Executive Director
   Blind People Association
   Dr. Vikram Sarabhai Road
   Vastrapur
   Ahmedabad (Gujarat)
2. National Association for the Blind
   State Branches Department
   11 Khan Abdul Gaffar Khan Road
   Worli Surface
   Mumbai 4000 25
3. National Institute for the Visually Handicapped
   116, Rajpur Road
   Dehradun 248001
4. The Poona Blind Men's Association
   Technical Training Institute
   109, Dr. Helen Keller Road
   Ramtekdi Hadapsar
   Pune – 411 012
5. Blind Relief Association
   Lal Bahadur Shastri Marg
   (Near Oberoi Intercontinental Hotel)
   New Delhi –110 003
6. Mitra Jyoti
   M-137, 9th 'A'
   Main LIC Colony
   Sector 11
   Jeevan Beema Nagar
   Bangalore 560 075
7. Audio Cassette Recording Studio
   Govt. of Institution for the Blind
   Braille Bhawan
   Jamalpur Ludhiana
8. Sruti Information Centre
   1398 Dr. Mukherji Nargar
   Delhi 110 009
9. ARUSHI
   E-7/Hx5, Arera Colony
   Bhopal 462016
10. Central Library
    University of Delhi
    Delhi 110 007
11. The Manager
    Computer Unit
    National Association for the Blind
    Sector V, R.K. Puram
    New Delhi 110 022
12. Electronic Media Production Centre,
    Indira Gandhi National Open University (IGNOU)
    Maidan Garhi
    New Delhi 110 068
13. All India Confederation of the Blind
    Braille Bhawan
    Setor V Rohini
    Delhi-110 085
14. Helen Keller Service Society for the Disabled,
    Vizhiyagam,
    Viswanathapuram,
    Madurai-625014,
    Tamil Nadu

ANNEXURE VII

List of Braille Presses in India

1. The Regional Braille Press,
   Ramakrishna Mission
   Blind Boy's Academy
   Narendrapur 743 508
   24 Paraganas West Bengal
2. The Director
   Sri Ramakrishna Mission
   Vidhyalaya College of
   Education
   Coimbatore (Tamil Nadu
3. The Secretary General
   All India Confederation of
   the Blind
   Braille Bhawan
   (Near Rajiv Gandhi
   Cancer Hospital)
   Sector V Rohini
   Delhi – 11000 85
4. The Manager
   Govt. Braille Press
   Tifra Police Line Road
   Bilaspur 495 223
   (Chattisgarh)
5. The Manager
   Regional Braille Press
   Govt. High Secondary
   School for the Blind
   Poonamallee
   Chennai 6000 56 (Tamil
   Nadu)
6. The Manager
   Government Braille Press
   Govt. Blind School
   Tilak Nagar
   Sayaji Rao Road
   Mysore (Karnataka)
7. The Manager
   Braille Press
   Govt. Institute for the Blind
   Jamalpur Ludhiana (Punjab)
8. The Manager
   Govt. Braille Press
   Near Govt. Blind School
   Vaishshta, Guwahati (Assam)
9. The Manager
   Braille Press
   National Association for the
   Blind

11. Khan Abdul Gaffar Khan Road
    Worli Surface
    Mumbai (Maharashtra)

10. The Manager
    National Federation for the
    Blind
    Braille Press
    Near Atamshudi Ashram
    Delhi Raod
    Bahadurgarh (Harayana)

11. The Executive Director
    Blind People Association
    Dr. Vikram Sarabhai Road
    Vastrapur
    Ahmedabad (Gujarat)

12. The Manager
    Kerala Federation for the
    Blind
    Kunuukuzhi
    Trivendrum Kerala

13. The Secretary
    LKC Sri Jagdamba Andh
    Vidyalaya
    Hanumangarh Road

Sri Ganganagar
(Rajasthan)

14. The Hony. Secretary
Red Cross School for the Blind
City Hospital Road
Behrampur 760 001

15. The General Secretary
Christian Foundation for the Blind India
Braille Press
2 Officers Lane GST Road
Pallavaram Chennai

16. The Poona Blind Men's Association
Technical Training Centre
109, Dr. Helen Keller Road
Ramtekdi Hadapsar
Pune – 411 012

17. The Manager
Central Braille Press
National Institute for the Visually Handicapped
116, Rajpur Road
Dehradun 248001